LEADER
shifts

JOSEPH W. WALKER III

LEADER
shifts

Mastering Transitions
in Leadership & Life

Abingdon Press
Nashville

LEADERSHIFTS
MASTERING TRANSITIONS IN LEADERSHIP & LIFE

Copyright © 2014 by Abingdon Press

Library of Congress Cataloging-in-Publication Data

Walker, Joseph W. (Joseph Warren), III, 1967-
  Leadershifts : mastering transitions in leadership and life / Joseph W. Walker III.
    pages cm
  Includes bibliographical references.
  ISBN 978-1-4267-8140-7 (alk. paper)
  1. Christian leadership.   2. Life change events.   I. Title.
  BV652.1.W346 2013
  253—dc23

                                                                    2013034699

Scripture unless otherwise noted is from The Authorized (King James) Version. Rights in the Authorized Version in the United Kingdom are vested in the Crown. Reproduced by permission of the Crown's patentee, Cambridge University Press.

Scripture quotations marked "NKJV™" are taken from the New King James Version®. Copyright © 1982 by Thomas Nelson, Inc. Used by permission. All rights reserved.

Scripture quotations marked (NIV) are taken from the Holy Bible, New International Version®, NIV®. Copyright © 1973, 1978, 1984, 2011 by Biblica, Inc.™ Used by permission of Zondervan. All rights reserved worldwide. www.zondervan.com. The "NIV" and "New International Version" are trademarks registered in the United States Patent and Trademark Office by Biblica, Inc.™

Scripture quotations marked (ESV) are from The Holy Bible, English Standard Version® (ESV®), copyright © 2001 by Crossway, a publishing ministry of Good News Publishers. Used by permission. All rights reserved.

14 15 16 17 18 19 20 21 22 23—10 9 8 7 6 5 4 3 2 1
MANUFACTURED IN THE UNITED STATES OF AMERICA

CONTENTS

FOREWORD

The first thing that happens when you meet my friend Bishop Joseph Walker in person is you immediately realize how bright he is; yes, just old-fashioned smart. And as with the classic definition of a pastor, the next thing you get through that smile is his personal warmth and love of people. But as you get to know him through the coming pages, you will find the journey of leadership his life has taken him on has uniquely qualified him to teach us about LeaderShifts.

There is nothing like intelligence and warmth combined with actual experience to create WISDOM. That is what this book is full of for those of us who lead and love to lead: wisdom. As a voracious reader, I have lost patience over the years for "experts" who have opinions and theories about things they have never done. My personal goal is to learn from bright doers, people who know what they are talking about because they have been there, done that, and got the T-shirt. My first pastor, L. H. Hardwick, says, "A man with an experience is not at the mercy of a man with an opinion."

As leaders or future leaders, you want to learn from someone like Bishop Walker and our friend Joseph in Genesis. As you turn these pages, you will see how to deal with leadership heartbreak and hardships. You will see how to use power appropriately and how misfortune tunes your gifts. Leadership is just plain bloody and uncomfortable, so it is not for the thin skinned or the faint of heart. In the coming pages, we are reminded that we can choose compassion and justice or we can choose bitterness and a victim mentality.

Leaders are readers. Leaders are action oriented. Leaders are true servants, serving from strength. The role models of the Bible and my friend, the author, live that before us, inspiring and instructing us to be great. Enjoy.

Dave Ramsey, *New York Times* best-selling author

INTRODUCTION

Each of us experiences shifts in life. Often when these moments occur, few of us are able to discern their true meaning. Nothing in life just happens. Everything that happens in your life is connected to a master plan designed by God. Every experience is significant in ushering you into your ultimate destiny. One shift prepares you to be propelled to the next shift. Whether those experiences are positive or negative, they are responsible for developing you and positioning you to walk in your God-given assignment.

Leadership evolves. We become the leaders that God desires us to be. God takes the raw materials of our life and fashions it for His glory. If you don't embrace the process of becoming, you will become bitter when challenges come into your life. Every real leader embraces challenges because they are a necessary part of transition. Transition is always difficult. Many organizations and churches experience unyielding discord because of their inability to embrace transition.

Some leaders shy away from transition for fear of rocking the proverbial boat. Growth occurs only in organisms and is not necessarily guaranteed in organizations. When you realize as a leader that there is a dream and a vision that resonates within you, that constantly stretches you beyond the boundaries of your comfort zone, you then understand the significant shifts that are necessary to make those dreams a reality. When organizations and churches understand what is necessary in order to transition from an antiquated existence to an innovative and relevant model, they become open to shifts necessary to bring this to fruition.

As a leader for more than twenty years, I've seen many struggles leaders and churches experience attempting to shift. Many churches are in conflict with their leaders' vision and feel that their legacies are threatened by a vision being "imposed" upon them. Many leaders are frustrated because they feel they are not appreciated and that their innovative ideas are met with cynicism and constant resistance. But this book is not just for church leaders and churches. I have discovered that the dynamics that exist in churches have implications for leaders and organizations from every walk of life. Whether you are a business entrepreneur, college student, or professional in any capacity, this book will help you realize your dreams. Though the assignments are unique, the challenges are universal.

I witnessed God bring Mount Zion Baptist Church of Nashville, Tennessee, from 175 members to more than 28,000 in twenty years. I saw firsthand how change affected people and how they struggled to embrace that change. As a leader, I experienced firsthand how change impacts leaders and how the demands upon leadership expand. I've learned valuable lessons on how to manage these shifts, and I believe that I can help others do the same.

The biblical story of Joseph is a powerful account of how God chose a person to grow into leadership and do something extraordinary. Joseph's story is powerful and insightful for any leader who desires to understand shifts. Joseph may have been thrown into the pit by his jealous brothers, but he ends up in the palace. He goes from prison to prominence. Who else but God could have orchestrated Joseph's rise to leadership?

God is at work in your life. There are things that God has shown you that will change the world. It's important to understand that seeing is only the beginning. Realizing the dream will require perseverance, focus, wisdom, and maturity. You will be tested, and your trajectory will be defined by your ability to learn the lessons in each shift. You must be willing to change from where you are to where God is leading you. If you are going to be an effective leader, you must be teachable and adaptable. You cannot be stuck in traditions that are no longer effective. Bishop Paul Morton says that **tradition is nothing more than frozen success**.

There are so many organizations and leaders who are struggling for relevance in a changing world. But the world won't wait. The world is moving rapidly, and only those who are willing to shift will have sustainability.

The landscape of leadership is changing. Innovative, out-of-the-box thinkers are taking over. People who embrace positive change and are willing to move beyond what has been and embrace what shall be will be successful. But this must be delicately balanced with an acknowledgment of the history and sensitivity to those loyal people who have sustained the organization to this point. Effective leadership does not impose new ideas upon old systems without a strategy that enables everyone in the organization to move forward together. It's not simply out with the old and in with the new. Successful organizations do not forget their history but rather commit themselves to using it as a bridge to propel them to their destiny.

As you read this book, I pray that you will be inspired to take the necessary steps to bring your vision to fruition. It is my hope that you embrace the inevitable challenges and see them as vital to your evolution as a leader. It is my hope that your church or organization becomes all you envision in accordance with the will of God. Wherever you are in the process, it is certain that you will arrive at the designated destination as long as you are obedient to God's will.

Whether you embrace them or not, shifts happen. How you respond to those shifts determines the kind of leader you will become. There is something powerful at work in your life. There is vision that is eager to bubble up out of your soul and that may wake you up in the middle of the night. But moving that vision from a great idea to a working reality will require diligence and intentionality.

You may think you know where your life will be in the next five to ten years, but I am convinced that when you embrace *LeaderShifts*, you will discover that your capacity is far greater than you dreamed. Joseph matured as he stewarded the vision God gave him. As he matured, the vision became clearer and his leadership became more effective. As you grow, your vision grows, changes, shifts, so prepare to shift. Prepare to be stretched. Prepare to impact the world.

CHAPTER 1

FROM CHOSEN TO CONSECRATED

CHOSEN BEFORE THE BEGINNING OF TIME

W hen you are chosen, you may have a sense of it from your childhood. For me there were indicators, but I chose to ignore them. Yet in spite of my attempts, the indicators were determined enough to endure the various seasons of my life. I remember realizing that there was something different about me when I was in the sixth grade. I was the class clown. I disrupted the teacher with various antics. Everybody laughed, so I thought, but the teachers had extended conversations about what to do with me. So they tested me for special education, only to be surprised that I was just a bored but gifted kid.

There was something brewing in me, but I was too young to really understand, so I acted out. Then came my sixth-grade teacher. She was a beautiful Caucasian woman with silky white flowing hair, and she took great interest in my personal development. She saw in me what I didn't see in myself. Although I was content being a clown, she never gave up and talked to me during those many after-school disciplinary sessions. The words she spoke triggered a realization that I was special and had been chosen to do great things. I believe God sends us angels who speak wisdom to encourage us at the right times so that we don't self-destruct. My sixth-grade teacher helped me shift from being a mediocre student to a more disciplined and focused person.

From that point on, I saw school as preparation for a larger assignment. Although I had a shaky academic beginning, I marched through the hallowed halls of Southern University Baton Rouge, Vanderbilt, and Princeton, gaining the tools necessary to embrace what I was chosen to do.

I was twenty years old when God called me into the ministry. I had every intention of becoming a lawyer, yet the call upon my life indicated that God had chosen me to serve His purpose as a pastor. There was no audible voice, but rather a certainty in my spirit that God was calling me to something more significant than I could have ever imagined. Parker Palmer asserts, "Before you tell your life what you intend to do with it, listen for what it intends to do with you."[1] No matter what God is calling you to be, listening to the deep call will allow your purpose to emerge and put you on a divinely inspired path.

You know when God is calling you, because every fiber of your flesh will reject and rebel against it; at least mine did. We all wrestle with our insecurities and inadequacies. Moses thought he was too old and that his speech problem made him inadequate. Jeremiah thought he was too young. Perhaps you are reading this thinking of all the reasons you are not qualified to do what God is calling you to do. You never feel worthy to walk in an assignment God gives, but during those times it's incredibly important to remember that you've been on God's radar since the beginning of time. God didn't just wake up and say, "I think Sally or Juan could do this. Let's see if they're available." No, God had you in mind since He laid the earth's foundations.

Many people go through life struggling with purpose, but the truth is that we carry purpose within us long before we actually say yes to it. God is a strategist, and He chose you from the beginning. God told Jeremiah, "Before I formed you in the womb I knew you.... I ordained you a prophet to the nations" (Jer. 1:5 NKJV).

It became increasingly clear to me that God had been moving in my life providentially, preparing me to carry out my assignment. Every event in your life is significant and is a part of the molding process of walking in purpose. Romans 8:28 declares, "And we know that all things work together for good to those who love God, to those who are the called according to *His* purpose" (NKJV). When I submitted to the voice of God, an indescribable peace came over my life. There comes a moment where you have to say yes to the fact that you are chosen. When you acquiesce to the divine plan over your life, you position yourself for limitless possibilities. You literally shift your will to God's will, and this shift begins profound change in you.

As this shift from my will to God's began to become markedly noticeable, I became more inquisitive about everything around me. I became curious and started asking questions: Why did this happen? What does it mean? How can that be? Why me? Although I enjoy being around people, I often felt alone in my inner journey. There were few people I felt could really understand what was happening to me. I believe that every leader experiences this. There were so many unanswerable questions. Why was I named Joseph after my father? I am not the first son of my father. I am the fourth son of five. I truly believe that I was providentially given that name not only as a gesture of succession of an amazing bloodline within my family, but also because of the spiritual journey my life would take. When I think about the life of the biblical Joseph,

3

I am fascinated at how God consecrated Joseph and used all his misfortunes to position him for greatness. God enabled him to lead his people to their destiny.

In this chapter, I will focus on Joseph's coat and what it means to be set apart. Leaders may be chosen, but they must also recognize that obstacles and misfortune can equip them for an even greater capacity to lead. Misfortune and obstacles create opportunities for self-development and help us exercise our gifts, making them stronger. But also through these experiences, we can learn a great deal about God, ourselves, and the people around us.

MOVING FROM ACKNOWLEDGMENT TO CONSECRATION

The first "shift" you will experience is moving from the acknowledgment that you are chosen to being consecrated as someone who is chosen. Being consecrated means being given the mantle of authority. When you realize you are chosen, it is humbling; yet there also has to be an acceptance that chosen people are often set apart by God to do great things. For me, it was difficult accepting being set apart, because being set apart also meant making some decisions alone and perhaps being lonely as well. Few people will ever understand the depth of your calling and the necessity of your consecration. James Baldwin says, "The price one pays for pursuing any profession, or calling, is an intimate knowledge of its ugly side."[2] This is why people often protest being consecrated. Unless you are willing to stand alone and apart from your crowd, you will never embrace being chosen and consecrated to do the work God has for you.

Everyone God uses He calls out of the crowd. God called Abraham from a place of comfort to go to a new place. Jesus called the disciples from their day-to-day routine to a life of following. If you are a social person, it can be difficult when you realize how small your new crowd will become. One of the most valuable lessons I learned in this shift is that God connects you with people who understand your "not yet." There are tons of folks in your life who embrace and affirm where you are now, because where you are now does not intimidate them or make a demand on them to change the dynamics of interaction with you. They are content where you are and where they are in the relationship. What you will discover is that once God shifts you into your "not yet," some will have difficulty adapting. For some, it will bring out negative feelings about you that they have suppressed. For others, it will be a revelation of their own inability to go where God is taking you. You cannot lose sleep when this happens.

I was deeply concerned and attempted to reach out to many people who were in relationship with me but left once I accepted my call. I wanted their approval. I wanted the familiar because it felt safe. It was then I was reminded of this true story. When the space shuttle flew into outer space, it was launched with enough energy and fuel to get it to its destination. There were two rocket boosters on the side of the shuttle, which were designed to fall off at a certain altitude. There was no system failure with the shuttle or with the boosters. They were engineered to respond this way. Their job was to boost the shuttle to a certain altitude and then fall away so the shuttle could continue into orbit. If they remained beyond their designed altitude, it would create drag on the shuttle and prevent it from reaching its destination. When you are chosen to do great things by God, some people in your life are designed to fall out at a certain altitude. It doesn't mean that they are bad people. It just reveals the fact that they were not designed to fly in your orbit.

The book of Genesis tells us that Joseph was given a coat of many colors. His father gives him this coat, distinguishing him from his other brothers. While this coat meant a lot of things, most notably this coat was an expression of special favor. There is nothing Joseph did to deserve the coat; rather, it was a gift from his father, who must have seen Joseph's potential. I became keenly aware when God chose me that I was not worthy to wear the coat of favor or bear the weight of the mantle of authority. Many of you are wearing the coat of favor your father has given to you. It is clear that you are different and that you have been consecrated for something greater than where you are. The reality of Joseph's coat, like yours, is that it is valuable—valuable enough to get the attention of others and stir up their jealousy and perhaps contempt. Joseph's brothers didn't get angry with their father for giving the coat but with Joseph, who wore it.

I remember when I first started pastoring Mount Zion Baptist Church of Nashville, Tennessee. I was a twenty-four-year-old neophyte fresh out of seminary. I came into this historical church with great ambition. Mount Zion was a few hundred members and a very proud people with a distinguished history. They loved the Lord and were eager for transition to take place, at least at the beginning. Often, organizations have to hit rock bottom before they can embrace the change necessary for growth. Mount Zion was different; the church knew it was time for a different direction, and I knew as a young leader that I was chosen to lead them, but I had not embraced the coat of consecration. Over time, I witnessed a transition in the church that involved several stages. I witnessed people struggle with change to the point of open resistance. I soon discovered that they were not fighting me; they were actually grieving the loss of the church as they once knew it. Just because you are chosen to do great things, it doesn't mean that you are insensitive to how what you do affects the people who are involved.

Initially, I was taken aback, until I realized that grief is a natural part of the growing process. Not only was I experiencing a shift as their leader, but also Mount Zion as a collective body was experiencing a major shift in understanding how to respond to a leader who was on the cusp of a mighty movement. The key to making the transition was not forcing the shift on them, but making the shift with them. I then witnessed the transition from the church being only a physical family into being a spiritual family. Mount Zion was a family church, and almost everybody was related. Many leadership positions were filled by people who had had them for years, so they controlled the direction of the church. When the church began to grow extensively, this dynamic changed. Now there were new faces and fresh ideas that would not be controlled by the "old guard" in the pew. This needed to be managed by me. It's not that the "old guard" had done a bad job. They wanted what was best for the church, but they knew only of their way of doing things, and they were frozen in their traditions.

One of the things chosen leaders need to do is realize the impact change has on folks who are there before the change occurs. For Joseph in Genesis, the impact on his brothers would be huge. For Mount Zion Baptist Church, it was similar. Regardless of age, economic status, race, or gender, people will struggle with new ideas that challenge existing ones. This is the point where you have to realize the responsibilities of wearing the coat of your father. As I mentioned earlier, it is a valuable coat. You cannot be like everybody else. You must be willing to stand alone and fulfill the assignment God has given to you. One of my struggles early on was that I wanted everybody to like me. I wanted everybody to embrace me as a young leader trying to make a difference within the community. I soon discovered that the coat brings contempt, which I experienced from within and from without. There were those in Mount Zion who resisted everything I did. They challenged every decision, and many of them left the church because they were unable to adapt to the shift. Even still, the greater opposition came from outside the church. I was very intentional about cultivating relationships; however, when folks are threatened by your coat of many colors, relationships quickly dissipate. I tried to fit in to many organizations and associations but was never comfortable. When you have been consecrated, you are drawn to those things that equip you in your assignment. You don't have allegiance to things just for the sake of accommodation.

The Mount Zion Church experienced explosive growth in the city. We were growing at a rate of 1,500 people a year. The more the church grew, the heavier the mantle of the coat became. We moved into the headquarters of the National Baptist Convention USA, Inc., reinvigorating the history Mount Zion had with this convention. Their acceptance of this arrangement was because of the long-standing support the church had given the convention. We paid our rent three months in advance. The church continued to grow until we were in overflow even in this massive building. Although we were experiencing great success, I knew that I had been consecrated for something different. I could have continued in this place of comfort or could walk in obedience to what God had called me to do. This is the spiritual intersection all leaders come to. Either you go the way of comfort or you take the road of conflict—the wide road or the narrow road. What I discovered is that the greatest change happens down the road of conflict.

Conflict is essential for change to occur in any organization. Many leaders miss the shift from being chosen to being consecrated because they fear conflict. Conflict is necessary if you are going to be effective as a leader. It works as confirmation that you are in the midst of a shift. Saul Alinsky states, "Change means movement. Movement means friction. Only in the frictionless vacuum of a nonexistent abstract world can movement or change occur without that abrasive friction of conflict."[3] I have experienced some of my greatest transitions as a leader when I have embraced seasons of conflict as opportunities, not hindrances.

Our spiritual DNA at Mount Zion as a ministry had shifted from the traditional Baptist expression to a more Pentecostal expression. People were joining our church from a variety of denominational backgrounds. They no longer held to their denominational upbringing but were drawn to the shift they witnessed at Mount Zion. My theology had also shifted, and I no longer embraced some of the tenets that I grew up believing. How I saw women in ministry and the gifts of the Spirit, for example, were forever changed. While I grew up with a theological position that women were not permitted by Scripture to preach, as leader and pastor, I ordained the first woman in the 125-year history of Mount Zion Baptist Church. The Baptist Church taught about Pentecost but did not necessarily embrace the power demonstrated in the book of Acts as relevant and active today in the local church. I saw people operating in the gifts of the Spirit openly within the Mount Zion Church, and I knew it would not be long before I experienced conflict within the Baptist Convention, so I aligned with the Full Gospel Baptist Church Fellowship under Bishop Paul S. Morton.

Full Gospel Baptist Church Fellowship was established to give Baptists a right to choose. In his book *Let Your Life Speak*, Parker Palmer says, "The people who plant the seeds of movements make a critical decision: they decide to live 'divided no more.' They decide no longer to act on the outside in a way that contradicts some truth about themselves that they hold deeply on the inside."[4] Aligning with Full Gospel allowed for an authentic expression of the shift that was brewing within me and Mount Zion. This fellowship was more in line with my coat, and I found others who shared similar experiences. Full

Gospel was viewed quite negatively at that time by the National Baptist Convention, and, consequently, we were asked to leave the World Baptist Center. Though it was a painful experience, I realized that being set apart carried a great price. This was not the time to lament; rather, it was the time to regroup.

We relocated to the campus of Tennessee State University in the Gentry Center Complex. This facility is where basketball games are played and graduation takes place. It seats more than twelve thousand people. It was there that our membership grew to exactly twelve thousand. Every leader must know that God is always at work behind the scenes on behalf of His people. What appeared to be just pure luck was clearly a part of a divine plan. The fact that this facility was available each Sunday for us to have worship was nothing short of a miracle. It was a tremendous blessing to be on that campus. This put us in the epicenter of those who would embrace change. Our church experienced its greatest growth in the Gentry Center. God reminded me that He had allowed a plant that had outgrown its pot to be repotted in one that could handle its true potential. I had every opportunity to be bitter and speak negatively about the experience with our move, but I had to be spiritual enough to know that God's hand was all in it. So often we get discouraged because we experienced rejection by people we know. When you are consecrated, you have to know that **setbacks are setups for comebacks**. God's plan for your life will prevail regardless of the opposition you experience. This is why it's important to be faithful to your assignment and not waver for popularity's sake. When you have the coat, there is greater accountability.

One of the most powerful revelations about shifting to consecration is the reality that you will never be the same. You will never be seen the same way again. Joseph moved from the ordinary ranks of being a brother to wearing the mantle of leadership as chosen by his father. The coat is not designed for people who are comfortable where they are. It is designed for those who desire to be stretched. Clearly God was stretching me. He was stretching me beyond the familiar and causing me to revisit old norms and create new ones.

As you read this book, perhaps you are being stretched. It is not an easy process. It requires tremendous resolve and dedication to the purposes of God upon your life. Joseph was being prepared to lead his people to their destiny. I remember distinctly coming to an interesting crossroads. Was I going to impress preachers or influence God's people? So often we seek affirmation from colleagues. We want to be accepted within certain circles. I wanted to be embraced. I wanted them to invite me to preach. I wanted them to look at me and be proud of what God was doing in my ministry. What I soon realized is that as long as I had that coat on and had shifted to consecration, my expectations were unrealistic.

One of the most valuable lessons you will learn as you shift from being chosen to being consecrated is the importance of identity and character. When you have been set apart, you must be sure about who you are in God and exude confidence in the call upon your life. What I discovered is that often my uncertainty generated skepticism in those who would eventually follow me. As a leader, you must be very sure that your identity is shaped by God and not by other factors that could dilute God's purposes for your life.

As a young minister, I was highly impressionable. I became a colleague of various ministers. Although there is nothing wrong with emulating certain aspects of others, it is unhealthy and unwise to lose sight of yourself in the process. My identity was being smothered by emulating others. All leaders have to carve out their own identities amid the influences around them. Joseph was clear about his identity. He did not allow the coat to define him; rather, he wore the coat confidently assured of his own self-worth and identity. The coat was confirmation of his father's belief in his identity and a reminder that he had the character necessary to wear it. Character is behavior on display, and many leaders must realize that wearing the coat demands strong character.

Joseph also had his flaws; many of them will be discussed later in this book. His character, however, is never in question. All leaders learn valuable lessons from mistakes; those mistakes test our character and steer it either toward righteousness or away from it. At some point as a leader, you have to realize that you are different. You will realize that there is a greater demand upon you from God, and I remember this moment for me early in my ministry.

When the Mount Zion Church was transitioning from the Gentry Center to the current Old Hickory location, I began to see a shift in how I was being perceived as a leader. For some time, the elder members of the church wanted a new facility but did not have the resources to make it come to fruition. It was a dream realized for many of them when we were able to build and occupy our Old Hickory location. What this move did was redefine their perception of me as their leader. Allow me to put this in context.

When I first got to Mount Zion, I was a young seminary student who eventually became their pastor at age twenty-four. They saw me as a young, energetic "little boy." This is the title many of them gave me. They used that term affectionately when referring to me, and I truly was their little boy—many of them became like mothers and fathers to me. I began the embryonic stages of my ministry in their midst. It was incredibly difficult for them to see me as a leader in terms of casting vision and giving directives. They saw me as a little boy doing his best to grow God's church. When the church began to grow and we were able to acquire the millions necessary to build and occupy a new facility, there was a shift in how they viewed me.

I went from God's chosen to God's consecrated right before their eyes. I am convinced that when people see your coat they may admire you, but when they see that you wear it well, they respect you. It was important that they understood that I was not caught up in the trappings of leadership but that I understood there was incredible stewardship involved. One of the mistakes I made early on was attempting to get them to respect me before I had earned it. The coat is an indicator that your heavenly Father sees potential in you. You must wear it and allow others the time to evolve into respecting you.

John Whitmore captures the essence of the evolution from admiration to respect in his description of the qualities of leadership. Whitmore writes, "Leaders of the future should be obliged to embark on their own journey of personal development to earn the title leader, in my opinion. We live in a world that seeks, even expects, instant gratification, but leadership qualities come neither quickly nor cheaply."[5] In 1992, Mount Zion extended me an invitation to become their pastor. But just because I held that position did not mean I had earned enough respect to be fully released according to my vision. Perhaps you are a young professional on a new job and your position is one of great responsibility. It is important that you don't allow the coat of your title to go to your head. Wear your coat with integrity and realize that it may take some time before those you are leading actually embrace you as their leader. You shift from being **a** leader to being **their** leader.

I am convinced that this is why consecration is so important. There is something that makes you unique. You are not like everyone else, striving to achieve goals of self-promotion. You realize that God has been at work in your life and that He has given you this coat in order that you might do something bigger. What consecration does is shift us to God's purposes for our lives. We have to be mindful that we don't allow ourselves to become consumed in reading our own press.

I remember once hearing God's voice as clearly as I have ever heard it. I was standing in the World Baptist Center in 1997. It was a year when many thought our ministry would never fill this massive place to capacity. When thousands came from across the city, it became apparent in that hour that God had shifted us from being chosen to being truly set apart for something much bigger. I stood at the altar thanking God for what He was doing, yet within me was a sense of pride and misguided confidence. I thought this would propel me to a place of respect and not just admiration in the eyes of those elder members. God said to me, "You are insignificant to the process; this is for my glory." I never will forget that moment because it refocused me on what was important: not the coat itself but the purposes for which I had been entrusted to wear it.

When you are chosen and shift to a consecrated leader wearing the mantle of authority, you must embrace your uniqueness. One of the main tenets of your uniqueness is realizing that whatever happens during the fulfillment of divine purpose should not be taken personally. I took every criticism personally. I lost many nights of sleep because I wore the coat too tight. You must wear the coat comfortably, loosely. What I mean by this is that although you have been called to do something great, **it's about God and not about you**. I've seen leaders fail horribly wearing the coat too tight. They lose sight of the call and consequently miss the beauty of consecration.

THE FIRST CALL IS ALWAYS TO GOD

When God consecrates us, He literally calls us to Himself first. We are always answerable to God first because we are under His authority. We often get caught up in doing the work of God but have no intimate connection to God. You can work for a company and do good work and never know the supervisor. God does not operate that way. He wants you to have relationship with Him. He will allow certain things to happen in your life to assure that you maintain an intimate relationship with Him. Think about this for a moment. If a person said, "Come here. I want to give you something," you would want to come close to the person to receive it. The first call is always to God and then to the assignment. When you wear the coat too tightly, you are so focused on the assignment that you leave your relationship with God to chance. What God is calling you to will require a deeper relationship with Him. This shift will require you to know God for yourself. Joseph had a relationship with his father, and you and I must have a relationship with our heavenly Father.

Let me say more about this. As I began to face the numerous challenges associated with transitioning a church, I realized then the significance of personal spiritual development. Often, leaders take for granted this area without realizing that it is an essential step to where they are going. You have to take time and build yourself up spiritually so that you have the strength and focus to fulfill your assignment. Jesus spent thirty years building Himself up for a three-year public ministry. When you consider the magnitude of your assignment, you cannot settle for a mediocre relationship with God. Those of us who pour out also need to be poured into or we become empty. Empty is when you are unable to receive revelation. It is when you have nothing to pour out to the people you lead and as a consequence you produce subpar work. God has not called you to average. Average is being on top of the bottom. He has called you to be on top of the top.

KEEPING UP WITH BUT NOT RUNNING AHEAD OF GOD

Shifting from chosen to consecrated definitely involves character, embracing your true identity, spiritual development, and intimacy with God, but also patience. This was a huge lesson for me. When you know that God has chosen you for something great, there is a tendency to get ahead of God and direct the affairs of your life. Remember that what God has chosen you for was done before the foundations of the world. The fact that He waited until now to tell you does not mean that today is the release date into the fulfillment of that purpose. God is a strategist, and He providentially allows things to happen at the right time in order to propel us into our assignment. What we will discover in the life of Joseph is that things will progress in their own time. All he has to do is walk with integrity.

I meet so many people who shift before God does. They are so anxious to see things manifest that they take it upon themselves to act out of sync with God. The Bible says in Psalm 37:23, "The steps of a good man are ordered by the LORD." This means whatever God allows is designed to take you one step closer to your destiny. Every experience no matter how joyful or painful is a part of the process. Patience is a true act of trust. It indicates that you trust God. I know you are excited and ready to move forward, but God knows the exact time, and you must trust Him. **Often, what looks like stagnation is really a divine delay.** I fly often, and what I have learned over the years is never to complain if my plane is delayed. I see people frantic and argumentative when the announcement comes that there has been a delay in departure. What I realize is that the delay is there to prevent my demise. If I boarded a plane with a mechanical problem that was not fixed, it would certainly crash, and I'd miss a lot more than my destination. I've learned to sit in the concourse and be productive until boarding comes.

No matter how long it takes, I patiently wait because I know the mechanics are working to ensure I arrive at my destination. God is at work behind the scenes navigating circumstances so that you reach your destination. Be patient and know He has a plan to get you where He has ordained you to be.

CONCLUSION

As you move through this first shift, remember that it is God's desire to separate you to Himself for purposes greater than you could ever imagine. As you follow Joseph's life, you will discover similarities that confirm you have been chosen for greatness. There is a leader in you with the capacity to shift during specific seasons to remain relevant, effective, and fruitful. The shifts will happen with or without you. The lesson is to come alongside God and join what He has already begun. This is how the journey begins.

CHAPTER 2

FROM NEARSIGHTED TO FARSIGHTED

MOVING FROM ME TO WE

The book of Genesis tells us that Joseph was a dreamer. He had the ability to dream and interpret dreams; however, he, like many of us, thought those dreams were for his own self-aggrandizement. Joseph had to learn to see beyond himself and visualize the bigger picture God intended for both him and his people. Kirk Byron Jones, in his book *Holy Play,* introduces the idea that dreams allow you to construct new truths and go beyond your "known perceptions and preference": "What dreams inspire in you from a place that knows no limitation will always surpass the offerings of your restricted rational reasoning."[1] Perhaps you are a dreamer and you possess this amazing vision about God's desire for your future. It's important to know that you must realize that when God gives us vision, we should never be nearsighted and limited as to how it affects us; rather, we must be farsighted and know the implications of the vision for numerous others.

This shift is very significant for leaders because it moves from "me" to "we." Everyone has personal desires and goals, but God always uses us for purposes greater than ourselves. I remember when I first realized I was a dreamer or visionary.

I had just completed divinity school at Vanderbilt, and God allowed me to experience something I never shall forget. I was blinded in the Spirit like Saul on the Damascus road, and when my eyes were opened, I saw my reality differently. I was seeing things. I would be in the car with people and they would see cow pastures, but I would see condominiums. They would see dilapidated buildings and I saw strip malls. It was not long before I realized nobody was seeing what I was seeing. I'm originally from Louisiana, and when people know that and then you declare you are seeing things, they think you are seeing voodoo or hoodoo. As comical as that might sound, I knew I was seeing what God was showing me. I eventually realized what was happening. God said to me that this was vision. He told me that He could not give it to me when He first called me but that He gave it to me when He saw me make an investment in my assignment. When you wear the coat right, you can be entrusted with vision.

When you have vision, it must be placed under divine supervision. If it is placed there, you will have provision and no division. By the way, you will never have a vision you can afford. If you see things and they are within your capacity to afford, they are not vision. Vision is always beyond your budget; it is always beyond your bank account. I tell people all the time that if it is God's will, it's God's bill. Perhaps you are reading this book and you know God has shown you something amazing, yet you are struggling to embrace it because you don't have the resources to see it through. Remember that God is a God of provision, especially where there is vision.

Joseph dreamed dreams, and God revealed to him his future. God reveals to him how he would be over his brothers and lead his people, but Joseph makes the mistake of allowing his ego to limit the true scope of his dreams. If you are going to shift, you must be willing to embrace the fact that God's vision for your life has corporate implications; a leader's vision is meant for the greater good of God's people. When I saw those things God revealed to me, they were larger than me, but they weren't just for me. I had to learn that the greatest threat to a dreamer is hubris or pride. The Bible says in Proverbs 16:18, "Pride goes before destruction and a haughty spirit before a fall" (ESV). There is a tendency for any leader to allow arrogance and pride to invade his or her life and corrupt the intent of the visions that God gives to him or her. C. J. Mahaney provides the paramount insight of what effects pride can have on those in leadership positions. He says that "pride takes innumerable forms, but has only one end: self-glorification. That's the motive and ultimate purpose of pride—to rob God of the legitimate glory and to pursue self-glorification contending for supremacy with him."[2] Each day, you and I have to guard against pride. Joseph was young and excited about the dreams God had given to him; however, he, like so many of us, allowed those things to trap him in his narcissism.

When God gave me visions, I was quite young. I was in my early twenties, and I was being entrusted with amazing revelations from God. When you are a young leader, you often are guilty of getting the big head. I was no different. I allowed myself to become prideful and ultimately got side tracked. I know and understand more than ever what the Apostle Paul experienced in 2 Corinthians 12:1-10. This is what he says:

> It is not expedient for me doubtless to glory. I will come to visions and revelations of the Lord. I knew a man in Christ above fourteen years ago, (whether in the body, I cannot tell; or whether out of the body, I cannot tell: God knoweth;) such an one caught up to the third heaven. And I knew such a man, (whether in the body, or out of the body, I cannot tell: God knoweth;) How that he was caught up into paradise, and heard unspeakable words, which it is not lawful for a man to

utter. Of such a one will I glory: yet of myself I will not glory, but in mine infirmities. For though I would desire to glory, I shall not be a fool; for I will say the truth: but now I forbear, lest any man should think of me above that which he seeth me to be, or that he heareth of me. And lest I should be exalted above measure through the abundance of the revelations, there was given to me a thorn in the flesh, the messenger of Satan to buffet me, lest I should be exalted above measure. For this thing I besought the Lord thrice, that it might depart from me. And he said unto me, My grace is sufficient for thee: for my strength is made perfect in weakness. Most gladly therefore will I rather glory in my infirmities, that the power of Christ may rest upon me. Therefore I take pleasure in infirmities, in reproaches, in necessities, in persecutions, in distresses for Christ's sake: for when I am weak, then am I strong.

I believe that God allows us all to experience situations at strategic times in our lives to bring us to a place of humility. In order to recognize the vastness of the vision and to fully embrace it beyond your own agenda, you must be humbled. We are only the vessels by which God blesses His people. You cannot be so nearsighted or focused on yourself that the vision stops with you. Zora Neale Hurston, in her literary work *Moses, Man of the Mountain,* provides a fictional retelling of the Exodus story that depicts the foresight Moses had by selecting Joshua as his successor to lead Israel into their land of promise. Interestingly, Hurston also captures the nearsightedness that others within an organization can have concerning leadership succession by expressing Joshua's hesitancy to take the reins of such a powerful movement. Her fictional character Joshua says to Moses, "You must live and cross over and govern us till the rod just naturally falls out of your hand. Everybody in Israel is expecting you to be there."[3] Looking past Israel's resistance to change, Moses sees far beyond the immediacy of crossing over the Jordan and knows that new vigor and fresh insight is needed to carry the vision further than the now. Hurston uses the character of Moses and the Exodus narrative to portray a paradigmatic shift that occurs when the visionary's eyes become dim and a new leader is needed. When this shift occurs, it is essential for the leader of a major movement to possess the prophetic insight to foresee the need to lead out by appointing a successor and not die out, allowing the vision to end.

THE VISION MUST OUTLIVE THE LEADER

One of the most important lessons any leader can learn is that vision should never die with her or him. If a vision dies with her or him, it is because she or he is nearsighted and not farsighted. When God gives vision, that vision must outlive the visionary. So often, we see great institutions and churches crumble through transition because the vision was so centered on the leader. An effective leader must be willing to help people realize that it's not about him or her. A great leader defers the glory to God and encourages others to embrace the vision beyond the life of the visionary.

It's a sad reality, but I've seen many businesses, organizations, and churches fail to progress beyond a particular leader. **We as leaders have a responsibility to cast vision that entails corporate ownership.** I have had church people ask me, "When are *you guys* going to build a school?" or "When are *you guys* going to open a day care?" These people who attend church every Sunday have not embraced the vision as something that they own, speaking of it rather as something that they passively accept, as though they had no relationship to it. You can tell when people feel engaged in the vision and see themselves as a part of it, because their language changes. A successful leader learns early that if the vision is ever going to come to fruition, the people the vision impacts must be participants and not spectators as it unfolds.

Here is a strategy of casting vision. It is something that came through trial and error but has been successful for several years. I am convinced that these principles will work regardless of your organization or business. I call them the 5 Cs of vision casting.

THE 5 CS OF VISION CASTING

1. Clarity

The prophet Habakkuk said,

And the LORD answered me, and said, "Write the vision, and make *it* plain upon tables, that he may run that readeth it. For the vision *is* yet for an appointed time, but at the end it shall speak, and not lie: though it tarry, wait for it; because it will surely come, it will not tarry." (Hab. 2:2-3)

What I discovered about vision is that those who receive it must be very clear about what the Lord is saying. There is no room for error or redaction. What God reveals to you is so significant that you must write it down as He gives it to you. God never releases vision that is complicated. Vision is always plain to the visionary and must be made plain to the participants. When you are a dreamer, you take great care in making sure those who will steward the vision understand what God is revealing. Again, this is why it's important for leaders to release hubris so that individual agendas do not taint the integrity of the vision.

Every vision God has given me has been very precise and clear. It was my responsibility not to assume that it would be as clear to others. I had to take great care in articulating the vision and providing space for people to ask questions, so that we would all move forward together with clarity. I've seen leaders cast vision and say, "That's it; let's do it!" This approach leaves many people confused, disillusioned, and maybe a little angry, because they are being told to support what they don't completely understand. I am convinced that I would have avoided many contentious situations in Mount Zion with the leadership early on had I taken the time and made certain that everyone clearly understood. You cannot assume that they will understand the intricate details, but they should understand the direction the vision is taking them. When you board a plane, you may not understand the details of flying a plane or the flight pattern, but you do have a clear indicator of your destination. It's called a boarding pass. On it there is a flight number, which assures you that you are on the right plane. There is a seat assignment, which tells you where to sit. There is time of departure, which gives you the expected time to take off. There is a destination, which gives you full assurance of where you are going. When God gives vision, the vision caster must be just as clear. God is not the author of confusion. Your vision will never advance if there is confusion in the organization.

2. Contextualization

Contextualization is the process of evaluating how things fit in the larger scheme of things where they are assigned. God always gives vision for a place. Regardless of how large or small that place might be, it must be taken into consideration. There is a history there. There is a certain ethos present. I've seen many young leaders impose vision upon an organization without studying the context. For example, I had to take into consideration that Mount Zion was more than 125 years old when I became pastor. The historical context of the church was significant, because it allowed me to put into perspective the responses of people. There were children and grandchildren of great leaders in the church who had influenced the community in positive ways and left indelible impressions. It was essential that the vision be sensitive to how it would affect that history and not eradicate the extraordinary accomplishments of its elders.

The vision that God gives Joseph was for Egypt, but its reach extended far beyond the context of this particular country. The vision God gave me would manifest in Nashville. Though the vision is global, its origin and launching pad is in a context that I had to study, affirm, and engage. Although Joseph was not a native of Egypt, he was called to be a great visionary for the Egyptian people. No doubt he studied the culture, learned to speak the same language, and developed an understanding of the ethos so that his vision could make the shift from revelation to manifestation. You cannot be successful as a leader or businessperson if you don't understand the context where the vision will come to fruition. You can have a great vision for a business and dream great dreams about how it should come to pass, but that business must be birthed in a community, and if you do not spend time understanding the people in that community, the history of it, and the trends within it, your product will never move and you will fail. Never cast vision without studying the context.

3. Collaboration

The third area is collaboration. This is an essential element of vision casting for any leader. If you are to be successful, you cannot operate in your own silo. One of the things I experienced early on was the temptation of doing it all by myself. I honestly felt that if God gave me a vision, I just needed to tell the people what it was and we would move forward. What I've learned through trial and error is that you need to surround yourself with capable people who can help bring the vision from theory to practice. When you work in collaboration, the vision has a better chance of being fulfilled. We often think that allowing people to chime in on the vision is a threat to the vision itself or will dilute the integrity of the vision. What I've learned is that when there are capable and resourceful people in the room, the vision is enhanced.

Mount Zion has an executive ministry team with the key leaders of each department or ministry. We work weekly in collaboration around the vision. When I share what God is leading us to do, I have folks at the table who represent every aspect of the ministry. There are things brought to my attention that I never would have considered had they not been at the table. For example, when I discuss the vision of a particular program, the leader of family ministries might ask questions about child care or bring to my attention the school testing schedule and how it might impact the date I'm considering. There is never a refuting of the vision but rather insight into how the vision can work best as we all work together. I'll give you another example.

My wife, who is a physician, has a great passion for underserved communities and making sure certain resources are distributed in those areas. To this end, she founded a nonprofit called Full Circle Healthy Community Coalition. The purpose of Full Circle is to identify health resources and connect those resources to people in their communities. She developed a website that allows people to locate what health resource they need to find and where it is located within their community. It all came about through collaboration. There were organizations doing amazing things in the community, but nobody knew about them in the faith community. They were struggling to get people involved and were at a crossroads. Many of them were working in their own silos and had grants to serve the community but could not get folks to come out. My wife saw this as an opportunity to manifest a true vision of collaboration. She encouraged them to continue doing the great programs but wanted them to use the connector website to reach the people they were desperately trying to reach. Now, through collaboration, their vision is manifesting, and her vision of connecting people to resources and resources to people has taken on a life of its own.

As a successful vision caster, you cannot be the smartest person in the room. You must be willing to surround yourself with brilliant, forward-thinking people who understand where you are going and who help you get there efficiently.

4. Counting the Costs

The Bible says in Luke 14:28, "For which of you, intending to build a tower, sitteth not down first, and counteth the cost, whether he have sufficient to finish it?" Counting the cost is an important part of casting vision, because this gives you an opportunity to assess strategy and timing. The vision is for an appointed time. As I mentioned earlier, when God gives vision, He gives provision. That provision comes through proper planning. We often want it to fall out of the sky, but if you don't have a plan to fund the vision, it will lie dormant for years. I've seen churches have building fund programs for more than twenty years with no sign of construction in view. If you are to be effective in casting your vision, you must assess the cost and develop a plan that gets you where you are trying to go. When we launched our building fund years ago, we put a plan in place called Project 2000. This plan served as a gauge and helped us determine when we would be able to break ground on the facility. Each member was asked to give $10 above tithes and offering to the vision, and those funds were earmarked for the building. Through the faithful support of these efforts, we were able to start construction on a $20 million facility in 1999. In 2003, we acquired another facility located across town; this purchase allowed us to have worship as well as retail space for $7 million. Because our $10-a-week plan was so successful, we continued it, and we were able to pay that facility off in three years.

We are now one church in three locations and launching the next phase of the vision. Our goal is to do it with 80 percent of the money in hand and raise the remainder as we build. We also plan to eradicate all existing debt prior to starting the new project. This is counting the cost. Though the vision is ambitious and we trust God completely, we still have to use wisdom and be good stewards of our finances. I've seen many churches and organizations move too quickly and not count the cost. Many of them have experienced foreclosures and financial turmoil. The Bible says that things should be done decently and in order. Our mantra is intelligent fiscal management. This means studying the trends and knowing when to engage the vision. There is a delicate balance between stretching people's faith and overstretching reality. As a leader, I always want to be sensitive to the financial realities of the people I serve, while at the same time challenging them to operate in a level of faith to see vision come to pass. If you find yourself having desperation offerings and using gimmicks to convince people to support vision, you did not properly count the costs.

5. Christocentricity

The fifth area of vision casting is Christocentricity, meaning that the vision has, at its core, values that are Christian. God will never give a vision that does not promote Christian principles and call attention to Christ. As I mentioned earlier, my encounter with God reminded me of my insignificance to the process. It was truly for His glory. When the vision centers on Christ and no other personality, it is positioned for longevity. God will not share His glory with any of us. Vision that is nearsighted attempts to place personal ego in the way of God's glory. I use ego acrostically to mean Easing God Out. Many people have leadercentric or personalitycentric visions, and when those people are not long in place, the vision struggles to survive.

One of the most powerful examples of Christocentric vision casting I have experienced is that of Bishop Paul S. Morton. He is the founder and presiding bishop of the Full Gospel Baptist Church Fellowship and has served in this capacity for more than twenty years. Bishop Morton has maintained from the beginning that this vision was a God movement and not about him. In 2010, Bishop Morton announced publicly that he will step down as presiding bishop in 2015 and allow a successor to take over the movement while he serves under the new leader. Needless to say, this was an unprecedented decision because many leaders who begin organizations or lead them die in the role. Bishop Morton is a farseeing visionary who recognizes that the future belongs to those who are open to positive change. He has given us a powerful paradigm of Christocentric vision by allowing someone else to function in his position so that the vision God has given him might remain relevant in generations to come. He refuses to let Full Gospel die, especially because of his own ego.

When it's about Christ, you have to be willing to get yourself out of the way. We often want God to join us in what we are doing, rather than find out what He is doing and join Him in His work. There is a song Bishop Morton sings called "Don't Do It without Me," in which the narrator asks to be a part of God's work, no matter what it is. I believe that should be our desire. When vision is Christ centered, we are mindful of two things in particular. The first is that His people are always edified. Vision makes people better. It moves people from despair to destiny. It shifts people from oppression to liberation. Any vision that oppresses or stifles people is not Christ centered. It is nearsighted and unfruitful. Secondly, God is always glorified. Within the vision, the outcome is always attributed to God. No one takes the credit, but collectively there is a common acknowledgment of the God who initiated the vision and brought it to pass. When this happens, the vision is certain to survive.

Raymond Rasberry wrote a song entitled "Only What You Do for Christ Will Last." He says, "You may build great cathedrals large or small, ... but only what you do for Christ will last."[4]

VISIONS SOLVE PROBLEMS

The dream that Joseph had was huge. It was something that would change the world. Within every visionary there is something that God wants to accomplish. I strongly believe that every vision solves a problem. Every dream is a solution to a problem God wants solved. We are often called not to places of ease and comfort but to places of conflict in order that God's will might manifest through us. Those who seek the easy path will never be entrusted with great vision. I remember the particular problem my vision revealed to me.

In Nashville there were so many churches, but few at the time were able to attract college students. When students are in college, they are at a pivotal age, because college challenges their minds and they are exposed to many new experiences that either draw them closer to God or drive them further away. If there is no spiritual reinforcement, students lose spiritual focus and often stop attending church. After college, many continue this trend in the workforce. God gave me a vision to minister to this demographic, but there was a problem and nobody knew how to solve it. One of the things I could not do was listen to the naysayers, and there were many of them. They told me that it was fruitless to invest in college students and that I would never build a ministry on a transient population. Others said that college students would never be serious about ministry because students use college as a retreat from the rules and values of their parents in an effort to experiment and engage in self-discovery. If I had listened to the negative reports, my vision would still be just a vision and not manifesting today. I immediately implemented the 5 Cs, and we began canvassing the university campuses engaging the students. We identified a need and began to implement creative ministries to meet them. One need was transportation, so we began sending buses to the campuses. This was a real blessing because many students who never would have attended church now had a way to get there. Secondly, we recognized that many of them would miss lunch if they came to church. The student cafeteria closed at 1:00 p.m. for lunch, so that meant missing a meal. When you are a college student, that's a big deal. We counted the costs and deemed it necessary to provide free meals for the students. When we did this, the college ministry grew beyond our expectations. Hundreds, then thousands of students began to attend our church on a regular basis.

Today there are more than three thousand students who attend our church from eight different campuses. We continue to invest because the vision demands that we do. There is no greater reward than traveling across the country and seeing students who were affected by the ministry of Mount Zion, still mindful and grateful of how the church ministered to their spiritual and physical needs while in college. Many of them stay connected virtually to our ministry and give to the ongoing vision so that other students can benefit from the blessing they received. That's how vision works. It always solves a problem. Just as Joseph's vision solved a problem of famine in Egypt, your vision is designed to solve a problem in the context where you are.

OUT OF THE BOX

One of the most interesting things I have discovered about dreamers or visionaries is that they are out-of-the-box thinkers. When you have vision, it always stretches you beyond your capacity and allows you to trust in God's ability to make it happen. There are some people who have small vision, and that is problematic in light of the fact that we have a big God. God gives big vision. I've heard it said on numerous occasions that "you can't be big if little has you." This is a true statement that reveals a powerful lesson. The reason many people have small vision is that they have never been exposed. I believe vision is exposure.

God allows you to be exposed to things that can inspire and ignite passion in you to do much greater than where you are. This is why it's important to connect with people who are doing what you desire to do. One of the saddest realities I experienced was when others leaders were criticizing the growth of Mount Zion rather than inquiring about why we were growing. If two fishermen are in the water and one is catching fish and the other is not, it makes sense to ask what tackle the successful fisherman is using. We often allow jealousy and other factors to prevent us from gleaning powerful lessons from others.

From early in my ministry, I made it a point to take our church on trips to expose them to where God was taking us. If people don't see more, they will never aspire to more. I made it a point to attend every conference I could that would expand my thinking and sharpen my vision. I wanted to rub shoulders and learn from folks who had traveled the path I was embarking upon. Just because God gave you a unique vision does not mean someone else has not received a similar vision in another context. You don't have to always reinvent the wheel. You can learn great lessons from others. I've learned things to do and not to do by putting myself in a position to be taught.

CONCLUSION

Every successful dreamer must be farsighted. The dream is not just about you; it's about so many other people. Their destiny is tied to how you steward the vision. People who have never been born yet will benefit from your obedience to vision. Generations to come would walk into Egypt as privileged guests because of Joseph and the manifestation of his dream. When you understand the significance and scope of your dream/vision, you will make it a point to always walk in wisdom concerning it. Self-aggrandizement and self-promotion around God's vision is a recipe for disaster. There has to be an intentional effort to think beyond yourself and embrace true purposes of the vision.

Little did I realize that more than twenty years later the vision God gave me would influence so many lives. When I see the fruit of the vision, I recognize that it is so much larger than I am. One of the most amazing things about vision is that it is contagious. I've seen people duplicate the vision in their businesses and organizations. I've had pastors who came out of Mount Zion implement the same principles in their own ministry.

Vision duplicates itself. This is what Jesus did with the disciples. He duplicated Himself. His ministry and vision was so powerful that He assured them in John 14 that they would do even greater works than they had seen him do. The student should always take the vision further than the teacher. That's how vision lives on from generation to generation. There is no greater reward than watching others benefit from what God revealed first to you.

All of Egypt will be blessed because of Joseph. We are mindful of our investments and make critical financial decisions about our future because of Joseph's vision. There is something within you that will change the world. You have to be willing to be farsighted rather than nearsighted. There are enough nearsighted people on the planet. You are unique. You have a powerful assignment that will influence ages to come.

CHAPTER 3

FROM OPPOSITION TO OPPORTUNITY

By now if you are reading this book and have embraced the fact that you are a dreamer or visionary, this next shift comes as no surprise. One of the common realities of every visionary is opposition. Every leader has to learn how to deal with conflict and opposition if he or she is going to be successful. Leaders have to find ways to get buy-in from others despite inevitable envy and jealousy. This chapter will help you understand the sources of opposition and how to effectively deal with them.

OPPOSITION ROOTED IN JEALOUSY

Joseph experienced jealousy from his own brothers. You should not be surprised that much of your opposition will come from familiar people and places. When Joseph received the coat from his father and informed his brothers about his dreams, they became envious of him. This is one of the most difficult seasons to navigate through. Those who oppose you do so for a variety of reasons; yet, in order to see your vision come to fruition, you must shift from opposition to opportunity. You cannot get stuck being focused on the opposition so much that you miss the big picture. I always tell people that **you can't**

37

focus on what you are going through; rather, you must focus on what you are going to.

Opposition to your destiny has its foundation in spiritual warfare. The Devil wants to prevent God's purposes from coming to pass in your life. He uses opposition rooted in jealousy to do it. I discovered some painful lessons in the early years of my ministry. The first lesson was that some people were opposing me because what God was doing in my life exposed their unmet expectations. When the church began to experience growth and much of that growing population was young people, people hurled labels and titles that were inconsistent with who we really were as a church. We were called cult, fad, pop culture, fly-by-night, to name a few. These names were given to us by jealous people who had the same opportunity to attract youth and young adults and were frustrated that they did not succeed and we did. You have to embrace the fact that often your enemies' jealousy has little to do with you and more to do with their own insecurities. Jealousy will cause people to degrade you and label you in order to minimize their own failures. Some people scream at the darkness rather than light a candle. Because you have chosen to take advantage of this season and walk in it, you have positioned yourself for greater things.

MISUNDERSTOOD MOTIVES

As a leader establishing a new paradigm, you must recognize that creating this new shift will not be free of opposition or despair. The opposition must be faced head on, despite the feelings of discouragement, disappointment, and despair; the courage to create must be the overarching inspiration to overshadow feelings contradictory to your destiny. In his book *The Courage to Create*, Rollo May says, "Kierkegaard and

Nietzsche and Camus and Sartre have proclaimed that courage is not the absence of despair; it is rather, the capacity to move ahead in spite of despair."[1]

Jesus experienced opposition from the community that He engaged. They labeled Him and ultimately crucified Him. I found great comfort in knowing that opposition was not some strange thing that had happened to just me, but it truly was what Peter declares when he talked about the fiery trial that comes to try us. Moses experienced opposition; Nehemiah experienced opposition. Throughout the entire Bible, there are countless examples of leaders fulfilling their assignments and simultaneously experiencing opposition.

The opposition I experienced outside the church was the easiest to handle. I felt that those folks didn't know me. They had no context for understanding my vision and my passion for my assignment. It was relatively easy to deal with. What became most difficult was the opposition I experienced within the church. It came from those I had invested in and whom I truly believed understood my heart. What I did not expect were a series of issues to show themselves. When your opposition is from outside, it's easier to understand the source. When it's from within, it becomes more complicated. What I discovered was that many people were opposing me because they misunderstood my motives. When people question your motives, it creates a great deal of cynicism and hesitancy. Although I was their pastor, it would take some time before they knew my heart.

I've learned that **people won't trust your hand until they see your heart**. In other words, they will not completely support your efforts until they are certain your motives are coming from a good place. Ronald Heifetz writes concerning the "intimate understanding" Gandhi had of the people he was called to lead: "For Gandhi to challenge these ways of life demanded knowing them deeply, by experience, by operating close to the frontline, where the stakeholders of India lived. Gandhi could speak to people, to their hopes, fears, weaknesses, and needs because he spent time knowing them."[2] Likewise, it was very important to me as a leader to get buy-in from those I led. I had to be intentional about developing relationships and listening to people's fears and expectations. I carved out time and took folks to lunch so that they would not define me based on their perceptions or the perceptions of others. I wanted them to know me. I wanted them to know that I was passionate about creating a caring and innovative community of faith that would literally change the landscape of the church in our city. Not only did I develop relationships, but I also held small group meetings with members of the church to hear their concerns and garner support for the direction God was taking the church.

So many leaders fail because their motives are misunderstood. You cannot draw a line in the sand and say, "I don't care what people think about me." You have to care. These are the people who are instrumental in making the vision God gave you come to fruition. Although their opposition is painful, you must remember the fact that it could be rooted in misunderstood motives.

REDISTRIBUTION OF POWER

Another area that spawns opposition is the redistribution of power. This is huge because there are people who hold tremendous influence in the church. Sometimes power can be seductive and create a mind-set where people rest the case on their point of view. Robert Greene in *The Concise Art of Seduction* speaks to the seductive nature attached to power: "The siren call of seduction is irresistible because power is irresistible, and nothing will bring you more power in the modern world than the ability to seduce."[3] This was very apparent in many of the meetings at Mount Zion. Some people were vocal in their opposition. Persons in these positions of power have given in to the seductive nature of power and have believed their overpowering voice was needed to speak on behalf of the people in their sphere of influence.

When I first shifted my board of deacons to a deacon ministry format, it created a real stir. In the Baptist Church, deacon boards carry tremendous power and influence and often have the power to approve things on behalf of the church. The vision God gave me was to get back to the biblical definition of what it meant to be a deacon. Consequently, there were no legislative powers but rather spiritual responsibilities of praying for the sick, supporting members in crisis, and serving Communion. This shift was extremely difficult for some because they had held power for years, and I was developing an infrastructure that moved away from chairpersons to a team leadership approach. Not surprisingly, this redistribution of power generated major opposition. There were times the church business was at a standstill because some leaders would not come alongside certain projects. I've been an advocate of shared leadership for years. I feel that when people work in teams rather than hierarchically, things get done more efficiently. I knew that if this was going to work, I had to get buy-in.

So I had strategic meetings with those individuals who were directly affected by this shift and explained to them the reason for this new approach. I listened to their concerns and reassured them that they would be a part of the leadership teams going forward. People want to feel connected to progress and know that their opinion matters in the scheme of things. This revealed to me what I believe was the most serious reason for opposition—exclusion. People who were strongest in their opposition were experiencing feelings of being left out. There was a sense that the church was moving forward without them.

Often, when the wheels of progress are moving, there is a tendency to become insensitive to the things they run over. Without meaning to, we were running over a lot of people, and as a result some great people were disillusioned and some were running away. People who had been in that church all their lives were choosing to stay home because they felt excluded. If you don't get buy-in from people like this, you can never accomplish vision. When this happened to me, I realized that I had to look differently at the opposition and make the shift to opportunities. There were some amazing opportunities, and it was important for me to maximize the moment.

OPPORTUNITIES FOR TEACHING

One of those opportunities was teaching. I used this opposition as a teaching moment and spent months educating the church on this biblical blueprint and model of ministry. I didn't realize the spiritual assumptions people had and the long-held theological positions they protected, many of which were nonbiblical. There were traditions that had greater influence than biblical truths. They were loyal to information they had "caught" rather than were taught. Ways of doing things that had been passed down for years without any biblical context were motivating decisions. I first had to "unteach." Carter G. Woodson, in *The Mis-Education of the Negro*, said,

> Philosophers have long conceded, however, that every man has two educators: that which is given to him, and the other that which he gives himself. Of the two kinds the latter is by far the more desirable. Indeed all that is most worthy in man he must work out and conquer for himself. It is that which constitutes our real and best nourishment. What we

are merely taught seldom nourishes the mind like that which we teach ourselves.[4]

I was very intentional in Bible study, teaching fundamental biblical truths and creating opportunities for people to open their Bibles and see for themselves. People should come to truth on their own. I often say that revelation is the apprehension of truth at your own level of comprehension. One plus one equals two. Some people get that revelation in the first grade, but for others, it takes a little longer. The truth is there, but we arrive at it based on our individual level of comprehension. If you are not willing to teach and orient people to new ways of doing things, they will oppose it based on their loyalty to what they are used to.

This meant that I had to be present in order to impart into the lives of the people who would support the vision. I restructured my schedule to reflect my priorities. I know a lot of great preachers who pastor, but their ministries never experience growth and they are always in conflict. I strongly believe their focus is wrong. They may travel all over the country and world and never be at home taking part in the life of their church. My church knows where I will be on 98 percent of the Sundays in the year. They know where I will be for more than 90 percent of the Wednesday night Bible studies. They see my investment in their spiritual development and my concern for their growth, and they, in turn, support that vision put before them, because they have a biblical frame of reference that has been explained.

OPPORTUNITY TO REFINE THE CULTURE

The next opportunity I discovered in the opposition was in redefining the culture. Every organization has its own culture, and that culture is rooted in years of existing in a particular way.

Joseph's brothers had a certain culture, a particular way of relating with one another. Now that Joseph had dreams of greater things, that culture, his relationships, would inevitably change.

For Mount Zion, this was a great opportunity to redefine who we were to be going forth. Would we be a church that was power driven, insulated behind its four walls? Or would we be church engaged in progressive ministry that welcomed new ideas and was open to positive change? These were critical questions. We chose the latter. As a result of teaching, people became receptive to what God was doing. I witnessed a culture shift within the church where the idea of family extended beyond the biological family units that existed for generations to a spiritual family that embraced the gifts and resources of others who might not share the same historical context. This allowed us to grow multiculturally and have a greater impact on the city of Nashville. So often organizations see themselves in their own bubbles and limit their potential.

When the culture of Mount Zion began to change, our focus changed. Organizations have great pride, in some sense rightfully so. Mount Zion is a historic church with great stories of accomplishments. The opposition I experienced could not be tied to me as a leader, so I had to be intentional about taking the attention off of me. The focus had to be God's will for the organization. If Joseph's brothers truly understood what God was doing through him and how his life would save their people, they would not have harbored the jealousy they did. Often, people who are jealous of you and oppose you have no idea of the plans of God for you and for them through you. They often see what's in front of them and seldom see what's around the corner. As a leader, you must recognize this and put aside resentful feelings. Although it was difficult bearing the brunt of my enemies' opposition, I had to stay focused on what my assignment was.

In football there is a play called a timing pattern. The quarterback drops back into the pocket when the ball is shifted. The receiver must go down the field fifteen yards or so and cut across seven yards. The quarterback is prepared to throw the ball to a spot, not the receiver. The receiver must get to that spot if he is to make a completion. The defensive back or opposition is determined to prevent this play from unfolding. When the ball is shifted, the defensive back is allowed a legal hit at the line of scrimmage. The opposition gives his best hit there because he wants to disorient the receiver and throw him off his route. Whenever God releases you into something great, the enemy will always hit you with his or her hardest blow.

As you read this, you might be able to identify how this has happened in your life, how that traumatic situation occurred right after God promised you something awesome. If the receiver is great and determined to get to the "spot," he absorbs the initial blow and continues to run his route. That's what happened to you. If you are reading this book, I believe you have survived that blow of the enemy and now you must continue to run your route. As this play unfolds, the receiver's back is facing the quarterback while the ball has been released and is now in the air. The ball is headed to its destination, and the receiver will not see until he turns in that spot. This is why it's called a timing pattern, because every step has been calculated and every tactic of the opposition has been factored in. There is a belief in the huddle that no matter what, the receiver has the capacity to get to that spot. That's also the reason God has entrusted you with such a great destiny—just like Joseph. God believes in your ability to get to that spot. There are things that heaven has released in your care, but they are available to you only when you overcome the opposition and get in position to receive them.

This leader shift is essential to the manifestation of your

destiny. A lot of people allow opposition to discourage them, and they are unable to see the opportunities in their midst. Perhaps you are reading this book and you are tired and frustrated by the opposition. Perhaps the opposition has worn you down and you feel you don't have the energy to continue pushing toward your destiny. You must remember what Paul says in Galatians 6:9: "And let us not be weary in well doing: for in due season we shall reap, if we faint not." You must be willing to outlive what's trying to outlive you. Opposition will forever be a part of your life. You must be spiritually strong enough to see opportunities in the midst of it.

CONFRONTING OPPOSITION

There are things I've learned over the years about dealing with opposition. As a pastor for more than twenty years, I feel like a veteran in this area. Allow me to share them with you. The first thing I've learned is that you must be willing to confront it. Early in my pastorate, I avoided conflict and opposition. I honestly did not want to deal with it and felt it was counterproductive to what God was telling me to do. I've learned since then that avoiding opposition does not make it go away. If you neglect it, it will affect the growth of your organization. **It will not only affect it; it will also infect it.** When infection sets in, you don't experience growth; you experience swelling. Just because a thing gets big does not mean it's growing healthily. There could be infections causing swelling. If you don't face it, you can't fix it. I had to be willing to go through the tough task of addressing the opposition and working on solutions that were beneficial to the success of the organization. You can't put your head in the sand and just believe it's going to get worked out. You must develop strategies and solutions that work.

Confronting opposition does not have to create irreparable damage to the organization. If done effectively, relationships can be strengthened as enlightenment takes place. This is an opportunity to curtail assumptions and make certain that people come alongside the work God has given you to do. There is no place for passivity. Leaders who are effective are determined to address each issue carefully and not lump them into generalizations. I take every concern and criticism seriously. Let me be clear. This does not include the salacious personal attacks upon my character. I refuse to minimize what was important to the persons I served. Each concern has to be confronted and addressed and taken through the arduous process of mediating meaningful solutions.

Perhaps you have concerns in your organization that have the potential to fester and cause infections that threaten its growth. It is critical that you carve out time and deal with them. Don't make the mistake I did. I became so busy moving forward with vision that I didn't pay attention to detail. I've learned that when driving a car you can't turn without tapping the brakes. You have to pause before you make significant moves within the life of your organization and make sure that you get a pulse of how it is affecting the people involved. In his book *Leadership without Easy Answers,* Ronald Heifetz writes, "We need a view of leadership that provides a practical orientation so that we can evaluate events and action in process, without waiting for outcomes."[5] The brief pauses allow you to evaluate the organization's progress and create solutions to potential problems to avoid hindrances to the growth process.

OPPOSITION CAN BRING GROWTH

The next lesson I learned from opposition is to grow from it. When opposition comes in your life, it should change you.

Every experience should be a teaching moment. It should create opportunities for personal growth and development. Not only were the members of my congregation growing, but I was as well. What opposition does is help you get a better picture of where you are spiritually, emotionally, and relationally. My reaction to opposition initially was not ideal; therefore, I knew I needed to grow spiritually to a place where I could address it from a healthier perspective.

Often, we get a gauge of where we are spiritually when we encounter conflict and opposition. If you find yourself reverting to old behaviors, it means you have some growing up to do. I wanted to lash out and give some folks a piece of my mind. I am certain you've felt that way from time to time. Rather than descend into a place inconsistent with my Christian values, I regrouped and spent more time developing my personal prayer life. I realized that as a leader I had to set the example, and I could not allow myself to be brought down to a level beneath my convictions.

So often we get so busy doing the work of the Lord that we don't allow God time to work on us. I can truly say that opposition increased my prayer and devotional life. I also had to grow emotionally. Often, our emotions get the best of us in heated situations. What the enemy will do is use our emotions to throw us off our game. I tell the people in my church that much of our commotion is a result of losing control of our emotions through a lack of devotion. I was an emotional wreck when opposition reared its head. I naively believed that everyone would just embrace what God had given me to do. But when that did not happen, I took it personally, and it cost me a lot of sleepless nights. When you are emotionally affected, you cannot give full energy and focus to your assignment. The enemy uses this to create breaches in your vision and ultimately derail your destiny. I had to talk to mentors and counselors to work through the impact of opposition upon my mind. If you respond purely out of your emotions, you will make unwise decisions. I had to grow in this area, and opposition gave me ample opportunity to do just that.

USE OPPOSITION TO YOUR ADVANTAGE

I also learned to use the opposition to my advantage. This is so important if you are to make the shift from opposition to opportunity. Whatever lessons you learn should propel you into your destiny with greater clarity and energy. Rather than shun the opposition, I realized that it could be used to my benefit as a leader. By spending time meeting with folks who had concerns and working through those issues, I developed powerful and meaningful relationships with key stakeholders. At our church, we have now developed meaningful relationships and alliances that are essential in getting things done. Now people who felt excluded see themselves as an integral part of what is happening in the life of the church. If it were not for the opposition, the conversations never would have occurred. We moved from talking at one another to talking to one another. Now everyone embraces opposition as opportunities for growth rather than viewing them as threats to the life of the organization. We all matured to this point.

OPPOSITION OPENS LINES OF COMMUNICATION

One other way we used opposition to our advantage was that it allowed us to pay close attention to detail within the organization and maintain open lines of communication. Our infrastructure is now designed to accommodate a culture of transparency and engagement. We are using it to our advantage and becoming a better organization each day. Every leader must realize that there are amazing opportunities hidden in opposition. Although a great deal of your opposition may have demonic origins, I believe that it also has providential implications. Whatever God allows is always designed for our benefit.

In order to be a successful leader, this is the shift that must be made. Opportunities are not always easily seen. It took months, even years in some cases, to realize they existed. I pray that as you read this book you will not become so inundated with what is coming against you that you miss the opportunities that can work for you. Even after twenty years as a leader, I am still learning to see opportunities, but you never will come to a place where jealousy subsides and opposition ceases. If you are continuously moving forward into your vision, you will most certainly experience more of the same. For every new level, there is a new devil. I've heard this statement and said it quite often over the years, but the more I've experienced, the more I've seen it come to pass. It is going to be important that you embrace who you are and where God is taking you, because the opposition is a part of it.

When I think about President Obama, I often think about the constant opposition he encounters. I must admit that in my lifetime, I've never seen a president experience the level of opposition he has. Nevertheless, I have watched him attempt to work, forging alliances and relationships to get things done. He has attempted to use opposition to his advantage. I've watched him grow as a leader, and he has inspired millions of other leaders.

SOME WILL NEVER SUPPORT YOUR VISION

If there is one thing that we can learn, it is that there will be some people who will never support your vision. You have to know when to engage and when to disengage. Unfortunately, there were moments in my past where I had to disengage, because the energy I was putting into certain relationships proved unfruitful and detrimental to the organization's health. If you find yourself more focused on naysayers who are determined not to change rather than invested in those who are attempting to work with you, you set yourself up for failure. My mother always reminds me that there are always more for you than there are against you. There comes a time where you have to shift your energies toward people who want to work with you. You should never expect everyone in your organization to agree with you all the time. That's not realistic, nor is it healthy. You need conflict. You need opposition because without it you never birth fresh opportunities.

In 1997, we experienced a great opportunity from opposition. Previously the Mount Zion church leadership struggled through a series of growing pains. All of the areas I mentioned in the previous chapter were manifesting within the life of the church. There were many days when I felt we were at a stalemate and would never shift to the place I had envisioned. The church was growing fast, and we were doing multiple services. People were literally waiting for the next service, standing around the building. We needed to move to a larger facility, and I anticipated a big fight brewing in opposition to it. As I mentioned earlier in the book, we moved to the World Baptist Center headquarters building, and how we got there is the real story. I stood before the congregation during a church meeting and shared the need to relocate from the historical Jefferson Street location. I was braced for a fight because I knew this was a huge move. But I did not anticipate what happened next. The eldest and most influential member of our church stood up and made a motion that we move our services to the World Center to accommodate the growth. Here was a man who in past years had struggled to embrace the pace of the changes and had led some of the opposition. Now he was making the motion to move the services to a larger facility. I stood there with tears in my eyes as they voted unanimously. God reminded me in that moment that because I had cultivated relationships over the years and had allowed people to see my heart, this was happening. It was a moment that forever changed the history of the Mount Zion Baptist Church. More space meant more capacity to do ministry, and the rest is history. It all happened because we confronted opposition over the years and cultivated a new culture within the church. Consequently, an opportunity was birthed.

PUT IN THE TIME

There are some amazing people in your organization. Their resistance can be understood if you are willing to put in the time. The easy thing to do is to write them off and move forward with your vision and remind them that it will happen with them or without them. The challenging thing is to bring them alongside you and recognize like Joseph did that all of Egypt will be saved one day—not some but all. What's inside of you is for all the people, not for a selected few. Some will embrace it and others never will. To be a great leader, you must try to bring folks alongside what God has shown you. Leadership is not easy in this regard, but you are not reading this book to take the road often traveled. You must take the road less traveled and be willing to shift from opposition to opportunity.

There are hundreds of untapped opportunities awaiting you. The opposition is nothing more than a bridge to get you to them. You cannot get bogged down in tactics of the opposition and allow it to throw you off your route. You must get to your spot and recognize there is a big picture. It is much bigger than those who oppose you.

Don't give up, whate'er you do;
Eyes front, head high to the finish.[6]

This poem by Edgar A. Guest, called "See It Through," speaks to the essence of shifting from opposition to opportunity. As you lead, remember there are hidden treasures buried beneath the mire of chaos and conflict that, once found, can yield great dividends for the life of your business, organization, or church. The names of your opposition will change as your organization grows, but at the core of it all, there are lessons to be learned. Never stop learning and you will never stop shifting. Stagnation is the enemy of success. Your opposition is confirmation that something groundbreaking and life changing is upon you. Remember, it's not about you. Don't personalize the attacks. It's about the lives your vision will affect. Knowing this should motivate you, as it has me, to make the shift from opposition to opportunity.

CHAPTER 4
FROM THREAT TO PROMISE

I f God allows something, it is designed to bless you, even if it doesn't seem so at first. I have spoken to millions of people around the world, and it continues to be a fact that God confirms continuously in my life. Joseph's brothers saw him as a threat; as a result, they conspired against him. Yet this conspiracy also launched events that would eventually make Joseph a formidable leader. Joseph was marginalized by those who were threatened by him, and he suffered terrible injustices, but in the end he knew that God was with him. Leaders are often threatened with failure, misperceptions, and false witness, to name a few, but in order to be effective as a leader, you must be able to shift from every threat to the promise God has made over your life.

As you read this chapter, you may be dealing with people who even threaten to end your ministry. The first thing I want you to know is that you are not alone. One of the most amazing realities I have noticed as I travel is that cutting-edge leaders in most cities are often under attack by those who are threatened by them. Pastors talk about this all the time. There is an incredible sense of loneliness when you are doing transformative ministry, because the gatekeepers of the status quo often marginalize and in some cases demonize you.

Let's examine why Joseph was a threat to his brothers. When he shared with them his dreams, they were threatened by the idea that they would have to serve Joseph as leader. He clearly indicates that he would be over them, and often when it appears that your trajectory propels you to positions of power and influence, some people become threatened by that. One lesson we should learn from Joseph is to be careful who you share your dreams with. When God has made you a promise, you have to be strategic about who and how you release that vision. Some people don't have the capacity to embrace what you are about to embark upon. As a young pastor, I made the mistake of sharing everything God was saying to me with anyone who would listen. Little did I know I was infuriating some folks privately, because, rather than see me as excited about the promise manifesting through me, they saw it as a subtle attempt to declare I was better than they were. There is a deeply rooted need for a leader to share his or her vision to avoid feelings of isolation. Dreams and vision exist in our private thoughts and are birthed out of a personal exploration of the searching of self for God. Howard Thurman encapsulates this concept in his book *The Search for Common Ground*. He writes, "There is something so private and personal about an act of thought that the individual may very easily seem to be a private island on a boundless human sea. To experience one's self is to enter into a solitary world that is one's unique possession and that can never be completely and utterly shared."[1] He further states that a paradox exists within this isolated setting: "A person is always threatened in his very soul by a sense of isolation, by feeling himself cut off even from fellowship with peers or family. Yet he can never separate himself from his fellows, for mutual interdependence is characteristic of all of life."[2] Although it is natural to desire to share the stirrings of your inner being, sometimes you have to keep your dreams to yourself until the right time. God has a way of surrounding you with the right people to embrace and propel your vision, but you have to be patient and wait for those folks to show up.

Joseph's brothers were so threatened by his dreams that they conspired against him. Their sinister plot to leave him in a pit and mislead their father, Jacob, into believing Joseph was dead was simply a means of getting rid of their brother for good, so they thought. Perhaps while you are reading this book you should not dismiss the possibility that there are plots in motion now to get rid of you by those who lack the capacity and spiritual fortitude to see what God is doing in your life. You should never be surprised when these attacks come. You should expect them.

When Jesus walked the earth performing miracles and ministering to people, there was a plot in motion by the religious establishment of that day to get rid of Him. He was aware of it, yet He continued to fulfill His assignment. If Jesus had to experience this, you and I definitely will. There are five reasons to consider as you deal with those who are threatened by what God is doing through you.

TERRITORIALISM

The first reason people are threatened by you is territorialism. When I talk about territory, I am referring to turf wars that exist within any organization. I have seen this on many different levels in ministry. Early in my pastorate, I saw people hover over ministries as if they owned them. Their ownership issues did not allow for growth because these people were threatened by new people who brought new ideas. I view the church as a system of transformation and innovation. The people who engage the system come from a variety of backgrounds. This is implicit in who we are as a faith community. We declare,

"Whosoever will let them come." So people come to the system from different walks of life with different ideas on how to make that system better. The goal of the system is to release those gifts as well as transform the lives of those who engage it, so that the outputs from the system look different from the inputs. If the outputs look the same as they did when they first engaged the system, there is a system failure. This is what we were experiencing within our ministry early on. It forced us to examine why the system was failing. What we discovered was that there were people who came in with great resources and talents, yet those who held positions were marginalizing them for fear they would "take over" what they had been doing. The sad truth is that in many organizations this paradox exists. We want new people to join us, but we want to remind them who's in charge of certain things. We place limitations on their ability to fully assist the organization and cause immeasurable frustration.

I have a friend who shared with me what happened in his church. He wanted to expand his media and marketing department. He asked some of his new members to assist in those efforts. The persons who were currently serving in this area were faithful, yet limited in their ability. There was an overwhelming response by the new people, and the pastor was excited about the possibility of fresh ideas being implemented within his current media department. There was a lady who had just moved to the city who had extensive training in media and marketing. In fact, she was recently hired by the city to lead their marketing initiatives. She was quite excited about getting involved in her new church and viewed this invitation as God ordained because media and marketing were her passion. Once she began attending the meetings, however, it was apparent early on that turf wars were in full effect, but nevertheless she began sharing innovative ideas in the meetings. Those who held positions were lukewarm at best. She kept sending ideas because she loved her church, yet there was no response from the team. When the team did engage her, the most they asked her to do was pass out fliers. While she did not view this as beneath her, she was quite frustrated that her ideas and her experience were not being maximized. She ultimately stopped attending media meetings and began sitting in the back during worship. She would come in, hear the word, and leave early. This is a classic example of what happens in many organizations, even the church. The resourceful and innovative people are often seen as threats to the people who hold positions. When you are gifted and resourceful, you will frequently be viewed as a threat to those in positions of power. This has little to do with you and more to do with those who are threatened by you. You have to know how to deal with it and focus on the promise God has made you.

I've also seen this happen in my own life. When I began my pastorate, I experienced ridicule and marginalization from a few other pastors who felt I was infringing upon their territory. In most cities, pastors have a nomenclature that exists among themselves. You are certain to hear claims of a city belonging to a certain leader. The leading pastor in the city usually gets to claim the city. For example, this is Brown's city or this is Anderson's city. When a new kid on the block comes with the potential to outgrow the existing leader, there is a threat that this will no longer be that person's city. As petty as this might sound, there are deeper implications to consider. The leading pastor is also a gatekeeper, and often whenever politicians run for office, they must meet with this person. Whenever huge initiatives are undertaken by a city, this person is at the table. There is a great deal of influence with the leading pastor or pastors in a city. Anything that is a threat to that potential threatens their seat at the table. This political and social capital is a valuable asset to those who network in order to get things done. The position leading pastors have in a city is what Ronald Heifetz refers to as "moral authority"; it is what King and Gandhi both possessed.[3] This type of authority, although it does not carry the breadth of leadership that formal authority gives, does allow these leaders to be on the frontlines engaged and informed about the issues of the people. Moral authority provides lead pastors a seat at the table to function as the voice for the people of the communities they serve.

What I encountered was something I didn't anticipate. I didn't realize the influence that was bestowed upon a leader when his or her church grows. Growth in the eyes of some represents a person's ability to galvanize folks around issues. There were longstanding organizations that carried the weight in the city in regard to the religious community. If you wanted a seat at the table with people who could get things done, you had to be connected to those organizations. My schedule would not allow me to connect as I would have liked; however, it wasn't long before I realized that I didn't need to be connected. People were coming to me for advice, input, and collaboration about community projects. Because Mount Zion touched every aspect of the community, this became somewhat of a threat to those organizations that used to be called upon first to get involved with those initiatives. Territorialism is a real issue that effective leaders must deal with. People can be protective of the spaces and places of influence they have historically held. It is essential that as you encounter these "turf wars," you continue to shift to the promise of God over your life.

You cannot get bogged down worrying about the tactics and plots of your enemies. You will waste needless energy. I experienced my greatest success in ministry when I shifted from being concerned about people viewing me as a threat to realizing there was a great promise over my life. You will experience marginalization. It comes with the territory—no pun intended.

As I mentioned in the previous chapter, I felt isolated and misunderstood. Labels were attached that were quite painful, yet I had to continue moving toward the manifestation of the promise of God over my life.

It took great energy and creativity for Joseph's brothers to devise a plan to get rid of him. A great part of that plan was to convince Jacob that Joseph had been killed. In other words, the enemy wants to create false perceptions about your reality. He or she wants to mislead people into believing you are not who you say you are. **Threatened people threaten people, just as hurt people hurt people.** We must remember that no matter how people cling to their so-called turf and refuse to allow others a seat at the table, ultimately all belongs to God—everything! Whatever we have, it is from stewardship through a powerful and intentional relationship. God is the owner, and if we keep that in perspective we will be able to overcome those who are threatened by us because of what they assume is theirs. Again, it all belongs to God.

SHIFT OF ATTENTION

The second thing that causes people to be threatened by you is a shift of attention. The fact that Joseph's dreams and promise would shift the proverbial spotlight away from his brothers and put it on him was enough to incite their negative response. This was Joseph's season to come out of obscurity. It's not that Joseph sought the attention; it was a by-product of the great thing that God would do through his life. You will discover this the closer you get to the manifestation of the promise. When it is your season, it can bring a great deal of attention to you. You have to know how to handle the attention so that it doesn't change who you are.

There were seasons, and continue to be moments, when I

saw articles about our church in the paper. These articles were highlighting the positive things we were doing in the community. We were on the radio, television, and the Internet. As we continued to get exposure from various media outlets, it created a buzz in the city about our ministry. People began visiting our church in great numbers. We experienced what I like to call free advertisement. When your vision becomes the buzz and attention is being drawn to what you are doing, it will inevitably become a threat to some. Joseph's brothers were threatened possibly because all the chatter and attention had shifted from them to him. When you are focused on the promise of God, you never do what you do for attention; you do it because God has called you to do it. It is important to remember, however, that it inevitably draws attention. When you are positioned to meet needs and do something that has never been done before, it becomes a hot topic.

We see this happening in Matthew 4:23-25:

> And Jesus went about all Galilee, teaching in their synagogues, and preaching the gospel of the kingdom, and healing all manner of sickness and all manner of disease among the people. And his fame went throughout all Syria: and they brought unto him all sick people that were taken with divers diseases and torments, and those which were possessed with devils, and those which were lunatick, and those that had the palsy; and he healed them. And there followed him great multitudes of people from Galilee, and from Decapolis, and from Jerusalem, and from Judaea, and from beyond Jordan.

It is very clear that Jesus was meeting needs. His ministry was personal and powerful. He taught the people and ministered to them. As a result of his effectiveness, the Bible says His fame went throughout the region. Consequently, they brought to Him others who had the same conditions as they did, and He met their need as well. Jesus' ministry generated a great deal of attention, and this caused many of the religious leaders to conspire against Him. The fact that the text says that when He left their temple the people followed Him is an indicator that their loyalty was to a new paradigm of ministry rather than the old. When you consider what God was going to do through Joseph, it is clear that he would represent a new model of leadership. You cannot prevent attention shifting toward you. The world is looking for change that matters. It is looking for leaders who will do what has not been done. When you are one of those leaders, you become a threat to those who are not.

Those who seek attention and popularity are often misguided and self-absorbed. As an effective leader, you will be amazed at the attacks levied at you over something you could do without. Most great leaders would rather lead discreetly, and they don't read their own press. They recognize that the same pen that celebrated them can be the same pen that crucifies them. Jesus spent a lot of time telling folks not to make mention of Him after He performed miracles. You will never be threatened by a person's success and the attention he or she is receiving if you do what you do for the glory of God.

When your attention is focused only on your own agenda and aggrandizement, it taints the true purposes of your assignment. You can work hard and become successful, but the underlying question is: Why did you do it? Did you do it to be celebrated by the media or by people? Or did you do it for the glory of God? I wake up every day with great intentionality and declare that whatever I do will be for the glory of God. I cannot control the attention being shifted in my direction, but I can control how I respond to it. I make a conscientious effort not to let it go to my head. If you do that, it will define you, and you will position yourself to be threatened by others when the attention shifts away from you to them.

Let me say another thing about attention. In many cases, people use attention to affirm the legitimacy of their assignment. The more people are paying us attention, the more significant we think we are. Joseph's brothers were conspiring not simply because of the attention he was receiving but also because of the lack of attention they experienced. Whenever you allow attention to validate you, you position yourself for disappointment. Seasons come and seasons go. Significance can survive seasons. What I mean is that even if your name is not in the spotlight, your work can still be productive and affect those around you. Attention cannot be the gauge by which you measure effectiveness. I have seen this in the church too long. We see people on television every week, and we make assumptions that they have "arrived." I've seen young pastors strive to get on television because it seemingly affirms them that they have arrived and are significant. You must remember that you are significant even if you are not getting the exposure you feel you deserve. Let me tell you a true story that happened to me.

When I visited New York City for the very first time, I rode the subway. I'm from Louisiana, so this was a new experience for me, and I knew it would be exciting. My host guided me to the subway station. We descended down a long stairwell and entered the subway. While we were moving on the subway, the Lord began to speak to me about visibility and attention. While we were moving, there were people above us who were oblivious to our presence. They were walking and throwing paper on us with no idea that we were down there. God said to be like the subway. Although people may not recognize you, respect you, or affirm you, keep moving toward your destination. There is a season when God will keep you in the subway in order to develop you and mold you into what you need to be before He releases you into a season of great attention. You have to maximize your time in the subway. Perhaps you are reading this book and you are clearly in the subway. You are moving, and quite rapidly at that, yet attention has not shifted to you. Remember that attention can be fleeting at best. You must maintain a level of productivity and progress. **It doesn't matter who doesn't affirm me, as long as God has confirmed me.**

THE WHY NOT ME SYNDROME

The next reason people are threatened by you is the why not me syndrome. People have a variety of personal expectations. When those expectations do not materialize when people think they should have and they witness your things going your way, it becomes a threat. They are not likely to feel secure about their own future and their visions coming to pass. Remember, Joseph was only seventeen years old when he received his vision. Imagine what it feels like to be much older, with what you dream about having yet to manifest. All of a sudden, you are witnessing someone much younger walk in his or her purpose past you. You might be wondering if your dreams are ever going to happen for you. This could be as simple as being a bridesmaid in your fifth wedding and wondering if you will ever be the bride. There is no limitation on where and how this can manifest in your life.

I was a young pastor whom God was doing extraordinary things through, and I was the most surprised about how God chose to use me. Some of the things we did were threatening to some churches because they were declining and unable to grow. Here I was, this young, energetic, progressive person ready to fulfill my assignment. Mount Zion was my first church, and I witnessed God give us growth that never had been experienced in the city of Nashville. It was a surreal yet exciting time. There were many who were threatened by what was happening through me as a young pastor. There were those who had been pastoring as long as I had been alive. Some shared with me years later that they struggled with their own churches. They had tremendous vision. I strongly believe that until you support others doing what you are desiring to do, you will never reach your goal. The reason I am able to accomplish the things I do today is because I celebrated those who had done it before me. Joseph's brothers were struggling through the why not me season.

This is the season when you as a leader must realize that other people's insecurities should not cause you to lose focus. Some folks will always be threatened by your success because it brings to the surface unmet expectations they have been dealing with for years. Joseph's brothers were struggling with why they didn't get the coat. They were struggling with why they did not dream the dreams he did. They were struggling with his youth and his potential to do things they would never do in their lifetime. The only thing they knew to do was conspire to get rid of him. You cannot own the issues of others struggling with unmet expectations.

You must accept the fact that as long as you are walking in your assignment and fulfilling your dreams, you will always bring out the insecurities of folks around you. They will mistake your confidence for being cocky. You cannot allow others to define you. You must be clear about who you are and what your assignment is. You cannot own the failures of those who squandered the opportunities that were before them. You must continue to see to it that your dreams come to fruition and move forward with an awareness that you will be a threat in this area. As a young pastor, I had to realize that the growth of Mount Zion had nothing to do with the decline of another congregation. We were accused of "stealing members." I thought that was the most hilarious thing I had ever heard. How do you steal a grown person? We never went out recruiting church folk; we evangelized the unsaved, and as a result, many folks united with our congregation. Some were from other churches, but we never recruited them. We were just meeting needs. There were people from other churches who resented the idea that our church was growing and doing the things we were doing. I couldn't wrap my mind around that because I assumed regardless of the church we were all on the same team. I am certain you have complete familiarity with this kind of resentment. The why not me syndrome is very real, and the more you accomplish, the more you will encounter it.

YOUR ANOINTING

The next reason people will be threatened by you is because of your anointing. When I refer to anointing, I am talking about the presence and power of God upon your life. Joseph had the favor of God upon him. His brothers were disillusioned by the favor on his life. Although there was ceremony to celebrate his anointing, he was clearly moving forward because his Father's hand was upon him.

People are often confused by the anointing upon your life. I am convinced that whenever God gives us an assignment, He gives us an anointing to fulfill it. The anointing empowers us with the supernatural strength to do what we could never do in our natural state. Although I am a trained theologian and have been to some of the best schools in the world, I am able to accomplish my assignment only because of the anointing. Intellect is good, but it only takes a person so far. It is the anointing that gives a person the strength to preach four services every Sunday, three on Wednesday, and travel across the world as I do. When you are anointed, people are threatened by it because they make comparisons. I know there are people who can preach circles around me. There are people who have more administrative gifts than I. Often, when people see you excel in areas where they feel more equipped, they are threatened by it, and they are mystified as to why you are successful. You must remember that it is the anointing at work in your life. God has enabled you to fulfill your assignment.

The anointing of God also attracts. People are drawn to the anointing. Wherever Jesus was present, there were great multitudes, because He was the anointed one. When God has His hand on you, people are drawn to that anointing. There were people who were threatened by the anointing on my life early as thousands were being drawn by that anointing. They thought it was my charisma or personality. They made the assumption that people were coming for every reason other than the anointing. This is why they prophesied doom and gloom and declared that our church growth would be short lived. However, it takes more than a personality to sustain an organization. It is a common belief that a charismatic leader is the driving force behind a particular movement in our faith tradition. But contrary to that belief, Anthony Pinn writes in *Understanding and Transforming the Black Church* that it is the Black Christian tradition and its value, the people, and their project that are much greater than any particular leader.[4] Here we are more than twenty years later and still growing by thousands each year because of the anointing of God.

I am thoroughly convinced that God has His hand on your life. You must walk in that anointing and not take any conspiracy against you personally, because your anointing also attracts adversity. Though the adversity comes, it cannot prevent God's purposes from coming to pass in your life. Joseph had gifts bestowed on him. The gift of prophecy was operative in his life. He spoke what God would do in his life. There are gifts in you that God has anointed for His purposes. You cannot allow those who are threatened by your anointing derail your destiny. Though they conspire, they will not be successful.

When you are anointed, it's like having oil naturally or spiritually poured from the crown of your head to the toes on your feet. You are completely immersed in the oil until you are greasy, slippery. Some people will look at you and wonder how you got out of every plot of the enemy. They will wonder how you escaped the conspiracies of your adversary. You are obligated to tell them this. Every time the enemy tried to get a grip, you kept slipping out of it. When I think about all the plots and plans of those who attempted to destroy me and my destiny, I recognize that it was the anointing on my life that kept me slipping out of their grip. I'm sure as you read this there are countless moments in your life when you have slipped out of some things as well. Remember that you are anointed, and walk in it with confidence.

SOME PEOPLE JUST DON'T LIKE YOU

There is one final thing that you have to remember when people are threatened by you. Face it: some people just don't like you. That's a hard pill to swallow, but I've learned this to be true over the years. Joseph's brothers plotted to remove him, but I would suggest that they were predisposed against him from the beginning. Just because you got the coat and the favor of your father, it is important to know that all that did was bring to the forefront feelings that were already there. There are some people who just won't like you. Some have never met you and have no desire to; they just don't like you.

I must admit that this is a difficult thing for me to deal with to this day. I consider myself a friendly person and quite relational. Once I truly believed that I could make everybody like me, but I soon discovered that the more God did in my life, the more some people just didn't like me. I'm certain there are a variety of issues that exist within them that contribute to their dislike. Jesus told His disciples that they would be hated by men for His sake. If people hated Jesus, you know they will hate you. What I had to do was shift beyond their feelings about me and focus on the promise that was before me. You cannot allow negativity to stifle your progress. You have a great assignment, and you must be willing to fulfill your assignment.

If you are a visionary reading this book, you need to come to a place where you say it's really okay if some people never embrace you. As I mentioned earlier, you cannot spend countless hours trying to persuade people who have rested the case on their point of view. My mother always told me that there are always more for you than against you. But it's difficult. I was guilty of being consumed with what my opponents were saying about me. I would be out around town, and I would be focused on the people who were rolling their eyes at me rather than be thankful for the amazing people God had placed in my life. Haters are haters, and you have to use them as elevators. In a real sense, God may promise to make them your footstools. The more haters you have, the more footstools you may have in the future. Get enough footstools and you have a stairway. Ultimately, those who despise you will be instrumental in elevating you to where God wants you to be.

The amazing potential on your life will always be threatening to some, but you must continue to focus on the promise of God, because this is the shift that sets you on a course for destiny. What you will discover in the life of Joseph and in your own life is that all of this is preparation for where God is about to take you.

CHAPTER 5

FROM SERVANT TO STEWARD

Joseph was placed in a pit by his own brothers' sinister plot to get rid of him, but God providentially used Potiphar to rescue him. Although we may have humble origins, leaders can find ways to serve and show their gifts. This chapter will show how God can work in our lives amid schemes to destroy us. By serving with excellence and faithfulness, Joseph earned favor and was given power. Leaders can earn respect by serving and being faithful stewards of their own gifts and the gifts of others.

Joseph's pit situation was ordained by God to put him in a position to be discovered. **What I have learned over the years is that you have to see the hand of God moving in every negative situation.** Perhaps you are reading this book and you are in a pit of despair or brokenness, and it appears that liberation is nowhere in sight. God has a plan to get you out of that pit and establish you on the path of your destiny.

One of my favorite psalms is a vivid reminder of that. David declares in Psalm 40:1-3:

> I waited patiently for the LORD; and he inclined unto me, and heard my cry. He brought me up also out of an horrible pit, out of the miry clay, and set my feet upon a rock, and established

my goings. And he hath put a new song in my mouth, even praise unto our God: many shall see it, and fear, and shall trust in the LORD.

What David discovered is what those before and after him can also discover. God never allows us to be in a pit without a plan to get us out.

Joseph was about to be left for dead when slave traders came along. So not only did Joseph's brothers get rid of him, but they also made a profit off their scheme. But then Joseph is sold to Potiphar. Surprisingly, Joseph was inadvertently saved by being sold into slavery, and Potiphar is the conduit by which Joseph gets to Egypt. God always has someone to help get us to the place of destiny. Joseph is made to serve in Potiphar's house, and here Joseph teaches us the importance of being a good servant and steward even if your situation is not ideal.

I meet so many leaders who make the mistake of not giving their all because their context is not what they want. Even when we face overwhelming obstacles, we must stay focused on destiny. Ronald Heifetz writes, "Preserving a sense of purpose helps one take setbacks and failures in stride. Leadership requires the courage to face failures daily....A sense of purpose provides the ongoing capacity to generate new possibilities."[1] I believe God tests us to see how faithful we will be in undesirable situations before He releases us into the desires of our hearts.

We all have visions and expectations about where we want to be in life. Perhaps it's the ideal job or practice; perhaps it's the ideal home or school. Whatever it is, please know that before it comes to fruition, you have to prove your faithfulness. I learned this early in my pastorate. Every young pastor imagines his or her vision coming to pass. There is never a sense of contentment until he or she arrives at the place of manifestation of the vision. It's in the meantime that you will experience challenges like never before. You might find yourself on the job but not in the ideal position, or perhaps it's a house, but not the house you dreamed about. It's here that you become a great steward of the opportunity God laid before you. Being a servant in Potiphar's house is significant because it comes before stewardship.

One of the most important lessons any leader will ever learn is that of serving. I am where I am today because I learned how to serve before God made me a steward over anything. When I arrived at Mount Zion Baptist Church in September 1989, I was a seminary student eager to serve in ministry. I had no entitlement issues or expectations other than to find a place to serve. The pastor at the time, the late Dr. E. W. Roberson, embraced me and gave me that opportunity. I viewed this not as a chore but a wonderful opportunity for growth and development. I arrived to everything thirty minutes before he did. I took great pride in making certain the pulpit was in order. I was humbled to assist him each Sunday and to teach in whatever capacity he saw fit to allow. I was raised in church serving. One of the things that is so troubling in this generation is how so few people really want to serve. So many want to be served and believe that they can bypass the work of ministry and serving and experience elevation. This is a sad truth. Joseph was in Potiphar's house, and he served. Serving is essential to leadership.

There is a powerful revelation in Matthew 10:1-4 (NKJV):

And when He had called His twelve disciples to Him, He gave them power over unclean spirits, to cast them out, and to heal all kinds of sickness and all kinds of disease. Now the names of the twelve apostles are these: first, Simon, who is called Peter, and Andrew his brother; James the son of Zebedee, and John his brother; Philip and Bartholomew; Thomas and Matthew the tax collector; James the son of Alphaeus, and Lebbaeus, whose surname was Thaddaeus; Simon the Cananite, and Judas Iscariot, who also betrayed Him.

ESSENTIAL, IMPORTANT, OR INTERESTING

I once heard a prominent minister speak on the essentials of missions. He insightfully made the distinctions among what is essential, important, and interesting. "Water," he said, "is essential to the human body. Juices are important, and most other beverages, at best, are interesting."

When it comes to the matter of Christian leadership, it is critical that we make the distinction among leadership that is essential, leadership that is important, and leadership that is interesting. Leadership that is essential is defined by what is essential to Christian discipleship. Leadership that is important is defined by what we consider imperative or urgent to our cause. Leadership that is interesting is defined by what we like, acquiesce to, or are curious about. Counting money, paying the bills, or counting members is important. Dressing up in robes, singing well, performing, or presenting cute sermons is interesting. Too often, the twenty-first-century megachurch phenomenon has measured its successes with an emphasis on what's important and what's interesting. But when it comes to the matter of Christian leadership, nothing is more essential than for one's leadership to be defined by followship.

When leadership is placed under the microscope of biblical scrutiny, leadership is always defined by followship. Jesus didn't say, "Lead me, impress me, excite me, entertain me, buy me, count me, sell me, or do me." Jesus said, "Follow me."

Leadership that bypasses followship may be important; it may be interesting; but it is never essential. Essential leadership operates from the perspective that we lead best when we follow most. An insightful business leader noted, "In the twenty-first-century organization, all leaders learn to follow if they are to successfully lead" (see Douglas K. Smith, *The Leader of the Future*).[2]

Of interest in the biblical text are the words "when He had

called." The word used for "called" in Greek, *pros-kal-eh-om-ahee*, means to "call toward one's self." The word "follow" used in the other call narratives, *ak-ol-oo-theh-o*, means "to be in the same way with." Jesus calls leaders to Himself to be in the same way with Him. We may come up with some ways that are important. We certainly could come up with ways that are interesting. We probably need to note that the Devil will help us create some ways that seem extremely important and quite interesting. The Devil will literally seduce us into believing that our energies need to focus upon what's important and delude us into a ministry that promotes what is interesting. Yet the things we may lean toward that are important and interesting are not always essential. Essential Christian leadership comes from those who are called to be in the same way with Him. Following is being in the same way with Him who calls us to Him.

May I use a moment to confess? I want to confess that I have been guilty of measuring my leadership acumen by focusing on what's important. I confess to believing the church building is important. I confess to believing that responsible monetary flow is important. I confess to believing that providing a meaningful worship and attracting new members is important. I confess that I used some interesting props with God's name on them that would help me in achieving all my important matters. In fact, I sought to make our ministry more interesting than everybody else's. After all my important emphases and interesting activities, however, I lived with a relentless uneasiness that I was neglecting the essential. In my own spirit, God's Word and the Spirit challenged me to reconsider. Moreover, as I saw wonderful people coming up short and beautiful people doing ugly things, I became convicted over my tendencies to emphasize what's important and the promotion of what's interesting. God has helped me to see that for anything lasting and transformative to happen in my ministry, I need to be attentive to what is essential. Moreover, for me to lead as the Lord would want, I need to commit more faithfully to the discipline of followship. I had to face the reality that the essential leader is one who is committed to being in the same way with Him who calls us.

ESSENTIAL LEADERSHIP IS A RESPONSE TO AN AUTHENTIC CALL

The matter of essential leadership is worked out in our text. It is worked out first in the fact that **essential leadership is a response to an authentic call**. Again, the text says, "When He had called." For the Christian, an authentic call is a disciple's response to being summoned to be with Jesus. It's like the African call and response where one person provides the song line and the congregation repeats it with collective emphasis.

He calls; we respond. We don't make up a new song. We don't flip the script and do what we think is important or promote what is interesting. He provides the lead meter, and we respond by saying and doing what He says. Jesus called His disciples to Himself first before releasing them to their assignment.

Please know that what we do first is usually a clear indication of who we really are and what we are about. In other words, the real you, or the most authentic you, shows up in what you do first. A leader is at his or her best when his or her first response is to be with Him. Leaders cannot focus on positions and forget Jesus. What the Lord wants first is a loving relationship. It is within the relationship where we can really know how much He loves us and where He can determine how much we love Him. I used to hear the old mothers testify, "I know Him and He knows me." I wanted to be able to say, "He loves me and He knows that I love Him!" Our call is authenticated within the context of our relationship with Him!

WORKING FOR GOD

Essential leadership understands that we work for God and don't simply work with God. Discipleship is ultimately about being with Him. We deny ourselves to be with Him. We lose ourselves and then find ourselves by being with Him. In Him we "**move, live, and have our being**." Please note, every one of the disciples was not "all that". All of them had an issue, and some had more. He knew their imperfections when He called them. Yet in calling them, He set them on a path to living a more authentic life, engaging each of them in a more authentic ministry, and empowering them into fulfilling a more authentic life purpose. It's always a miraculous thing to watch God use people the world never imagined Him using.

The next time you feel like God can't use you, just remember:

—Noah was a drunk.
—Abraham was too old.
—Isaac was a daydreamer.
—Jacob was a liar.
—Leah was ugly.
—Joseph was abused.
—Moses had a stuttering problem.
—Gideon was afraid.
—Samson had long hair and was a womanizer.
—Rahab was a prostitute.
—Jeremiah and Timothy were too young.
—David was an adulterer and a murderer.
—Elijah was suicidal.
—Isaiah preached naked.
—Jonah ran from God.
—Naomi was a widow.
—Job went bankrupt.
—John the Baptist ate bugs.

—Peter denied Christ.

—The disciples fell asleep while praying.

—Martha worried about everything.

—The Samaritan woman was divorced (more than once).

—Zaccheus was too small.

—Paul was too religious.

—Timothy had an ulcer.

—Lazarus was dead!

BEING TEACHABLE

Essential leadership also proves that it is teachable. Jesus took twelve men on a didactic journey. He declared that He would make them something that they were not. He would give them the skills to be effective in their new assignment. When leaders are called and commissioned to fulfill an assignment, they have to be willing to learn new skills necessary to complete the assigned task. Marshall Goldsmith, in his book *What Got You Here Won't Get You There*, sheds light on the behavioral characteristics of successful people. He notes they are confident, committed, and consistent contributors to an organization. However, they may have a tendency to get stuck celebrating past successes, which leads to "success delusion" and resistance to change: "All of *the* delusions are a direct result of success, not failure. That's because we get positive reinforcement from our past success, and in a mental leap that's easy to justify, we think that our past success is predictive of great things in our future."[3] Those who were called to walk alongside Jesus were already doing great things, but in order to do the "greater works," they had to have a willingness to be taught by the Master a new way of doing business.

Leaders who follow leaders know that it's not about tenure, titles, or turf. It's about being teachable. So often leaders miss this because they claim tenure, titles, and turf. It's hard to be teachable when you pull rank (tenure). It's hard to be teachable when you employ self-imposed exemptions based on your title. I'm a pastor, overseer, bishop, and so on. It's hard to be teachable when you claim turf. You feel like whatever is happening is diminishing your glory. It can be a God thing, but if it's not your thing, you disengage. God will not share His glory with anybody. Teachable leaders learn to do well. They realize that they don't know it all.

REMOVAL FROM YOUR ARENA OF COMFORT

The text allows us to see that another aspect of **essential leadership is a removal from the arena of comfort**. When Jesus called the disciples to be with Him in the same way, they had to leave from where they were. To go with Jesus in the same way He went, they could not stay in the places where they were most comfortable. They had to leave some stuff: their ships, occupations, business concerns, family arrangements, relational patterns, ideological beliefs, and treasured religious assumptions. Let me put it like this: you will never be more than **what** you are by staying **where** you are. Who we are is always a direct result of where we are. Your who-ness is always connected to your where-ness. Following always results in our going places we would not normally go.

The psychologist John Bowlby wrote extensively on attachment. He noted that our current relational patterns are profoundly influenced by our early attachment patterns. Many of us suffer from attachment disorders, and it shows up in all areas of our lives. We are holding on to things that are not really good for us, that do not help us or allow us to progress and fully develop. There are no people more prone to attachment disorders than religious folk. We cling to unhealthy relational patterns because of unhealthy God attachments. We tend to theologize what we believe is important and interesting and miss out on what's essential.

On one occasion, Jesus called a disciple, and when the person balked, Jesus' response was to tell him to let go and let the dead bury the dead. This presents us with a striking revelation of leadership. There is one paradigm that follows the casket and another that follows the Christ. The Christ is progressive, innovative, and purposeful. The casket is dead, resistant to change, and not relevant.

Churches not open to positive change—casket
Leaders who don't embrace innovation—casket
Reformations stuck in their glory days—casket
Let the dead bury the dead!

The Gospels provide us the stories of the making of the disciples. We are privileged to learn how the disciples coped with their removal from arenas of comfort. James and John left the powerful influence of Zebedee's household to become members of Jesus' inner circle. Andrew and Simon left the comforts of fishing to become fishers of people. Philip left farming to become a powerful evangelist. Nathanael left the confines of traditional religion to become an encourager of the faithful. Thomas left the prison of his own intellect to become a proclaimer of resurrection faith. Matthew left the offensive occupation of tax collecting to become a trusted member of the faith community. James the son of Alphaeus left the arrogant posture of self-delusion to become a humble follower of Jesus. Lebbaeus/Thaddaeus left the coldness of culture to become a compassionate follower. Simon the Canaanite/Zealot left the angry zeal of nationalism to become a world-changing believer in Jesus Christ. Even Judas Iscariot left his urban inclinations toward becoming a person of the world, although he tragically fell short.

Some of you can testify that you are not who you once

were as a result of following Jesus. Some of you even surprised yourselves, because you left the arena of your comfort to follow Him. I know my life has been one big surprise after another because one day I answered His call to leave my primary arena of comfort and follow Him!

AUTHORITY TO IMPLEMENT CHANGE

Where the text really allows us to see the power of essential leadership is in understanding what Jesus gives to those who are called to Him. Essential leadership is expressed when we receive **authority to exercise or implement change**. During his first presidential campaign, Barack Obama delivered a speech encouraging a mind-set of change for the American people. He said, "Change will not come if we wait for some other person or some other time. We are the ones we've been waiting for. We are the change that we seek"—in essence, essential leadership requires a leader to be the embodiment of change.[4] Mahatma Gandhi is often quoted as having said, "We must be the change we wish to see in the world."

The word *essential* is the adjectival derivative of the word *essence*. The word *essence* comes from a Latin word meaning "to be more at," the "nature of," or even "more of." When Jesus gave the disciples power over unclean spirits, He was literally giving them more of who He was, His essence, so that they might do more of what He does. He had power over unclean spirits; so would they. He had power to cast them out; so would the disciples. He had power to heal all kinds of sickness and disease; so would the disciples. Jesus was literally duplicating Himself in those who followed Him.

The essential leader allows the One he or she follows to be duplicated in the ones who follow him or her. Paul said, "Follow me as I follow Christ Jesus." Like the disciples, we duplicate

81

ourselves into destiny. Jesus does not want anyone's life limited by unclean spirits, sickness, or disease. Leaders who follow are given authority over the life-limiting powers of unclean spirits, sickness, and disease.

Please know, my brothers and sisters, that there are some spirits and sicknesses that are far more dangerous and limiting than physical sickness and disease. There are some life-limiting forces that go deeper than physiological and emotional sickness and disease. The Catholic priest Father Booth notes in his book *When God Becomes a Drug* that there are spiritual forces at work that affect church people exclusively. We have people in our congregations, even in our pulpits, who have serious religious disorders that are keeping them from their destiny. They can't think for themselves. They are rigid and unbending. They see themselves and others as worthless. They view the world as hopeless and themselves as shameful. Their religion is more magic than faith. They are trying to be perfect rather than faithful, and their God is more judging than loving. More significantly, we have structural evils that perpetuate this kind of unhealthy spirituality. Some of our people use their religion to hurt people, oppress people, abuse and even destroy people. Some of you who don't follow leadership, always challenging the pastor, criticizing the bishop—you need to be careful. Leaders who don't follow duplicate themselves into a destiny where they will reap what they sow.

God needs leaders, essential leaders who do more of what Jesus does—cast out evil spirits and heal all kinds of sickness and disease. Jesus had authority to change limiting-life situations and facilitate new-life realities. The disciples walked into their destiny by following Jesus. Simon becomes Peter, "the Rock Man"; Andrew the limited becomes Andrew the resourceful; James and John become sons of Thunder, "servants who roar," by following Jesus. Philip becomes the first martyred evangelist; Thomas the double-minded becomes Thomas the single-minded; Matthew the despised becomes Matthew the adored; Labbaeus/Thaddaeus the cold becomes Thaddaeus the warm-hearted; Simon the angry becomes Simon the focused; even Judas the betrayer becomes known as having a part in the ministry of Jesus.

Every plant needs sun. A small plant is in the shadow of a big plant. Once the big plant is removed, the shadow is removed. The small plant struggles and withers away. It never had any sunlight, and it can't take the heat. Jesus wants us not to walk in His shadow but to walk in His footprint. The weight of who He was left impressions, directives, and stories.

THEN COMES PROMOTION

When you develop the ability to serve faithfully, as Joseph did, you will discover that God will promote you. This is where the shift happens. Joseph is now a steward over all Potiphar has. He served faithfully, and now he has been entrusted to oversee the affairs of the house. Proverbs 18:16 says that your gift will make room for you. Joseph, in the intermediate place of his destiny, is in a position of great authority. As I served at Mount Zion in those early days, Dr. Roberson gradually entrusted me to preach and teach more regularly. There were times when I would preach twice a month. I would teach Bible study three times a month. The more he saw me serve, the more he trusted me. In order to be a good steward, I had to remember I was not the owner of what I was being entrusted with. I had to remember that, though these opportunities were coming frequently, he was the pastor and I was a mere servant available to do whatever he needed done.

You cannot allow greater responsibility to go to your head. You must remember that the more you are trusted, the better a steward you must become. Joseph walked in humility in Potiphar's house and was a good steward of what was entrusted in his hands. All great leaders are great stewards. Stewardship requires a great deal of responsibility, and Joseph understood that.

When that opportunity opens up for you, regardless of the circumstances surrounding it, you must step up to the plate and be a great steward. This would be significant in Joseph's future. His integrity in all areas would soon be tested. Joseph took great pride in managing what he was responsible for. You cannot do lousy work and expect elevation. You must serve in a spirit of excellence. A spirit of excellence means paying meticulous attention to detail in every assignment and ensuring the final product represents God in a way that brings Him glory. This requires going over and beyond to be organized, focused, faithful, and above board. Sadly, I've witnessed leaders who don't value the spirit of excellence. Things are thrown together at the last minute, and there is no forethought as to how what they do will benefit the Kingdom and bring glory to God. We have adopted the spirit of excellence in the Mount Zion Church. There is no church growth where the spirit of excellence doesn't exist. There is no growth in your business if you don't take seriously operating in the spirit of excellence in every capacity.

When you think about the trajectory Joseph was on, it gives you a reason to serve and be faithful where you are. One of the reasons I wrote this book is that people often see where you are but have no understanding of where you come from. They have no knowledge of your humble beginnings and your willingness to serve in situations that were not ideal. Joseph's promotion in Potiphar's house occurred because he could be trusted. What leaders desire are people who can be trusted. There are a lot of talented people who are deficient in the trust department. The fact that Potiphar would turn the affairs of his house over to Joseph meant that there was such a trustworthy servant spirit upon Joseph. Trusting God is only half of it. The real issue is, can God trust us? Joseph doesn't complain about where he is; he just serves faithfully. He does his job in a spirit of excellence, and for that he is rewarded.

As you are reading this book, God is calling you to greater service and has plans to summon you to stewardship once you have proved you can be trusted. When you serve faithfully, it gets noticed. Joseph doesn't have to apply for promotion, nor does he have to petition Potiphar; it happens organically because he just serves. You have to get beyond how others view your servitude. There were many young ministers who saw me serving at Mount Zion and laughed at my level of service. They thought I was taking it too seriously. They called me a busboy. I left no stone unturned. I was committed to seeing every task completed on time and in a spirit of excellence. Many who laughed at me are still wandering in the wilderness twenty years later without a place to minister and use their gifts. Again I say, if you can't serve, you are not ready to lead. **So many people want to go right to boardroom, but nobody wants to serve in the mailroom.** I was willing to sweep the floor, take out the trash, or do any other seemingly menial task in order that God's house would represent Him and that the services we provided would bring Him glory. I was not too big to do small tasks. When you are a servant, you just serve where you can.

Today I recognize that I must be a good steward of this awesome opportunity God has given me to lead His people. The larger the church, the greater the responsibility is. I study harder than I have before. I pray and prepare with greater intensity, because I realize that God has entrusted me with leading His people at this level. If you cannot be faithful on one level,

He knows you will not be faithful at the next. I am convinced that the habits and patterns you develop will go with you where He takes you. I was a serious servant; therefore I am a serious leader. You must take what you do seriously and not come to the moment of ministry unprepared. You cannot expect God to give you an amazing job when you don't produce at the level of expectation. Serving shifts you to stewardship. Every day I wake up, I promise God that I will give Him my best.

Joseph set an amazing precedent in the house of Potiphar. He came in at the lowest level possible. He quietly worked his way up and allowed his work to speak for him. If you stay connected to God's assignment for your life, you will produce wherever you are. Jesus said in John 15:1-8,

> I am the true vine, and my Father is the husbandman. Every branch in me that beareth not fruit he taketh away: and every *branch* that beareth fruit, he purgeth it, that it may bring forth more fruit. Now ye are clean through the word which I have spoken unto you. Abide in me, and I in you. As the branch cannot bear fruit of itself, except it abide in the vine; no more can ye, except ye abide in me. I am the vine, ye are the branches: He that abideth in me, and I in him, the same bringeth forth much fruit: for without me ye can do nothing. If a man bide not in me, he is cast forth as a branch, and is withered; and men gather them, and cast them into the fire, and they are burned. If ye abide in me, and my words abide in you, ye shall ask what ye will, and it shall be done unto you. Herein is my Father glorified, that ye bear much fruit; so shall ye be my disciples.

Your productivity is not tied to a zip code or a certain environment. You recognize that you have been rescued for a reason, and you become grateful for the opportunity. You could have been left in the pit and died, but God providentially orchestrated events so that you would have the opportunity you have. That should generate an attitude of humility, service, and gratitude.

MOTIVATED TO FULFILL THE ASSIGNMENT

I've learned that grateful people are those who don't have to be reminded of their responsibilities. They are motivated by their passion to fulfill the assignment of God upon their lives. They produce in any environment. Jesus said in Matthew 23:11 that the greatest must first be the servant. This is the call upon your life as you read this book. Complaining about the context you are in is not going to solve the problem. Can you be faithful in a scenario you didn't envision and yet produce at a high level that brings glory to God? Can you prove to God that you are worthy of elevation? Are you up for the challenge? This is what LeaderShifts are all about. They are about you understanding that where you are is a moment divinely ordered by God to put on display your integrity of service and stewardship. This is a moment ordained by God to see if you will be faithful. The stage is set to see if you will maximize this moment or trivialize it. How you serve in Potiphar's house will speak volumes about you as a leader.

CHAPTER 6
FROM ACCUSED TO RIGHTEOUS

When leaders develop the capacity to serve in integrity, as Joseph did in Potiphar's house, that integrity will be tested, perhaps even accused. All leaders can be tempted and naive about the trappings of success. Leaders must protect and maintain integrity despite temptation and accusation, as Joseph did when Potiphar's wife accused him of indiscretion. Every successful leader must be above reproach and strive to live righteously.

I remember an old wise man telling me that the more successful you become, the greater the target you become. Satan takes aim at folks who are impacting the Kingdom in positive ways. Joseph was excelling at a rapid pace within Potiphar's house. What happened to him is nothing short of what happens to most successful leaders. Potiphar's wife presented him with an ungodly proposition, and when Joseph stood strong in his integrity, she accused him of an indiscretion. Although nothing happened, she publicly proclaimed that Joseph had done something to her. This story reveals so much about the Devil's agenda and successful leadership. How you deal with accusation will speak volumes about your preparedness for promotion. There are several things that every leader needs to know as he or she shifts from the accused to the righteous.

POWER IS SEDUCTIVE

The first is that power is seductive. Whatever is said of Joseph, it is clear that his advancement in Potiphar's house could be viewed as the possession of power. In *The 48 Laws of Power*, Robert Greene asserts, "As your reputation for independence grows, more and more people will come to desire you, wanting to be the one who gets you to commit."[1] The more you advance in your career, the more attractive and seductive that power becomes to certain people.

Pastoring over twenty years has revealed this truth to me in more ways than are imaginable. When our church began to grow in the early years, I was somewhat naive of the attention it brought from the opposite sex. Often, you can be so consumed in your work that you are not aware of the subtle things taking place around you. What I was naive about early on became very apparent in 2005 when my first wife passed away. I was thirty-seven years old, pastoring a church of more than twenty thousand people. We were on worldwide television, and I was preaching around the world. I often joke that it was during that time of widowhood that I discovered there is a thin line between the voice of God and schizophrenia. I had never in my life heard so many people say, "The Lord told me you were my husband." During this very interesting time, I experienced a season unlike any other. There were letters coming from women all across the country. Many had convinced themselves that they were my soul mate. I had never met them, and yet they were planning our wedding. Some even relocated to Nashville and declared that they were sent there to marry me. The attention got so bad that in some cases I was stalked across the country. I am sharing this because I recognize it had nothing to do with me. It was the seductiveness of power. These particular women were struggling with a series of issues, and insecurity was the chief among them.

When people have insecurities, they often attach themselves to power and powerful people for affirmation. Robert Greene writes in *The Concise Art of Seduction*, "Religion is the most seductive system that mankind has created.... Religion humanizes this universe, making us feel important and loved."[2] It is very important when you are experiencing these attractions as a leader that you remember it's really not about you. It's about what you represent. It's about your position and power. Some people are so attracted to power that they will do whatever they can to connect with it. This is one of the areas that most folks in church are aware exists but seldom want to discuss. I think it is important to discuss it here because if you are going to be a transformative leader who shifts from accusation to righteousness, you have to be aware of this dynamic.

I have counseled many young leaders who are enamored by the sudden attention they are receiving. Many are flattered and often find themselves flirting with danger. If you are a glutton for attention, you will fall prey to this scheme of the Devil. Your desire for attention coupled with another's desire to connect with the perceived power of your position is a recipe for disaster. Joseph was a leader of integrity, and although he excelled in Potiphar's house, he was not a glutton for attention.

Let me say another thing about power and seduction. What I have discovered over the years is how leaders become surrogates of sorts in the lives of those they lead. When you are greatly admired, there is a good chance you fill voids in the lives of some of those you lead. This is not done intentionally; it just happens as a result of your effectiveness. For example, a leader who speaks life and encouragement must realize that some listeners could be in a situation where they only hear it when you speak it. Nobody in their lives encourages them and reminds them that they are fearfully and wonderfully made or that they can achieve what they put their minds to. Consequently, leaders become surrogate fathers, mothers, sisters, brothers, husbands, and even wives. Whatever deficits exist in the lives of certain people are filled by those who effectively lead. Though this is an unfair expectation, if you talk to leaders around the world they will tell you that it truly exists. You have to be able to understand the source of the seduction. I make the assumption that there was something missing in the life of Potiphar's wife that she felt Joseph could fill. To become an effective leader, you cannot fall victim to this ploy of the enemy. You must do what Joseph did and maintain your integrity regardless of the issues of others.

ACCEPTING WHAT YOU CANNOT CHANGE

You have to accept what you cannot change. Potiphar's wife could not handle rejection, and, as a result, she accused Joseph of something he did not do. She accused him of attempting to seduce her when in fact it was not the case. As a leader, you must understand that as you navigate through life, you cannot control what people accuse you of. Although you walk in integrity and do all you can to maintain transparency, you must accept the fact that some people will say and do whatever they desire to do to discredit your anointing. Joseph was accused! I understand this in a very real way.

In 2012, I experienced one of the most challenging seasons of my life. I, Joseph, was accused. I was accused of things I did not do. We live in a litigious age, and I discovered in a very real way that people can sue you for anything. Dealing with accusation is extremely difficult because it tests your resolve. We live in a country where the law says we are innocent until proved guilty, but in this age of social media and Internet blogs, whenever leaders are accused, they often are guilty until proved innocent.

I never could imagine the sweltering accusation leveled at me as a leader. Although I never have, nor ever will, profess to be a perfect leader with an unblemished past, to see things written about me that I knew did not happen was very difficult. It was big news in Potiphar's house that his wife had accused Joseph of an indiscretion. Although there were people in the house who knew Joseph and could testify to his integrity, many believed the accusation. One of the most painful things about being accused was watching people who I had assumed knew my heart and my integrity for more than ten or fifteen years believe a scathing lie with no concrete evidence to prove it. What this showed me is that when you are accused, it reveals to you the real nature of the relationships around you. The people who left were already predisposed by their own hidden negative perceptions of me and used this as an opportunity to do what they ultimately wanted to do.

You cannot be naive and assume that the people who are attached to you are connected to you. A trailer can be attached to a truck but not be connected to the truck. Although it is attached, it is not a part of the truck. There are people in your life who are attached to you for a variety of reasons, but when you go through rough spots, they will detach from you. Those who are connected to you are people who believe in you and see their destiny tied to what God is doing in your life. I learned that although I could count a lot of people who attended my church, there were fewer whom I could really count on. Often, when people walk out on you, they have walked out emotionally long before they do it physically. This can be very challenging for any leader. It was very clear to me that I could not control being accused, nor could I control their perception of the events that were unfolding in my life. One of the most powerful lessons you will learn in these kinds of moments is this: people who know you know you, and those who don't really don't matter. You cannot spend precious time trying to convince people you are not what the accused say you are.

YOU CAN CONTROL HOW YOU RESPOND

You can control how you respond. In the biblical story, you will discover that Joseph never attempted to defend himself. He stood firmly on the truth, trusting that God would defend him. One of the statements I continually reminded myself of during my ordeal was this: **a lie has wings and the truth has legs**. Though the lie gets there quicker, it can't stand. The truth may take a long time, but when it shows up, it will stand. What you must do as a leader is have the patience in the midst of accusation to wait on the truth. When you are a person of integrity, you don't have to give a rebuttal. There were so many people wanting me to give my side of the story, but God told me to stand still and that He would fight my battle. My attorneys were doing what they were ordained to do, and I had to do what I was ordained to do. They would fight in the courtroom, and I would fight in the throne room. My prayer life went to another level because I realized that if I was going to respond in ways that brought glory to God, I had to remain spiritually focused on what God called me to do. Too many leaders get in trouble when they get too emotionally involved in accusation and spend countless hours answering every blog, defending every lie. You have to recognize that you cannot control what they say about you, but you can control how you respond to it.

I never will forget what one of my dear friends shared with me. He said to me when I was in the midst of this season that you can't quote silence. This was one of the most powerful and helpful statements for me to hear at the time. There were people pressing me to make a personal public statement, but what my friend's words indicated was that you cannot fuel your enemy by responding to things that have no merit. They wanted to try this case in the media because they knew it was weak and had no merit in court. If I had taken the bait and sparred with them in the press, I would have given credibility to their case. I had to remember Exodus 14:14: "The LORD shall fight for you, and ye shall hold your peace." I put this on the door of my office, made it my screen saver on my phone, and confessed it every day through the entire ordeal.

In the midst of this, I witnessed that my church continued to grow and that people were amazingly supportive. Never underestimate the confidence of the people who follow your leadership. I knew I pastored an intelligent and mature congregation, but this experience confirmed it beyond a shadow of a doubt. I have seen leaders experience accusation and have watched it tear their congregations apart. I've seen huge exoduses from churches where leaders were accused. I am thankful that Mount Zion stood with its leader. I honestly believe that people watched how I chose to deal with the situation. They watched me continue to preach God's word even when lies were being printed in the paper and on blogs. They watched me pray for thousands each week on a prayer call when news stories were airing about the situation. They had seen me go through the loss of my first wife publicly as well, and many had drawn strength from my strength. This situation was another opportunity to see how their leader would represent the Kingdom on this platform.

PLATFORMS FOR HIS GLORY

I believe God gives us platforms for His glory. When we experience crisis, we either make Him look good or embarrass Him. This is what happened with Job. When God allowed the Devil to test him, God put His reputation on the line. God was declaring that Job would make Him look good, going through what others could not. Gustavo Gutierrez says this regarding the character of Job: "The problem of speaking correctly about God amid unjust suffering is not limited to the case of Job, but is a challenge to every believer."[3] Job is the character witness utilized in demonstrating how to speak of God correctly. The hidden revelation of how to speak well of God during severe adversity is unlocked by the character of Job, causing a paradigm shift in which "an entire social and religious order is hereby turned upside down."[4] Throughout his entire trying ordeal, Job maintained his integrity of speech concerning God. God could trust Job with trouble.

As an effective leader, you have to ask yourself, can God trust you to represent Him when you are under attack? Will you do that which brings glory to Him, or will you embarrass Him? I chose the former. Beyond a few updates on the case, I never drew attention to it. Rather, I continued to walk in my assignment and trust God to work it all out. My preaching became more intense, and my commitment was taken to another level. What the Devil wants to do is to hinder the assignment upon your life. I had to remember that every day I woke up, there were precious lives depending upon what God would say through me. I had to remember that God chose and consecrated me for something that would influence the Kingdom in a powerful way. I refused to neglect my responsibilities because of accusation. Every time my members showed up for church, I was there. When they came to Bible study, I was there. I kept my preaching appointments and all of my meetings. I was not going to give the Devil the victory while I sat on the sideline feeling sorry for myself. I had to step up and be the leader I knew I had the capacity to become. As a leader, you cannot get off course fanning flies.

Once, when I was driving my father in the car, a fly got in. I had one hand on the steering wheel and a newspaper in the other hand, swatting the fly. I was putting our lives in danger and risking not arriving at my destination because I was consumed with swatting a fly. There are many leaders who waste time and risk not making it to where God wants them to be, all because they swat flies rather than drive toward their destination.

YOUR CHARACTER IS ON PUBLIC DISPLAY

There is one more thing about Joseph's response that we should note. Nowhere do we see Joseph becoming vindictive toward Potiphar's wife. When you are being accused, your character is on public display. I remember telling my congregation that no amount of hate could hate the love out of me. **When we harbor vindictiveness, it is like drinking poison and hoping the other person dies.** Your assignment is too great to allow accusation to sidetrack you. You can control how you respond.

MANAGE THE SCRUTINY

You have to manage the scrutiny. The most difficult part for leaders is when your name has been tarnished by accusation. Joseph's name was golden in Potiphar's house; now, with this accusation, it was tainted. Leaders who are serious strive to make sure their name is good. I always wanted my name to be good, and I did everything I could to make sure it was. Just like Joseph, I would soon discover that when accusation comes, scrutiny comes.

When you are under the spotlight, you have to be able to remember who you are. Joseph is Jacob's son. Joseph is Abraham's great-grandson. Joseph has been chosen and has the favor of his father upon his life. You have to remember what God says about you when others say all manner of evil against you.

It was difficult going places and having people speaking under their breath, having conversation about me while I was present. The scrutiny is designed to break you. It is designed to cause you to live in shame and guilt over something you didn't do. I remember praying fervently, and the Lord said to me, "Stop worrying about your name and lift up My name. Then and only then will I restore your name." That was perhaps the most powerful and pivotal moment in my life. While I was scrambling trying to save my name, God reminded me that He would protect my name. Scrutiny is going to come, but when you know who you are in God, you aren't sidetracked by it.

One of the questions every leader who shifts from accusation to righteousness must ask himself or herself is, why did certain things happen? Kellerman and Rhode make the following assertion concerning leadership strategies: "A necessary first step on the path to leadership involves self-reflection."[5] If you are not asking this question, you will miss valuable lessons in life. Regardless of the organization you choose to lead, you must know that when the inevitable accusations come, you must seek direction from God regarding what is required of you as a result. For me, it was a time of self-reflections and ministry evaluation.

MAKING ADJUSTMENTS

The final principle I want to share with you is the importance of making adjustments. What I realized is that this situation was an opportunity for me to look closer at the infrastructure of our ministry and make the necessary adjustments that would curtail this kind of event from ever happening again. I imagined Joseph being seduced by Potiphar's wife because he put himself in proximity to her, where it could happen. What this situation did for me as a leader was cause me to take the administration of our church through a season of closing all gaps. Wherever there were potential risks or gaps, we spent days and weeks closing them.

When you are moving fast toward the fulfillment of your assignment, you can take some areas for granted. We began revising certain policies and procedures, revamping some and finding assurance in others. We began redefining certain staff roles and expectations as well as training our staff in critical areas to prevent future exposure. The adjustments caused me to take nothing for granted. I examined everything that was associated with the church to make sure we were 100 percent compliant at all levels.

Often, God will allow a leader to experience moments like this in order to motivate her or him to pay attention to detail and bring things into order. This is what integrity is about. Organizational leader Brian P. Hall conducted a study on values and integrity as they relate to corporate performance and discovered that

> values not only underpin our beliefs but are also the basis for our morality. The values priorities we have chosen dictate our day-to-day decisions about what we see as right or wrong. When people in leadership are made explicitly aware of their own values priorities and those held by the group or team they work with, they become more conscious about their decisions and what the criteria for their choices are.[6]

It is not just about your personal lifestyle; it's about your business practices as well. So much has happened since we made the necessary adjustments in our ministry.

The cases against me were dismissed out of court in October and December of 2012. It took a while for the truth to show up, but when it did, it stood. Allow me to say a word about this. When the accusations began, it was blasted across the media. But when I was vindicated, it was a news blurb. You cannot expect the same attention to be given to your victories as to your accusations. This taught me the importance of staying true to my assignment for the glory of God. When we made those adjustments, our ministry began to experience unprecedented growth. This was and continues to be an amazing season birthed out of a painful season of accusation.

I am convinced that one of the greatest lessons I've learned is the importance of establishing new order. These situations cause your mode of operation to change. You are no longer naive concerning the people around you or their capacity for causing harm to your organization. You put in safeguards and systems to protect the sanctity of the organization. Often, these lessons are passed down to other leaders by those who have learned through the painful experience of accusation. This is why I am sharing candidly in this book, because I want leaders to understand the potential threats. I have developed certain criteria for those who work alongside me in ministry:

- The first requirement is that people have references. You cannot have people working closely with you without a sense of their track record.

- Second, we look at their faithfulness in ministry beyond the position. Are they committed to the vision of the church (church attendance, Bible study, tither, volunteer)? This gives us an indication of their commitment level. If they have strong commitment prior to being given a position, they will not leave the ministry if they are removed from the position.

- Third, we want people who are teachable. People who are willing to learn have the capacity to enhance any organization.

- Fourth, we look for people who are grateful. People who know how to say "thank you" are often humbled by opportunities rather than feel entitled to them. We want people who pray for the organization and its leader. These kinds of folks serve with good intentions rather than ulterior motives.

- Fifth, we look for people who invest in our vision. You cannot invest in people who have divested from you.

- Sixth, we trust the Holy Spirit's direction regarding the people around us. You can have talented people who are not anointed to walk alongside you.

- Seventh, we look for people with the capacity to walk with us into our "not yet." We oftentimes allow people to get close to us who can handle where we are, but we need people who can navigate where God is taking us. In short, as you progress in your vision, take nothing for granted.

The shift that Joseph makes from accusation to righteousness happens because his integrity is not shaken by accusation. One of the things I set out to do early on in my ministry was to get it right. When I mention righteousness, I am referring to what is pleasing to God. I have seen so much in ministry. I remember being exposed to great men of God in my early twenties. I was sitting at tables that any young preacher would covet. The Lord told me then that He was exposing me to teach me valuable lessons. Those lessons would be twofold. They would be lessons on what to do and what not to do. I set my course on doing those things that were pleasing in God's sight. I was determined to get it right and be a leader who would inspire others. Joseph's example of integrity is one that speaks to any leader with similar aspirations.

INTEGRITY WILL SUSTAIN YOU

You must remember that your talent or gift may take you to places of influence, but your integrity is what will sustain you. Many leaders make the mistake of focusing on their gift or talent and spending too little time developing integrity. Joseph's integrity was defined by a simple yet profound act. It was his ability to say no. Whenever you are presented with things inconsistent with God's will for your life, you have to have the ability and strength to decline. It may come with a price, but ultimately it pays huge dividends.

Life is always about choices, decisions, and consequences. Every day you wake up you will be presented with choices. As a leader, you must have the spiritual discernment to examine those choices and determine which decisions you will make. Those decisions can have long-lasting implications. Whatever is said about Joseph and Potiphar's wife, we know based on the Bible that it was a false accusation. Joseph did not do it or try to cover it up to protect his reputation. He did not cut a deal so that it would work in his favor. He stood on his integrity because from the very beginning he made the right decision. He knew the consequences would be on his side. My grandmother would say, "If you do right, right will come back to you." Martin Luther King, Jr. once said, "Although the arc of the moral universe is long, it bends towards justice." Although it may take time, right consequences will follow right decisions.[7]

This is such a pivotal time for leaders around the world. With scrutiny and continuous attack, many leaders are intentional about making right decisions. These decisions have to do with the people they have around them, employ, and empower to carry out tasks on behalf of the organization. Nothing should be taken for granted.

When shifting to righteousness from accusation, you must be mindful of your own capacity for failure and make certain that you guard against anything that could compromise your integrity. Progressive leaders must be extremely careful how they manage the day-to-day grind of the responsibilities associated with leadership. Leadership is demanding, and becoming successful at it requires long hours and often grueling schedules. When you put this into context, you will discover that many leaders are suffering silently and are vulnerable to the schemes of the Devil.

LEADERS BLEED TOO

When a pastor suffers, his family suffers. The reality is that there are many leaders and their families who are suffering in silence in their own silos. This silent suffering has far-reaching implications on how effectively the pastor can provide a powerful witness of the gospel of Jesus Christ. There is an amazing revelation from the cross of Calvary: "My God, My God, why hast thou forsaken me?" (Matt. 27:46). This statement from Jesus discloses the reality that many leaders deal with. Regardless of the anointing, position, and title, no leader is exempt from having his or her private pain in Gethsemane manifest into a public spectacle at Calvary. The amazing paradox of Jesus' pain is His ability to minister while bleeding. He is pouring out while blood is running out. **The challenge for any leader is having to be strong at his or her weakest point.** Jesus was a victim of accusation and a tainted court system. He was a victim of a world system that refused to embrace that which was spiritual and different. Yet in the midst of it, He prayed, "Father forgive them; for they know not what they do" (Luke 23:34).

Please know that I am sharing this reality not as an admission of a burden but as an acknowledgment of the weight of the call upon us as pastors and leaders who bleed. The assumed and sometimes stated contract to which most adhere is an absolute burden on ourselves and our families. Kirk Byron Jones says in his book *Rest in the Storm* that most pastors are expected to carry out the following duties:

1. Preach and lead worship at least four Sundays a month.

2. Administer Communion to the congregation on the first Sunday of the month.

3. Conduct funeral services for members of the church. The pastor will contact the bereaved family as soon as possible following the death and meet with them prior to the service.

4. Train leaders.

5. Teach weekly Bible study.

6. Twenty other things.[8]

Jones contends that such a schedule causes the pastor to inflict "self-violence," and this violence wreaks havoc on the pastor and his or her family life.

Eleven percent of the adult population is divorced. Twenty-five percent of adults have had at least one divorce. Divorce rates among conservative Christians are much higher than those of atheists and agnostics. With the amount of drama in the church, there seems to be a problem not only among pastors but also in the pew.

Many leaders cannot shift from accusation to righteousness because they develop unhealthy approaches to ministry. These pathological approaches often produce breakdowns in their families, ministries, physical bodies, minds, and moral and spiritual lives. It seems that in this time of technological genius and access, we have failed to create opportunities for self-development and spiritual renewal among leaders. Many leaders have become so enthralled and entangled in the pursuit of ecclesiastical celebrity and fame that they have left their first love. Many have been led astray as a result of believing in their own power and might more than they believe in the mandates in the word of God: "To whom much is given, from him much will be required" (Luke 12:48 NKJV).

Perhaps you are reading this book and you are bleeding right now as a result of the self-inflicted wounds of self-pursuit and selfish ambition. You cannot fall into the trap of mimicking the lifestyles of those who are poor examples. You must be willing to follow the examples of those who raise the standard of character, integrity, wholeness, and humility, which brings everlasting promotion and prosperity. I've seen so many leaders get caught up in the trappings of the illusion of success. Power, positions, and titles that satisfy the ego all produce leaders who lose sight of the true purposes of God in their lives. To top it off, many leaders are overworked. Even though they may be physically, mentally, emotionally, and spiritually exhausted, they are unable to stop because of their commitments, expectations, expenses, people, and personal paralysis. Many harbor indifference to what is going on within their human-made kingdoms.

If you are unhealthy, you cannot be vulnerable enough to make the shift from accusation, even your own, to righteousness. Righteousness must become a standard in the midst of accusation. Whether or not Potiphar's wife tempted Joseph, it is most certain that if he had had the proper structures in place, where she would no longer have access to him, he would not have been accused. Yet, some of the most valuable lessons in life are learned in the most difficult situations of life. Joseph's integrity sustained him on his way to the fulfillment of his destiny, and although circumstances appeared to be working against him, it all shifted toward a righteous plan ordained by God before the foundations of the world. Every shift in the life of a leader prepares him or her for the next.

Allow me to share with you something the Lord revealed to me as He was vindicating me. He assured me that nothing happens to me unless He allows it. He showed me two pieces of glass. One was clear, and the other had a texture. He revealed to me that the textured glass had been tempered. The tempering process involves intense heat in order to prepare the glass to be used differently from the clear glass. The clear glass was weak and could be easily broken. He revealed to me that the tempered glass had been through a process of heating whereby the glass was strengthened and positioned to carry greater weight than the clear glass could.

Perhaps you can identify an accusation and difficult circumstances that surround you now. God is allowing this situation to temper you like glass so that you can carry the weight of the assignment He is about to take you into. I knew that was the case for me, and I'm confident it is God's desire for your life.

CHAPTER 7

FROM CHAINED TO UNLEASHED

As a result of an accusation, Joseph was thrown into prison by Potiphar. Joseph did nothing to deserve this unfortunate turn of events; it was a part of a providential plan of God to propel him closer to his destiny. There are different types of prisons and different kinds of chains we wear. Leaders will always experience imposed limitations, whether by rules of their respective institutions or even just the limitations of time and money. Some people are on jobs where they are limited or isolated, while others are in relationships where they are limited. Leaders strive to help others to unleash their full potential.

SERVING IN A CONFINED CONTEXT

This shift is important because you must understand the importance of working through limitations and still being productive in your assignment. Personal crisis does not prevent purpose from manifesting in the life of a real leader. Joseph's prison experience reveals some valuable lessons for those who seek to lead successfully. The very first lesson it reveals is the reality of serving in a confined context. I've helped numerous leaders work through situations where they felt in bondage to tradition and stagnation. When you are a visionary and have a desire to operate with progressive leadership, it can be incredibly frustrating to operate in places that limit your potential.

During my early years at Mount Zion, numerous factors sought to place limitations on what I felt God was doing through my life. Tradition was the prevailing factor. If there is anything people are passionate about, it is their traditions. Not all traditions are bad; however, when they are perpetuated for the sake of tradition rather than progress, they become problematic. I came in with a vision to move the church forward, and some of the things I proposed ran right into tradition. There were some people who didn't mind integrating new ideas as long as the ideas didn't conflict with their traditions. As you can imagine, this became a challenge as we attempted to move forward.

Many leaders are struggling in a context of confinement where the rules of the prison are rigid and unbending and their creativity is being stifled. Every leader experiences this and must discover ways to be effective despite the prison. Joseph was in prison, and yet he continued to fulfill his purposes while there. He interprets dreams in the prison. Although he has been locked up, his gift has not been locked out. When you are committed to your vision manifesting, limitations are viewed as opportunities that unleash the gifts that reside in you.

Often, God allows us to get into situations that seek to limit us in order to sharpen the gifts that are in us. If gifts can evolve in places like that, they can evolve anywhere. Your gifts often bear the most fruit in the worst situations. It was during those early years at Mount Zion that I learned to be creative and implement unique strategies to work within a system that was not willing to shift easily. There are five things that you will experience in this shift. The first is the "I'm innocent. Why am I here?" season.

"I'M INNOCENT. WHY AM I HERE?"

Joseph really was innocent, but nevertheless he found himself in an oppressive situation. Often, when gifted and anointed leaders find themselves in limiting contexts, there is a sense that they are being punished. I've had several friends who have struggled being in churches where they felt God was punishing them. As unfortunate as this might sound, it is more common than you can imagine. Many leaders are suffering from depression because they view their appointment as a sentence. All the vision and enthusiasm that comes with it is often quashed when they end up in organizations that punish them for progress. Many of these leaders are depressed because they can't see past the current reality of their struggle. There has to be some level of optimistic hope of their vision soon becoming their new reality. Some may see this seeking of success as delusional. But executive coach Marshall Goldsmith asserts that the delusion of success is not necessarily a bad thing: "If we had a complete grip on reality, seeing every situation for exactly what it is, we wouldn't get out of bed in the morning. After all, the most realistic people in our society are the chronically depressed."[1] Whether you are a pastor, a CEO, or anything else, if you are placed in an oppressive context designed to limit your capacity for growth, it can be a difficult assignment. The key to avoiding the pit of despair during the prison season is to remain focused on the vision.

I've seen some churches never grow beyond a few members and have difficulty keeping pastors because of their inability to change. The sad reality is that many churches are on the verge of extinction because they cannot attract progressive and effective leadership. The leaders they do attract feel punished by a system that places a small premium on advancement. There is a great deal of shock for leaders who find themselves in a situation like this. It is very important that you know you are not being punished; rather, you are strategically positioned in order that you will be prepared for the next level. I believe that every successful leader has spent time in places where he or she asked: "Why am I here?"

When I first became pastor of Mount Zion, there were many days I asked that question. I was struggling because I had invested in myself by preparing for ministry and then I was called to a church that at that time was content to penalize progressive and innovative ideas to move forward. What I encountered was the next thing you have to deal with in limiting contexts: the keepers of the gates.

CONFRONTING THE GATEKEEPERS

In Joseph's prison, there were guards, or keepers of the gates. These persons are there to protect the system and make sure there is little deviation from the mode of operation. In every organization, there will be keepers of the gates. There are always those persons who are positioned to make sure things stay the way they always are. They prevent any attempt at liberation. Their sole purpose is to maintain incarceration. Whether it is a board or a family, every leader has experienced this group. I'm sure that as you are reading this, you've already thought of names of some gatekeepers. This is a difficult group to deal with when you are attempting to implement new ideas into an organization.

Martin Luther King, Jr. experienced keepers of the gates during the civil rights movement. He was advised to wait and slow down the progress toward social change. In response he wrote, "Human progress never rolls in on the wheels of inevitability."[2]

During the ministry of Jesus, it was quite clear that the religious leaders of the day were keepers of the gates. Anything that threatened the sanctity of the status quo was quickly condemned and punished. The keepers of the gates say things like, "This is the way it's always been." They find comfort in things remaining the way they have been. Prisons thrive off of redundancy and routine. Prisoners do the same thing every day in an intentional and methodical way to maintain the order of the prison. Some organizations have developed the same system. I've seen churches do the same thing the same way for years. Everyone wants change, but nobody wants to change.

What keepers of the gates often don't realize is that the whole world is passing them by while they are preserving rituals and patterns that have no relevance. **After all, you can't have an eight-track ministry in an iPod generation.** There is a way to preserve the gates yet introduce innovative ideas that can move the institution forward. This is the transformative gift of leadership. What Joseph did in the prison had never been done before. You have the ability to do something in your limiting context that has never been done before.

What I have discovered is that most institutions want to grow. The struggle is often in preserving those things that are important to the organization while engaging in new ways to operate. It takes great patience as a leader to walk an organization through this shift. It's easy to demonize the keepers of the gates and declare they have no desire to see the organization transform, but that would be a cop-out. Those folks are just doing what they have always done. They would not do it if they were not invested in the organization. They have a desire, as you do, to see progress. A successful leader cannot impose his or her will upon the keepers of the gate. That's like breaking out of prison, because although you are out, you are never free. The goal is to assure those who keep the gates that what they are protecting is important to you as well and is an integral part of where your vision is headed.

I made certain at Mount Zion that I didn't demonize the

keepers of the gates. Many of them had been in the church longer than I had been alive. It was important for me to hear their stories and become sensitive to those things they held sacred. A perfect example of this for us was the hymns of the church. Our church grew rapidly, and it was during the emergence of more contemporary gospel music. Many of the hymns that were dear to many folks were not being integrated into the worship. I must admit that I felt that those songs were counter-progressive and that to embrace them would be to maintain a loyalty to tradition that was the enemy of innovation. This was my way of thinking as a leader. Anything that reminded me of the "Old Mount Zion" I felt was not progressive. So in an effort to move the church forward and keep pace with the growth, I intentionally divested from those things. Wisdom ultimately prevailed, and I realized that the hymns should be integral to all we do.

There was a group of folks in our church who were being exposed to new, more contemporary forms of music, but the songs that were meaningful for them, which had been songs of victory over the years, were never sung in worship. I realized that I was breaking the hearts of the keepers of the gates. When an organization grows, it must grow in a balanced way, and I understood this. I eventually put the hymns back in our worship, and to my surprise, the entire church has embraced them as a meaningful part of the worship experience. It's amazing to see the young people look forward to this part of the worship experience. If you visit our church today, we still sing a morning hymn every Sunday. This is just one example of many. If leaders are to be successful, it is essential that they properly engage those who keep the gates.

Another thing about those who keep the gates is their positioning in the system. They are the first point of contact. If your leadership style engages them and seeks to work with them, you will create a welcoming environment conducive to growth. If not, the tension that exists in the organization will be the first thing people are introduced to when they engage your church or business. If you are going to be successful, you have to give the gatekeepers something. Your vision cannot be a big eraser that wipes out everything that existed prior to your arrival. There were things they were doing that were effective long before your arrival.

I've also learned that this group can teach you a lot. The gatekeepers can teach a new leader the lay of the land and help him or her navigate through the context even if it is limiting. You need to forge alliances if you are going to be successful in this kind of place. You need people who can advise you on the best ways to get things done.

One of the things Joseph's prison ordeal reveals is that he would be a man in authority, but he was also under authority. And effective leaders must be teachable. You must be willing to learn as much as you can and submit to others who can assist your vision in coming to fruition. It is helpful for leaders to coach people through letting go of the old system instead of demanding that the new paradigm be embraced. John Whitmore suggests that "it is often more productive to allocate time and focus to provoking and assisting people to let go of the old. . . . the new rushes in to fill the vacuum. Remove the blocks and the potential emerges."[3] It's very unfortunate to see leaders who have drawn a line in the sand and who are determined to do things their way without availability to words of wisdom or counsel.

The keepers of the gates may be preservers of the way things have been done, but they have a deep desire to see the organization move forward. There are some extraordinary people keeping the gates. If you are going to see your vision come to fruition, you need to create opportunities for engagement.

PRISON ENVIRONMENT

The next experience is the prison environment. When Joseph goes to prison, his entire environment changes. He was just promoted in Potiphar's house, where he enjoyed certain privileges; now he is thrust into an environment where things are completely opposite. When I refer to a prison environment, I am referencing the idea of becoming institutionalized. There is a mind-set that must be understood. Whenever you seek to do meaningful and transformative things in an organization, you should be aware of those who have been institutionalized by the theological, sociological, and operative constructs that exist there.

One of the most difficult things to do in a system where people are chained is change their minds. The Bible says in Matthew 4:16, "The people which sat in darkness saw great light; and to them which sat in the region and shadow of death light is sprung up." John 1:5 says, "And the light shineth in darkness; and the darkness comprehended it not." Second Corinthians 4:4 says, "In whom the god of this world hath blinded the minds of them which believe not, lest the light of the glorious gospel of Christ, who is the image of God, should shine unto them." What these Scriptures reveal is the lack of illumination in the mind. Where there is no illumination (knowledge), there can be no transformation. The problem is that when you are institutionalized, you begin to think that you have to make a dysfunctional existence normal in order to convince yourself that nothing is wrong with you. In other words, you are not the one locked up; they are the ones locked out. This way of thinking is prominent in many institutions that find it easy to criticize those churches or organizations that are experiencing growth and success, because to do so reaffirms that there is nothing wrong with them.

Consider this illustration. If you were to go to the movies at noon while the sun was at its peak and enter the dark theater, it would not be long before you became comfortable in darkness. Your pupils would expand to allow the maximum amount of light in. You would know how to find your drink and popcorn as well as navigate through the dark theater if need be. Imagine someone coming in late to the movie steps on your foot. Your first thought is, *You can't see?* You've been sitting in darkness so long that darkness has become normal, instead of light. This is what happened during the time of Jesus. He was that light, but those in darkness had difficulty comprehending it because they were institutionalized to the dark.

Effective leaders must be aware that this mentality exists if they are going to bring change into an organization. Years of being acclimated to a way of thinking is not going to be changed overnight. You must be willing to understand the environment if you are going to be effective within it. Some relationships in the prison would be instrumental in propelling Joseph to his destiny. He had to engage those in the prison and be intentional about developing friendships. If there is one profound lesson we can learn about Joseph's interaction with the baker and the butler in the story, it is that conversation took place. One of the reason leaders are not effective is that they don't know how to communicate in contexts like this. It is critical to your survival that you communicate with those in the organization or church. As simple as this might appear, I've seen leaders struggle in this area. Many operate in isolation and refuse to develop relationships. This weakness keeps leaders in their prisons of limitation and away from their destiny.

With the emergence of megachurches and technology, many leaders have lost the common touch in the hustle and bustle of doing ministry. I have seen leaders isolate themselves from the people they serve and have no intent to be involved in the lives of the people. They preach and go home. I remember promising the Lord from the beginning of my ministry at Mount Zion that regardless of how the church grew, I would always be a relational leader. More than twenty years and more than twenty-eight thousand members later, I still shake hands after service, perform weddings and funerals, and visit the hospital.

I believe that we are in a new day in the church, and in order for churches to be effective and grow, there will have to be a focus on the pastor building relationships and encouraging others to do likewise. The day of ecclesiastical celebrity is over. If illumination is going to break through the darkness of institutionalization, it will require intentional acts of relationship. Jesus walked among the people. He did not allow Himself to be isolated from them. Even when the disciples attempted to guard him from the crowd, a woman with an issue pressed her way to touch the hem of His garment. She was changed forever. Not just her physical condition but also her mind-set were changed when He declared that she was made whole. The ministry grew and people were changed because Jesus interacted directly with people.

This is an area that I am tremendously passionate about. I was able to get through one of the most limiting religious confinements because of my willingness to establish relationships. Mount Zion was known as one of the most traditional and stagnant churches in the city when I became pastor. I realized that regardless of how well I preached, the light would not be comprehended by the darkness unless I developed strategic relationships. What came out of those relationships was priceless. I learned how to transform a stagnant and limiting context by slowly integrating change at a pace that was palatable rather than pushed on the people.

If you are sitting in darkness and you've been there for a long time, your eyes cannot handle the brightness of a sudden flash of light bearing down upon your face. You automatically reject it. Though light is a good thing, your normal reaction is rejection, because it's too much at one time. You need time to adjust to the light. So often, leaders don't give people time to adjust to the light because desire to fulfill the vision outweighs the needs of the people whom the vision will impact. **It is true that where there is no vision the people perish, but it is also a fact that where there are no people the vision perishes.** I learned that the light needed to be gradually recessed so the people could receive it. I integrated change slowly and gave them time to adjust to it. After a period of time, I would introduce something else. I went at a pace sensitive to where they were, and they gladly embraced it because they were appreciative of my attempts to walk rather than run with vision. In every organization, there is an environment that must be understood. There is a language, a mode of operation, a culture of existing that has kept those in the organization feeling significant. Effective leaders must consider all of this if they are going to shift from being chained to being unleashed.

PRISON ID

The next area is that of prison ID. When I refer to this, I am talking about the identity and perceptions of those in the prison. Prisoners today no longer are known by their names; rather, they are known by numbers or as convicts. When you find yourself as a leader in a context like this, it can create a negative perception about you. So many leaders struggle with identity issues. Some leaders are struggling with ministerial low self-esteem. Who wants to be identified with an oppressive context? Who wants to be tied to an organization that prides itself on limiting your potential to advance as a leader? It's difficult being the leader of an organization that is not progressing while others around you are moving forward. I've counseled so many leaders through seasons like this.

I remember experiencing this in my ministry. When Mount Zion was a few hundred members, very traditional and fighting over change, it had a great impact upon my identity. When I would tell people where I pastored, they would look like they felt sorry for me. This greatly affected my self-esteem as a leader and tainted my motives for wanting the church to grow. I wanted the church to grow because I needed to be validated as a leader. My self-steem was directly tied to the growth of my church rather than the assignment on my life. I've since learned better, but many leaders fall into the trap of comparison and lose sight of their calling.

Not every church can be mega. Not all ministries will have million-dollar budgets. Success is not measured in numbers or dollars but rather in the fulfillment of the assignment God has given to that leader for that place. So often, leaders become caught up in the perceptions of other people. Joseph was in prison, but prison was not in him. You can be in a difficult context, but it should never determine how you perceive yourself. Although Joseph was in prison, his gift of interpreting dreams was what he would be remembered for. His identity would not be defined as a convict; rather, it would be defined as dreamer and dream interpreter. Never allow your context to determine your content. You must be sure of who you are regardless of the challenges in your organization. It takes a unique person to be assigned to a place like that. What's inside of you is designed to transform into what God desires. Not many people can handle that assignment. You were called to greatness.

Allow me to say another word about comparison. I discovered that when I compared myself to others, it created a misguided perspective. Your assignment is different from what others are doing. Often, we see the success of others in their context and covet what they are doing. We use them as a measuring rod for our own success. While in some instances there are certain aspects of their success that we can learn from, we do more harm when we juxtapose their model against our own. There are so many variables that can contribute to someone else's success that may not exist where you are. Demographics, economic environment, and population are just a few. I remember marveling at a great ministry in California and attempting to impose the same ideas upon Mount Zion. I was using their model as my model for success. What I soon discovered is that Mount Zion had its own dynamics, and what would make it successful was determining what things worked and what things did not. You cannot just use someone else's template to build a successful model of your own. Nashville is not Los Angeles. It was imperative for me to discover soon what my identity and the identity of our church would be before I created a carbon copy of someone else's vision and struggled to make it work in my own church.

Let me be clear. There are effective models of ministry that we can learn from. There are powerful programs and models that can help propel your organization to the next level. What I am suggesting is that when you compare your success to the success of another, your identity as a leader can be compromised. So many young preachers see preachers on television and become carbon copies of what they see. They have not taken into consideration the anointing of that leader, what that platform may have cost that leader, and the current contextual situation of that leader. They take a model that costs millions to manage and impose it upon a context that can barely pay its electric bill. You have to embrace where you are now and be willing to work hard to get where your vision is designed to take you. You can't walk in someone else's assignment.

I've seen pastors have multiple locations that they never should have started. They struggle to fill up one service and yet place an undue burden on their membership to start another location. Without counting the cost, they are motivated by competition and the illusion of success. As a result, they have two locations, but neither is growing because the motivation was wrong. I've seen ministries go on television too soon. The leader's insatiable desire for notoriety and success pushed the church into going on television without having the necessary pieces in place. As a result, the telecast is done poorly, the quality does not represent the kingdom of God in excellence, and the financial burden on the church jeopardizes the integrity of the vision. **You can do a good thing, but you have to ask yourself if it is a God thing.** Ministerial ID is important, and when you are confident in who you are, you don't despise small beginnings. You embrace the challenge head-on, and it motivates you to do what Joseph did. He was productive in prison.

PRODUCE WITHOUT EXCUSE

As we have seen, Joseph was in a context that sought to limit his capacity and punish him, yet he was able to thrive. The fact that he interprets dreams in prison is an indicator that his gift did not become dormant. It flourished in a difficult context. Often, the greatest in us comes to fruition when the worst is happening to us. One of the most important lessons any leader can learn is how to produce without excuse. You cannot make excuses for your context. Even if it is not the most ideal situation, you must still function and be effective within it. I hear so many leaders complaining about the limitations they are experiencing. They spend countless hours and days chronicling the challenges rather than making full use of the opportunities.

In the biblical story, the baker and the butler had their

dreams interpreted by Joseph. What Joseph did in prison was instrumental in getting him out. I am still benefiting today from the decision I made twenty years ago when my context was not ideal. I could have despised it, chosen to be passive, and waited to be moved to something better, but I chose to be as productive as I could be, and it has yielded great dividends. This is an opportunity for you to maximize the moment and bring change into the prison context. There is a need in the prison that, once met, will providentially position you for the next step toward your destiny. You have to give 100 percent in prison before you can be entrusted to the palace. I preached just as hard with two hundred members as I do with twenty-eight thousand. There is no difference for me. I worked just as hard then as I do now, because I am motivated by what is inside of me. I knew that my gift needed to flourish in a place where others would have given up. Perhaps as you read this, your gift is being ignited again. I hope so.

You must remember that what you do now has lasting implications. Remember what Jesus said in Matthew 25:23, "His lord said to him, Well done, good and faithful servant; you have been faithful over a few things, I will make you ruler over many things. Enter into the joy of your lord" (NKJV). **You have to think big in a little context.** I often say that you can't be big if little has you. I use this phrase because many leaders fail to embrace the possibilities in difficult contexts. You have been anointed and appointed, and wherever you are, you are to be fruitful and productive. One of the most powerful words spoken over Joseph's life was at the bedside of Jacob: "Joseph is a fruitful bough, even a fruitful bough by a well; whose branches run over the wall" (Gen. 49:22). This is confirmation that wherever Joseph is, he will be productive. No wall of limitation or oppression can prevent his gift from flourishing.

CONCLUSION

You will experience places where you are confined by circumstances. But it's in those situations where you have to realize that your gift has positioned you to go over the walls of confinement and be productive despite circumstances that may not be conducive. This is how you shift from being chained to becoming unleashed. It probably won't be in a place of comfort and ease. It will happen in a place of stress and strain. When you are experiencing your greatest challenge and being confined by the limited capacity of others, remember you are called to this. You are called to go over the wall and produce without excuse. You are destined for greatness, and regardless of the context, you will always be effective.

CHAPTER 8
FROM CONCEDING TO SOLVING

J oseph is confined to prison for some time. However, God is in the plan. When the butler is freed, Joseph requests to be remembered. When Pharaoh had dreams that nobody could interpret, he sent for Joseph. The butler informed Pharaoh that in his prison was a man who had a gift of interpreting dreams. Regardless of your location and situation, when God gets ready for you, He will make provisions for you to be found. Pharaoh conceded his need for help, but so did Joseph. Joseph put his trust in God. There was a problem, and Joseph was the only one who could solve it. There is something within us that manifests at the right time. Leaders are born to solve problems. Regardless of where we find ourselves, God allows our gifts to glorify and serve His purpose. This problem solving helps position leaders to serve effectively and gain respect for their abilities and gifts.

One of the things I've learned is that God is always active in the life of His people. He is not passively sitting by observing the affairs of our lives. He is providentially engaged in every component, navigating circumstances so that His will comes to pass. Joseph's gift flourished in prison, and therefore it gave him greater credibility in the palace. If he had not been productive, the butler would not have referenced him when Pharaoh's dreams could not be interpreted. When God is moving, concessions have to be made. Pharaoh conceded that he needed help. With all of his resources, this was no small thing. Joseph concedes his need to be remembered in the prison. His concession is used to connect his gift to Pharaoh's need. Both require great humility. Pride can be destructive, but humility can create opportunities for you to be released into your destiny.

This scene in the story reveals to us some valuable lessons that every leader should know. Nothing just happens. Everything happens with purpose and on purpose to bring God's will to pass in your life. I remember the very day I came to Mount Zion. I had just gotten to Nashville in 1989 to attend Vanderbilt Divinity School. Because church was very important to me, I knew I needed to find a fellowship to unite with, and then I needed to get involved. I drove down Jefferson Street, which is a historic street in Nashville with numerous churches on it. I was immediately led to this red brick building on the corner of Eleventh and Jefferson. I went in and sat to the rear. It was prior to service beginning. As I sat in the back, an elderly lady was very kind to me. I never shall forget her words. She said, "Are you a minister, young man?" I said, "Yes I am." She then took it upon herself to introduce me to the pastor of the church. I was warmly received, but I must admit that the first worship service was unlike what I was accustomed to. I thought I would visit another church the next Sunday, and I did, but in the midst of that service I left and went back to this quaint little church on the corner. I joined that Sunday, and the pastor embraced me in ways I never could have imagined. I began teaching Sunday school and getting involved. He allowed me to preach after being there three weeks, and the people were so receptive to my message. I knew this would be home for me. I often think about how God was navigating my steps. Psalm

37:23 says, "The steps of a good man are ordered by the LORD and He delights in his way" (NKJV). I often think about where my life would be had I not returned to Mount Zion. Although at the time it was a different experience, I felt deeply that God had sent me there to serve, and as a result, I am the pastor today. God is always in the plan. We have to obey Him.

WAITING FOR YOUR CHANCE

Joseph's shift from conceding to solving involved waiting until his chance came. This is an important lesson for leaders. Joseph was in prison and others were released before him, yet he patiently waited for God's will to manifest in his life. As I mentioned in the previous chapter, there will be those moments when your context will confine you and prove oppressively limiting. You have to realize that it is not a terminal stop but rather a temporary one. You have to serve and remain patient until things turn around. When you remember your assignment and what God said to you when He first chose and consecrated you, it will keep you when you grow weary of the redundancy of your situation.

I've witnessed so many leaders who allow their frustration and impatience to ruin any chance of things turning around. I almost made that mistake in my ministry. When Mount Zion was opposing change and I felt like I was in a prison of tradition and resistance, I applied for a church in California as a way to escape. The church was so interested in me coming to pastor that they made me a verbal offer to come be their pastor before I had even preached there. I was so excited until I prayed about it. Yes, I was led completely in my flesh and frustration, and I realized that God would not release me to go. Here was a congregation in California excited about a young pastor coming to serve them, and I had to call and decline.

When you know you are out of the will of God, you never have peace. I often wonder about how I would have missed my assignment by stepping out of God's will for my life. Maybe you are reading this book and opportunities are presenting themselves, and they look more attractive than the situation you are currently in. You have to be very clear that you don't confuse opportunity with assignment. Opportunities will come and go, but assignments will last. Although you are weary in your current placement, you have to wait until your change comes. Remember the words of Habakkuk 2:3: "For the vision is yet for an appointed time, but at the end it shall speak, and not lie: though it tarry, wait for it; because it will surely come, it will not tarry." You have to develop the endurance to remain faithful until you are released into the next phase of your assignment. When you are waiting for God to release you into destiny, this is a period of "expectant waiting." Kirk Byron Jones says, "Though waiting is an important recurring theme in Scripture, it is never trumpeted as an ideal or perpetual state. Waiting culminates in coming, in breakthrough. And the breakthrough is often sooner rather than later, sometimes surprisingly and abruptly so."[1] Though the vision tarries, it will come. As leaders, we simply have to learn how to expectantly wait. So often we want to hurry God. We have our own timetables, and we have the audacity to place demands upon God. If things don't develop at the pace we intended, we take matters into our own hands, which causes great detriment to the vision.

It's important to remember that God is a strategist. There are a series of things taking place behind the scenes, lining things up for your assignment to manifest. While it may appear that nothing is happening, a lot is occurring on your behalf. Pharaoh is having dreams he cannot interpret. This is going on while Joseph is in prison. I believe God gave Pharaoh dreams that were outside the usual scope of his men's ability to interpret, because this is about Joseph's destiny. These were no ordinary dreams; they would have a profound impact upon the future of Egypt. Joseph could not be released until Pharaoh dreamed.

There is a divine order involved in being released into destiny. A sequence of things must transpire in order for it all to make sense. This is why you must understand that you were born to solve a problem. The assignment on Joseph's life would come to fruition because there was a problem in Egypt that nobody could solve but Joseph. There is something in you as a leader that is so unique that you have to embrace it. You are not called to replicate what has been; you are called to solve new problems that others have struggled to solve. None of Pharaoh's interpreters could make sense out of the dreams; the answers to the dreams were inside of Joseph.

Every effective leader who shifts to solving problems understands his or her assignment. God will put you in a context where there is a significant problem, because He has given you a system. There are systems in you that will change the destiny of a people. God has gifted you with a unique plan to rescue a generation from a perilous predicament. Effective leaders do not create problems; they solve problems. God placed within me a system to attract youth, college students, and young adults to church. This was a problem in my city, as it is in a lot of cities. Most churches struggle to attract this demographic, and my arrival to Nashville was meant to solve this problem. God had given me a vision, and I knew when the time was right I would be released to do it. I could not move forward while serving another person's vision. I had to wait until God would release me to do it. You can have great vision and plans, but you must be patient and wait to be released before moving forward within them.

God had shown me years before what it would take to get this demographic in church and engaged in ministry. The system of developing creative ministry, busing kids in from the college campuses, feeding them after service, engaging in meaningful and relevant worship, and doing cutting-edge ministry was in me long before it manifested in the ministry. God will always align you where the problem exists. I've seen leaders transform cities because the leaders had systems in them for the unique problems that existed there. Whether it was building exceptional schools, low- to moderate-income housing, or community centers, they were solving problems that others had difficulty solving. It doesn't make one leader greater than another. It just means that every leader needs to discover what problem he or she is called to solve. Once you understand that, it becomes easier to chart a course of preparation.

STAYING FOCUSED ON YOUR MISSION

One of the most powerful things about the ministry of Jesus is the fact that He clearly stated His mission. He was clear on the problems He was sent to solve as well as the anointing upon Him to accomplish the task: "The Spirit of the Lord *is* upon me, because he hath anointed me to preach the gospel to the poor; he hath sent me to heal the brokenhearted, to preach deliverance to the captives, and recovering of sight to the blind, to set at liberty them that are bruised" (Luke 4:18). Jesus would operate only in assignment because He understood the problems He was sent to solve.

Jesus was not called to meet every need. He was called to fulfill His assignment. This is a critical lesson for leaders to learn, because many leaders take on every problem and often experience burnout. They attempt to boil the ocean. When Lazarus died, there were a lot of other people dead that day.

They were not Jesus' assignment. Though there were other problems present in the cemetery, Jesus spoke to Lazarus because He understood specifically what He was sent to solve. This is why He called Lazarus by his name. Jesus had so much power that if He had merely said, "Get up," the entire cemetery would have obeyed.

Although it is noble to chase problems, if you are going to be effective, you must understand how to focus your energy on your assignment. Listen to what the writer of Hebrews says in 12:1-2:

> Therefore we also, since we are surrounded by so great a cloud of witnesses, let us lay aside every weight, and the sin which so easily ensnares *us*, and let us run with endurance the race that is set before us, looking unto Jesus, the author and finisher of *our* faith, who for the joy that was set before Him endured the cross, despising the shame, and has sat down at the right hand of the throne of God. (NKJV)

You have to run your race or focus on your assignment. I cannot run someone else's race. You will never fulfill your calling if you are working daily fulfilling someone else's. Every day you wake up, you must remember to run your race.

One of the most fascinating revelations God gave me as a leader was knowing how He called Moses. You remember that God called Moses out of a bush that was on fire but the fire did not consume it. There was a clear problem. Pharaoh had enslaved God's people. There were a series of things that led to Moses being called. He was raised in Pharaoh's house and he also was good at tending sheep. These would serve as important lessons for the fulfillment of his assignment. When God gave Moses his assignment, He was very clear. Moses was to tell Pharaoh to let God's people go. That's a simple assignment. The problem is present, and God places the answer in Moses.

All Moses has to do is obey God, and he will be successful in fulfilling it.

BURNING BUT NOT BURNED OUT

The remarkable thing in the text is the bush that is burning. It is burning but not burning up. God told me years ago this was a revelation about leadership and assignment. When there is a problem, God always gives an assignment. When you operate in that assignment, you should always have a burning for it, but it should never burn you out. The moment you step outside of what God originally instructed you to do, you run the risk of burnout. There are so many leaders who tire too quickly. They burn out trying to solve every problem and neglect the problem they are called to. I've seen what this looks like, and it is not a pretty picture. Leaders who are overwhelmed lose focus on their original task. They do a lot of things but none well.

Our churches are filled with folks who are doing too much. They are in church seven days a week, participating in every ministry and neglecting their home lives. Whenever churches or organizations create systems that allow people to easily operate in areas beyond the scope of their assignments, they often are unsuccessful. They are confusing passion with purpose. I've learned that "no" is an answer. I cannot serve on every committee and board. I cannot accept every engagement that comes across my desk. I have to go where I'm assigned to go. Though it is a noble effort, you will never be successful chasing problems. There are too many problems and only one you.

Most successful organizations focus on what they do best and do it well. The American Red Cross focuses on disaster relief and blood drives. They know the problem they are assigned to. St. Jude's Children's Hospital is called to the problem of cancer in children. They focus their energies and gifts on solving that problem. When you know you are called to solve a problem, you are not all over the place. You are very clear and focused. You have to know what God has assigned you to do and be willing to allow others to work in their assignments. I don't have to reinvent the wheel. There are leaders in your community who are solving problems every day. Support those who are solving problems. They are not a threat to you. They are living out what you need the courage to do.

YOUR GIFT WILL MAKE ROOM FOR YOU

When you embrace the fact that you were born to solve a problem, you must know that your gift will make room for you. The Scripture says in Proverbs 18:16, "A man's gift maketh room for him, and bringeth him before great men." This was evident in the life of Joseph. His gift brought him before the pharaoh of his time. This meeting would never have happened in his capacity as a prisoner, but he had a gift, and when the time was right and the problem presented itself, he was summoned to the palace.

When you are gifted as a leader, you don't have to manipulate situations to get to certain platforms. God will allow these moments to manifest based on what He has placed in you. Too many leaders spend time chasing platforms and relationships when, in fact, if they continue doing what they are called to do, those platforms will find them. I've often said of being in purpose that you don't have to chase stuff; it will chase you. There is an amazing gift of leadership within you, and it will open doors unimaginable.

The butler had the ear of Pharaoh. God always has the right people in place to connect you at the right times. These are meetings you can't schedule. These are appointments you can't just book. They are providentially made to happen. When they do, you are clear without any doubt that it is God who did it. I often think of how I got connected in the Full Gospel Baptist Church Fellowship. Bishop Kenneth Ulmer had heard of my work in the college ministry in Nashville and summoned me from the audience at the Louisiana Superdome. He took me backstage and introduced me to Bishop Paul Morton. Shortly after that, Bishop Morton's nephew began attending school in Nashville and united with our church. Because of this relationship, I was able to invite Bishop Morton to speak each year, and our relationship grew. I was given the opportunity to develop the college ministry on the national level, then serve over evangelism and then as bishop of senior pastors. I never lobbied for any position. Every position I have ever held in the Fellowship came to me. It pursued me. There was a problem; Bishop Morton saw God's hand on my life and knew the answer to that problem was within me. Again, there were systems in me to solve it, and as a consequence I am positioned where I am today.

If I had not focused on my assignment and maximized my gift, nobody would have known what my calling was. I often tell young leaders to do what they do with excellence so that when their time comes, there is room for them to do it. Stop worrying about how the position is going to develop. Don't lose sleep over the logistics. God's got a plan. Remember He's working. He is working behind the scenes making something happen. Every platform that the Lord has ever given me was a result of my gift making room. These doors open not for our own edification. They open up for the glory of God.

God allowed Joseph to be brought to the palace because it was necessary in order for His purposes to come to pass. This is why when these moments transpire in your life, you don't walk into them arrogantly with a sense of entitlement. You recognize that God saw something in you to trust you to serve at another level. Whenever arrogance shows up in a leader in the palace, the leader's tenure is short lived. I've seen God raise leaders up to levels they never imagined. Their gifts were extraordinary and made room for them. But many leaders became so consumed and intoxicated with celebrity that they lost sight of the reasons God made room for their gift. Now they have gone back into obscurity because they didn't manage the moment to the glory of God.

USE THE PLATFORM FOR TRUTH

The next thing that the story of Joseph teaches us is that leaders must use the platform for truth. Joseph was called to interpret the dreams of Pharaoh. This would have been an intimidating assignment for some, but Joseph was a man of integrity. He did not redact what God revealed to him. He explained to Pharaoh the consequences of his dream. He told Pharaoh the truth. God does not raise you up as a leader to compromise your gift in order to be accepted or popular. You must maintain integrity and do what God has called you to do. Joseph was not worried about the consequences of his interpretation. We see this in the prison when he gives the baker bad news. He is stern and unbending in his interpretation. As a result, they have much respect for him as a true man of God.

We live in a day when so many leaders compromise their God-given gifts. A part of our stewardship is remaining faithful to the original assignment no matter how painful the price. When you are faithful to your assignment, you gain the respect of those within the church and without. This is why the Bible says in Romans 12:1-2: "I beseech you therefore, brethren, by the mercies of God, that ye present your bodies a living sacrifice, holy, acceptable unto God, which is your reasonable service. And be not conformed to this world: but be ye transformed by the renewing of your mind, that ye may prove what is that good, and acceptable, and perfect, will of God." **When you conform, you cannot perform and therefore become spiritually deformed.** True leadership recognizes its ability to transform culture and affect change by remaining loyal to the assignment.

PLATFORMS ARE NOT FOR SELF-PROMOTION

One lesson that leaders need to learn is that these platforms are not opportunities for self-promotion. I've seen good people allow these moments to become all about them. They used the platforms to advance their desire for attention and popularity. It is important that we remember what the Scripture says in Isaiah 42:8: "I *am* the Lord: that *is* my name: and my glory I will not give to another, neither my praise to graven images." God is not in the business of sharing His glory with any of us. It is essential that we become good stewards of these moments and not exploit them for our own agendas. Joseph did not go to the palace with any expectations other than that of fulfilling his assignment. He was there to interpret a dream. If anything occurred as a result of that, it was not a part of his agenda. It was simply a result of his faithfulness. You cannot navigate on these platforms, posturing for positions and power. You must do the same thing you did while you were in confinement.

One of the things that cripples so many is their motives, and these motives derail many potentially great leaders. Certain platforms can be intoxicating. When you are in the spotlight and your gift is instrumental in solving problems and creating systems of change, you have to constantly keep it all in perspective. This is why it's important to stay grounded. First Peter 5:6 says: "Humble yourselves therefore under the mighty hand of God, that he may exalt you in due time." Every day when I do what I do, I am mindful that God could have chosen anyone else to do it. I realize my own inadequacies and am grateful that God has allowed my gift to be used at the level He has. John Calvin wrote, "It is evident that man never attains to a true self-knowledge until he has previously contemplated the face of God and come down after such contemplation to look into himself."[2] C. J. Mahaney in his book on humility says, "Every time I claim to be the 'author' in my life and ministry of that which is actually God's gift, I'm committing cosmic plagiarism." He goes on to say, "Whatever successes you experience in your life and ministry and vocation, learn to immediately transfer the glory to Him."[3] You cannot allow the platform to go to your head.

One of the things I have admired about Bishop Paul S. Morton is his humility. I've witnessed this man walk among kings and queens, and yet he has not lost the common touch. He has been elevated to platforms that many folks would die to get, yet you would never know it because of the spirit of humility in which he walks.

Joseph does what he is assigned to do without an underlying motive. Becoming a good steward of the platform means being truthful about God's assignment upon your life and being truthful to yourself.

SIGNIFICANCE OF THE MOMENT

The final thing I want to address in this chapter is the importance of understanding the significance of the moment. What Joseph says to Pharaoh has significant implications for the future of Egypt. Generations to come would benefit from the gift and systems Joseph communicates to him. Joseph's gift was setting in motion a savings plan for Egypt, so that in times of lack they would survive. This plan inspires many individual retirement accounts today. What many leaders don't realize is that what God is doing through you now will affect generations long after you are gone. This is why you should use the gift with integrity and not minimize its significance. An entire nation would be spared because of what God put inside of Joseph.

We often minimize our assignment as local when in fact it has global implications. I never in a million years would have thought that what God placed in me would impact the world in the way it has. I'm humbled to think that people all across the world who have passed through universities in Nashville have been affected by our ministry in a positive way. During the most formative years of their lives, our ministry kept them grounded and focused on achieving their goals. We prayed for them and kept them connected to God and His church. Many attribute their relationship to God to our ministry and still faithfully watch our virtual church each week. We've received countless testimonies from parents who have witnessed the change in their children while in college. There was a problem, and God placed the solution in the vision He gave me. As a result, thousands of college graduates around the world are spreading the good news of Jesus Christ because we shifted from conceding to solving.

Can you imagine the impact you will have on the world? The potential to bring positive solutions to lingering problems resides within you. When you were first chosen and consecrated, God had this on His mind. It was never a small vision. It was always huge and transformative. Before Joseph ever arrived in Egypt, events were in motion to set the stage for his gift to be used. The events that led to his arrival were unfortunate, yet they were necessary to deliver him to his destiny. A people and a nation would be grateful that Joseph lived. He went into Egypt as a prisoner and became honored as a prince. First Corinthians 2:9 reminds us, "But as it is written, Eye hath not seen, nor ear heard, neither have entered into the heart of man, the things which God hath prepared for them that love him." God's plans always manifest in the lives of His people. Jeremiah 29:11 says, "For I know the thoughts that I think toward you, saith the LORD thoughts of peace, and not of evil, to give you an expected end." God wants to use you in ways you can fully conceive. All you have to do is walk in integrity and remain humble, and He will bring it to pass.

CONCLUSION

You are a problem solver. You are gifted to do what others are unable to do, and you must remind yourself of that each day. You must concede the will of God and make yourself available in any capacity in which He chooses to use you. Nothing should be taken for granted, because in the least likely place your gift can spring forth. This is your season to walk in destiny and come forth. Everything you've gone through has positioned you for this moment. This is what has kept you up all night. This is what you've dreamed about. Kirk Byron Jones asserts that our dreams allow for the freedom to go beyond the limits of our present reality: "Dreams rain down imaginings that can inspire liberating new images of personhood and purpose. They are life openers, making it possible for you to conceive what you never dared to imagine."[4]

The time has come, and you must manage the moment to the glory of God. There are millions of people who would love to be in the position in which God has you now. Walk in it with boldness. Go to the palace and tell Pharaoh the truth. He needs to hear the truth because that's what will set the nation free. Don't underestimate the hand of God upon your life. You are a leader who shifts when God says to shift. You are anointed for this moment. Joseph's name literally means "God will add or bless." **When you walk into the fullness of your assignment, you shift conditions.** The strategies that God has placed inside you will have a monumental impact on the world in which you live. Joseph the dreamer and dream interpreter was summoned from confinement to change the world. He realized that more than ability was required for the task; it needed availability. A lie put him in confinement, but the truth set him free. Your gift is greater than any lie of the enemy. Remember what Isaiah 54:17 declares: "No weapon that is formed against thee shall prosper; and every tongue that shall rise against thee in judgment thou shalt condemn. This is the heritage of the servants of the LORD, and their righteousness is of me, saith the LORD." It doesn't mean that weapons won't be formed, but in the end they will never prevail over the purposes of God for your life. Joseph would change Egypt's history from one of financial ruin to one of financial prosperity. Through his obedience, we invest in times of plenty today so we can have resources in times of lack. We all should be inspired and as leaders be determined to see our vision through until full manifestation. Whatever the problem is that God has assigned you to solve, it awaits your gift, humility, courage, and availability to do God's will.

CHAPTER 9

FROM DIMINISHED TO RESTORED

As a result of walking in his assignment, Joseph was promoted in Egypt. His faithfulness and integrity gave him the valuable position of distributing bread to the Egyptians. He rationed out resources in order to secure their future during difficult economic times. It wasn't long before his own brothers showed up unaware of him being alive and in a position of such high authority. Eventually, they realize that it is Joseph, who once told them that one day he would rule over them. This chapter will address how Joseph was restored to a right relationship with his family. While he now has position and prestige, he uses his power to be humble and forgive the wrongs that his brothers did to him. It is God who restores us and propels us into destiny. Leaders must learn how to deal with insults others inflict and move forward in life.

DIVINE PROMOTION

Joseph's promotion by Pharaoh was not by chance. It was the culmination of a series of events that strategically positioned him to be exactly where God wanted him to be. No matter how tumultuous the path, it leads to the manifestation of an amazing promise. What we learn from Joseph's promotion are some critical keys that every leader should recognize. The first key is recognizing that what happened to Joseph was divine promotion. Although Pharaoh was in a position to promote him, it was God who ultimately orchestrated the entire event. The Bible says in Psalm 75:6-7: "For promotion cometh neither from the east, nor from the west, nor from the south. But God is the judge: he putteth down one, and setteth up another." It is God who promotes us in His own time and according to His own plan.

Divine promotion takes into consideration everything we have experienced in our lives. As I mentioned earlier, God doesn't promote as we do. We often promote people because of tenure or experience. Because people have been around a long time, we allow this to stand as credible proof of their readiness to be promoted to the next level. Longevity is not a good measuring tool for promotion. If a child is in the sixth grade for three years, he or she doesn't get promoted just because it's been three years.

There are certain criteria necessary for advancement. Consequently, when God promotes, He uses these criteria to deem us ready for the next level. Chiefly, it is our ability to pass the tests. Divine promotion is a result of consistently passing tests proving your preparedness. That's why leaders who have incredible trajectories have the greatest test. As you are reading this book, maybe you are being tested and it's beyond anything you ever imagined. This test is getting you ready for where God is about to take you. This test is about you proving you can manage the challenges that come with promotion.

When God promotes, He can promote people who don't have as much tenure as others; God will raise them because they have been tried and found faithful. Every elevation I have experienced has been by God's hand. Although He used human vessels to carry it out, it was very clear that it was divine promotion. When you experience promotion, only spiritual people will truly embrace it, because they recognize it is not something you lobbied or sought after; it sought after you. This is one way you can tell the assignment is authentic—it chooses you. Our authentic assignment emerges from the revealed knowledge of our authentic selves. Parker Palmer says, "Our deepest calling is to grow into our own authentic self-hood, whether or not it conforms to some image of who we *ought* to be. As we do so, we will not only find the joy that every human being seeks—we will also find our path of authentic service in the world."[1]

Let me explain in a very personal way what I mean by divine promotion. In 1993, I attended the Full Gospel Baptist Church Fellowship International Conference. I was just one year into pastoring my church and didn't really know as many pastors as I do now. This movement was the talk of the religious community. It was fresh, exciting, and cutting edge. More than thirty thousand came to the New Orleans Superdome, and so did I. I came with my best friend, Pastor Michael Caldwell from Houston, Texas. We were unable to attend the entire conference, but we made certain we attended the night Bishop Morton gave his address. We didn't have VIP passes like many pastors did, but I truly believe it was providential. I remember the exact seat where I sat that night. It was the very top seat facing the immediate center of the pulpit. I was literally in the nosebleed section among thirty thousand delegates with my back against the wall, dead center of Bishop Morton. No one was behind me, and everything was happening before me. At that time, I didn't know Bishop Morton personally, but I was so eager to hear the word that he would impart that night. It was an amazing message that reminded me God was doing a new thing on an old foundation. Something in me shifted that day, and I knew I would never be the same. As I mentioned earlier, my connection to Bishop Morton would be divinely orchestrated by a series of events beyond my control. Over the next twenty years, I served Bishop Morton's vision with passion and excellence because I knew this was a God movement. I had no aspirations within the fellowship because my church was more than enough to keep me busy at the pace it was going. Nevertheless, I was given appointment after appointment, and my relationship with Bishop Morton became closer and closer. I can't really explain this. I just remember the connection being like a father to son. God told me He was putting Bishop Morton's spirit in me. Mount Zion grew, in part, because I gleaned so much from how Bishop Morton grew Greater Saint Stephen's. I modeled our ministry and my personal pastoral approach after what God had done through him. I maintained my uniqueness, but clearly he had become my mentor.

I watched Bishop Morton go through so many difficult seasons, and I didn't understand their significance to divine promotion until I experienced similar events. Bishop Morton had a mental breakdown and became transparent as to why it happened. When his health was restored, Mount Zion Baptist Church was the first church he preached in. I never shall forget that message. He preached, "I'm coming out of this crazy house." It was a message about taking authority over the Devil and spiritual order. At the time, I thought it was just a coincidence that he preached for Mount Zion first after being cleared to preach again, but now I know it was a significant moment toward divine promotion. Bishop Morton lost his first grandbaby. I lost my first wife. He experienced Hurricane Katrina and the loss of his church and home. My house was hit by lightning, and it was the only house in Nashville hit that day. I was misplaced for months after the fire. Also, Nashville experienced a flood unlike anything it had experienced in fifty years. Bishop Morton was diagnosed with colon cancer, which was caught early. Today he remains cancer free. Within my ministry I experienced a cancer of sorts that attempted to extort me and scandalize my name, but thanks be to God He fought my battle and gave me the victory as well. Perhaps you are wondering what this has to do with divine promotion. I believe that these tests were preparing me for what has happened in my life.

For three years, Bishop Morton has been discussing his imminent retirement from his position as presiding bishop. He is an amazing leader who is determined to see his vision go forth and reach the next generation. Because he is officially turning his position over in 2015, he asked the Bishop's Counsel to cast votes on whom they would like to see succeed him and lead the Fellowship going forth. There are twenty-one bishops on the counsel. On July 5, Bishop Morton stood in Louisville, Kentucky, and announced that I (Joseph) had been chosen to succeed him as presiding bishop of the Full Gospel Baptist Church Fellowship. Talk about divine promotion. That moment was awe inspiring and humbling for me, yet I realize that it didn't start that night. It had been happening since I first attended the conference and sat in the nosebleed section. Imagine that. I sat in the top row, back to the wall in the New Orleans Superdome, and now I have been chosen by God to be the leader of this great organization. Only God can bring you from the nosebleed section to the helm of the movement.

. . . .

Perhaps you are reading this and nobody knows your name. What's important is that God knows your name. He has a plan for your life, and He can bring you out of obscurity into your destiny. Divine promotion is a God thing. Focus on passing the test and watch God do the rest. You don't have to politick or connive. All you have to do is be faithful, serve where you are, and watch God elevate you where and when He wants. When God promotes you, spiritual people are very clear that it is bigger than you. Joseph was a prisoner a few days ago, and now he is promoted in Egypt and responsible for more than he could have ever imagined.

SIGNIFICANCE OF THE DECORUM OF PROMOTION

The next key is to understand the significance of the decorum of promotion. When Pharaoh promoted Joseph to be prime minister of state, he took his signet ring from his hand and placed it on Joseph's finger. He also took his robe and put it on Joseph. Finally, he took his gold chain and put it on him. The signet ring gave Joseph the authority to acquire supplies and to validate documents in the king's name. The new clothes were extremely finely woven linen garments befitting his new status. The gold chain was an award to those who made significant contributions to the state. It also signified his office as the chief minister of the king. When we experience divine promotion, how we wear the promotion is important. I'm not referring to physical decorum but spiritual.

True leadership is wearing your office in such a manner that you don't abuse the privileges that have been extended to you. I've seen people come into leadership positions and completely change. Rather than wear their offices with grace and humility, they wore them with arrogance and pride. When God raises you up, your spiritual decorum should be appealing and draw attention to Him who has chosen you and not to yourself. Everywhere Joseph went, people knew he had on items that Pharaoh gave him. You could not see Joseph without seeing Pharaoh. When we lead effectively, it is impossible for people to see us without seeing God. Many leaders are guilty of letting their egos get the best of them. I often refer to ego acrostically as <u>E</u>asing <u>G</u>od <u>O</u>ut.

One of the most powerful words Jesus gives is when He speaks to His disciples in John 14. After Jesus informs them of His imminent departure, Philip raises the question concerning the revelation of the Father: "Show us the Father, and it is sufficient for us" (John 14:8 NKJV). The disciples are troubled that Jesus will no longer be present in the flesh, so they want evidence of the Father's presence to comfort them. Jesus tells them these words:

> Have I been so long time with you, and yet hast thou not known me, Philip? he that hath seen me hath seen the Father; and how sayest thou then, Show us the Father? Believest thou not that I am in the Father, and the Father in me? the words that I speak unto you I speak not of myself: but the Father that dwelleth in me, he doeth the works. Believe me that I am in the Father, and the Father in me: or else believe me for the very works' sake. Verily, verily, I say unto you, He that believeth on me, the works that I do shall he do also; and greater works than these shall he do; because I go unto my Father. And whatsoever ye shall ask in my name, that will I do, that the Father may be glorified in the Son. If ye shall ask any thing in my name, I will do it. (John 14:9-14)

What Jesus declared to the disciples is that it was impossible to see Him without seeing the Father. Whatever He is, it is because of the Father. His decorum of leadership was wearing the Father. What an amazing example of leadership. As leaders we must learn to get ourselves out of the way and recognize that we present something bigger than ourselves. Although we have on the garments of authority and prestige, we must realize the origin of those garments and be intentional that people see God before they see us.

THE DISCIPLINE OF PROMOTION

The next key is the discipline of promotion. Every effective leader must display discipline in leadership. It's one thing to see a vision but another to actually manifest it. Joseph interpreted the dream of Pharaoh and gave a strategic plan, but once he had the position, it would take discipline to implement. He had to organize the distribution stations and factor in the amount of people who would need bread against the necessary rations that his plan required. It would be no small task and would take a great deal of personal and professional discipline to work out. If there is one area that trips up many leaders, it is the lack of personal discipline. We get so distracted that we are unable to focus and be effective in the assignment we are called to. I've seen great visionaries who end up with the picture on the wall but nothing in the earth. In other words, they don't have the discipline to organize, strategize, and see their plan through to completion.

If you desire to be a transformative leader, it will require discipline. I have learned to be disciplined by making intentional moves regarding the implementation of the vision God has given me. You have to be a good a steward of time. Leaders don't have time to waste. Martin Luther King, Jr. addressed the people of his time who suffered from procrastination and social stagnation. He discussed this issue[2] and compelled the community to aid the process of time, not allowing things to just happen: "We are now faced with the fact that tomorrow is today."[3]

Time is money. Time is vision. You must be about your Father's business. You have to make certain that you are not meeting just to meet. You must spend your time collaborating with people who are critical to your vision coming to fruition. Disciplined leaders manage not only their time but also their resources. Joseph had to make certain that every resource was accounted for if the vision was going to come to pass.

Finances

One of the areas in which I've seen too many leaders struggle is that of resources. You must have discipline in your personal finances. Joseph had access to what Pharaoh had, which means his financial situation shifted. Please understand that I am not suggesting that there is a certain economic level leaders must be on to be successful. That is not the case. The point I am making is that leaders must be good stewards of their personal resources so that their financial motives and integrity are never questioned within the organizations they lead. If a leader has bad credit and is in debt over his or her head, how can he or she effectively lead an organization and maintain fiscal management of resources to get things done? One of the principles we employ in our ministry is called Intelligent Fiscal Management. Our church budgets, plans, and is accountable for the finances down to the penny. We make the best decisions based on our current financial situation and future projections without putting our church in a financially poor position. As a leader, I take great pride in managing my personal finances, so it is a natural progression in the organization I lead. When I look at projects compared to finances, I understand words like "not yet," because I do the same in my personal finances. If you just blindly spend and spend in your personal finances without any accountability, you will do the same in your organization as a leader.

Joseph would be responsible for the economic destiny of all of Egypt, and it required great discipline. When you think about what you are responsible for, it's a good time to work on financial discipline. Another area of discipline is prayer. What has kept me successful as a leader is the discipline of prayer. Prayer is communing with God. You can run the risk of moving at such a fast pace that you neglect this critical area.

Ronald Heifetz addresses the personal challenges that leaders at the pinnacle of success face and asserts that leaders need times of prayer and meditation; leaders need sanctuaries: "Working amidst the cacophony of a multiple-band dance floor, one needs a sanctuary to restore one's sense of purpose, put issues in perspective, and regain courage and heart. When serving as the repository of many conflicting aspirations, a person can lose himself in the role by failing to distinguish his inner voice from the voices that clamor for attention outside."[4] If you study the ministry of Jesus, you will notice that Jesus had a disciplined prayer life. He would regularly steal away and pray. Although His schedule was overwhelming and the demand upon Him as a leader was great, He realized that the only way to be empowered to do what He had to do was spend time with the Father. I am convinced that leaders who have the discipline of prayer are more effective because they are stronger spiritually and have a greater sense of what God is saying in their lives.

Prayer

Because of the magnitude of your assignment, it is impossible to accomplish it without prayer. When you pray, you seek the greatest advisor of all. As a leader, you will find many who will advise you on critical matters, but there are always those moments when you need to hear from God. I've learned to spend time in prayer early in the morning while the dew is still on the ground. I've learned to get up when everything is still and spend quality time with God. When I pray, I am declaring my need for God and my inability to function without His direction. What made Moses an effective leader is that He had the discipline of prayer. Can you imagine if Moses had listened to the people and taken a vote at the Red Sea? The discipline of prayer will sustain you as a leader during times of peace and times of struggle.

I was so blessed to learn the discipline of prayer from a great leader. My pastor, Dr. Harry Blake of Shreveport, Louisiana, instilled prayer in me at a very young age. During the 1980s, he had one of the country's largest midweek prayer meetings; I never missed one growing up. I saw this discipline of prayer strengthen him throughout his pastorate, and it continues to this day. I often wondered how he was able to bear such tremendous burdens and maintain his level of efficiency and excellence. I am confident it is because he is a leader who leads by the discipline of prayer. The Mount Canaan Baptist Church of Shreveport, Louisiana, is a model of a praying church transformed by the discipline of a praying leader.

THE DUTY OF PROMOTION

The next key is the duty of promotion. This is significant because Joseph's brothers arrived to receive their ration of bread. Joseph was in a position of authority and had it in his power to deny them if he so chose. Joseph ultimately realizes the need for restoration in his family as well as the divine mandate he is under concerning his assignment, and he gives them bread. The duty of great leadership is to recognize, regardless of your past issues with people or your current disagreement, that the duty is greater than the disagreement. You have to rise above petty behavior and pass out bread. If the vision is to come to fruition, everybody in Egypt must be saved from the famine. You can't pick and choose based on your hang-ups; you must stay faithful to the integrity of the mission. Herein lies a critical test for most leaders. We often harbor ill will toward those who have done us wrong and use our positions to punish them through retaliatory acts. When we do that, we diminish the assignment to a self-serving act rather than a God-given opportunity to bless His people.

Great leaders recognize that they are not leaders for some of the people but for all of the people. I had to learn this in ministry. I remember harboring feelings of resentment for those who fought me vigorously early in my ministry. I realized that if I was going to be God's leader, I could not make decisions void of those who opposed me; rather, I needed to include them in all we were doing. One lesson you will learn is that people who have done you wrong know it. Eventually, most will repent of it and apologize to you. This is what Joseph's brothers did. They knew they were wrong and were truly contrite. This is what the Bible says in Luke 20:42-43: "The Lord said to my Lord: Sit at my right hand until I make your enemies a footstool for your feet" (NIV). Just because people have done you wrong and are now a footstool at your feet doesn't mean you have to step on them.

The passing out of the bread is a powerful part of your duty as a leader. It implies that your vision is comprehensive enough to reach every person regardless of differences or shortcomings. God gave Joseph a vision for Egypt. Everybody in Egypt must get bread if that vision is going to come to pass. God has given you a vision, and you must ask yourself if your vision is a big enough tent to assist and empower everyone God has sent you to. You have to determine if you will use your position for payback and revenge or for the glory of God. I am reminded of the words in Romans 12:20: "Therefore if thine enemy hunger, feed him; if he thirst, give him drink: for in so doing thou shalt heap coals of fire on his head." God will always put you in a position to do your duty in the face of those who have done you wrong. Joseph was more concerned about restoration than he was retaliation. This is what allows him to make this shift from diminished to restored.

There were some pastors a few years ago who said some terrible things about me. Some of them wanted to see me fail. I was so devastated that some of my brothers in ministry could be divisive and negative. It hurt; however, I realized that I had a responsibility to what God had called me to do. I was invited to speak at a leadership retreat, and many of them were there. I openly shared what God had given me to share and even left principles on how to develop staff, grow a church, engage in multiple locations, and explore a variety of other infrastructural strategies. Although I knew some of my worst critics were in the room, I gladly shared this information to help their churches grow, because regardless of what they had done, they still needed bread.

I want to encourage you to examine those areas in your life that are preventing your vision from coming to its full capacity. Examine what areas could be limiting your ability to pass out bread to all. This will make you a more effective leader. Because Joseph was a man of prayer, he chose to do that which was right rather than what could have been perceived as popular. We live in a world that gloats in retaliation. We want to have that "see there" moment or that "good for you" moment. But God is calling you to a higher calling. You must embrace your duty and remember that all your enemies still need bread. What moves you from being an average leader to a great leader is your willingness to pass out bread. What you will discover is that you don't always get to choose who gets the bread. God does.

THE DECISIONS OF PROMOTION

The final key is the decisions of promotion. Every leader will have to make critical decisions if the vision is going to be implemented. Joseph had to decide who would assist in getting bread, how the people would be organized, and a host of other things. Decisions drive life. We live or die by the decisions we make. Where you are now is the end result of the choices you made and the efforts you put forth. It is a fact that success is the product of making accurate decisions. Many leaders fail because their decisions are ill advised and ill timed.

The decisions that Joseph made had generational implications. There are long-term consequences to the decisions you make as well. I've learned to think through my decisions and make certain that I have factored in every possible consequence before I act. Often, leaders are moved by their passion and emotions, compromising their decision making. You have to be levelheaded and make decisions that are in the best interest of the organization you will lead.

There are two kinds of decisions. There are those that are motivated by your convictions and those motivated by the crowd. There will be some tough decisions, but great leaders don't shy away from them; rather, they meet them head-on and follow their convictions. When you lead based on what's popular, you set yourself up for failure. You must follow your convictions and be willing to deal with the consequences of disappointing some people who have been faithful to you. You must remember that getting decisions right is far greater than pleasing people. When you make good decisions, you won't always be liked, but you will most certainly be respected. Ultimately, that's what's important. When people respect you, they will follow you. They see the God in you and not your personal agenda.

One of the most important decisions you will have to make is regarding the people you allow close to you. I think it is so important to understand that as you walk into your assignment and promotion as a leader, you should have some crowd control. The truth is that as you go higher, there will be fewer people who truly understand your plight. The lower you are, the larger the crowd, and the higher you are, the thinner the crowd. It doesn't mean anything is wrong with you; it just means that your standards have changed. I had to make small decisions about who could have my cell phone number. There was a time when I just gave my number out to anyone I met. In casual conversation, I just allowed people to have access to me. You can still maintain your relational spirit; however, you cannot allow everybody access into your personal space.

Another area where decision making is key is in finding mentors. I wanted to share this because I believe whom you allow to mentor you makes a statement about where you see your future headed. If you are mentored with dysfunction and small vision, you can't expect to have more than your mentor. If, however, you are mentored with innovative, out-of-the-box thinking and progressive leadership, you are positioned to be inspired, enlightened, and empowered. You should never come to this decision without prayer and counsel. How to establish your mentoring relationships is an important decision you must make if you are going to be successful in fulfilling your assignment.

One of the decisions I believe Joseph makes is the decision to get it right, because he truly desires to walk in this assignment with integrity and transparency so that God's will comes to pass. I pray this prayer every day. Although there are some things I realize I can't control, I ask God to give me the strength to get it right. I am committed to being one of His leaders who gets it—one who understands humility, integrity, and faithfulness. Every decision you make ultimately determines this. Do you want to get it right? Do you want to be a leader who represents God in a way that brings glory to His name? Do you want to pass out bread so that the entire community is blessed, not just some in the community? Do you want to transcend every negative and shift to every positive so that your assignment will manifest without a manipulated agenda? If you said yes, then you should pray and ask God to help you make the right decisions. It is true that we are often consumed with so much that our decisions are not completely thought through because of deadlines. It is very important in this day and time that even if your decisions are late, they are quality decisions well thought out before they show up. God will always honor your efforts when you take pauses and consider the implications of each decision you make.

CONCLUSION

Joseph shifted to restoration because he understood that his promotion was divine. He wore his spiritual decorum correctly. He embraced discipline, duty, and the right decisions. Each leader has to decide what kind of leader he or she is going to be. You have to decide if you will be average or exceptional. Bishop Morton always says that average is just being on top of the bottom. It is my prayer that as you read this book you are inspired to become an exceptional leader. I pray the passion for your success in my heart is felt on each page, because I believe there is an extraordinary assignment within you. That assignment needs to be birthed with the right attitude and spirit. You have to commit to doing what you have never done to get what you have never had. You will walk alone most times, but the journey will be exciting. The fact that you are committed to pleasing God and fulfilling His bidding will only position you for greater things up the road. Every day you wake up, there are choices, and your decisions determine your destiny.

CHAPTER 10

WHAT YOU MEANT FOR MY BAD, GOD MEANT FOR MY GOOD

The story of Joseph and how he ended up in the position he did is a testament to the will of God manifesting in our lives despite the obstacles that seek to prevent it. When I see Joseph, I see myself, and I'm sure you see yourself as well. The fact that he could have a series of unfortunate events ultimately work in his favor is encouraging to all who call themselves visionaries or dreamers.

One of the most profound statements Joseph makes is a statement of forgiveness. When he stands in a position to prevent his brothers from receiving needed bread, he takes the high road. When his brothers recognize that they at are at Joseph's mercy, they discover why their father favored him and God chose him. Joseph declares, and this is my paraphrase, "What you meant for my bad, God meant for my good." As you have read this book, I pray that you have come to the same conclusions in your life. Remember, whatever God allowed was designed to bless you. What doesn't kill you only makes you stronger.

Joseph evolved from a young man not fully aware of the magnitude of his assignment to a mature man who embraced it with integrity. This chapter will reveal how Joseph upped his level of integrity. When God raises us up, there is a stewardship of maturity we must display that brings glory to God. When the story begins, Joseph gets a coat from his earthly father, and he allows his identity to be shaped by that. As he grows in his relationship with God, Joseph's focus changes from the coat of his natural father to the crown of his heavenly father. Strong leaders must mature beyond the desire to please people and ultimately graduate to pleasing only God by living with righteousness and serving with humility.

WALKING WITH INTEGRITY

When Joseph walks in his leadership position, he does so by employing certain attributes that guide his life and serve as a model for you and me. The most important attribute is integrity. Integrity is doing what you said you were going to do. When Joseph realized the uniqueness of the dream upon his life, he saw it through until it manifested. This required integrity not only through the events that led to his promotion but also when he received it. It is essential that you and I live a life of integrity. Clayton Christensen says in *How Will You Measure Your Life?*, "It's easier to hold to your principles 100 percent of the time than it is to hold to them 98 percent of the time. The boundary—your personal moral line—is powerful, because you don't cross it. If you have justified doing it once, there's nothing to stop you from doing it again. Decide what you stand for. And then stand for it all the time."[1] It's easier to walk in integrity when you are on your way to the goal, but once you achieve it, it becomes more difficult to maintain. If you are going to be a successful leader, you are going to have to maintain integrity that assures people there is continuity between what you say and what you do. Joseph not only makes a statement of forgiveness but also engages in an act of forgiveness. His brothers get bread.

I've learned that people may not ever read the Bible, but they will read the lives of those of us who profess it. It is vital that our integrity permeates every aspect of our leadership.

The more God does in your life, the greater the distractions will be. The reason we see so many leaders fail is because they become too comfortable in the position and neglect integrity. One of the things I've done in my life to maintain integrity in leadership is have specific people in my life who can hold me accountable. Often, leaders fail because they attempt to operate solo rather than realize the significance of strategic relationships along the way. If you are going to be effective, you must have people who can tell you the truth.

When you are in a leadership position, there is the potential to disregard input from others because it makes you feel like you are diluting the power you have. Nothing can be further from the truth than this. Integrity is maintained when there are people who can help you stay focused on the purposes by which you are anointed and think through the consequences of every decision. Integrity does not mean you will not make mistakes. Every leader makes mistakes and learns from them, however truly successful leaders develop a regime in righteousness that sets a standard in their lives. When people interact with this kind of leader, they respect that desire to walk in integrity.

What has been of great help to me is having key people who call and pray with me and who are at liberty to speak truth into my life. There are times when leaders become so popular that nobody wants to offend them or seem disrespectful. This often results in leaders falling into satanic schemes. My accountability partners are folks who are willing to jeopardize their friendships with me by telling me the truth, because they are concerned about me fulfilling my divine assignment. If everyone in your life tells you "yes," you are setting yourself up for colossal failure.

Here is one final word about integrity. What I've witnessed among many leaders is their unending desire to create a positive image even though their personal integrity is in direct opposition to that image. The pressure of putting on your game face is huge. Every time you show up, you have to appear to have it all together, but we know many leaders don't. While you are trying to put forth an image of perfection, your internal dysfunctions are eroding your personal integrity. It's like detailing a car with an engine going bad. You can continue to wash it and shine it, but engine neglect will cause it to stop running and never reach the desired destination.

There was a time in my life when I felt the need to keep the outside polished, and I neglected those things that would sustain integrity. Every leader goes through those seasons. The higher God takes you, the greater the demand of integrity upon your life. There is more at stake now. What I realized as a leader was that it was important to put safeguards in place to ensure integrity at all levels of ministry. Mount Zion has a financial advisory board as well as an executive board, but there was a need for two boards higher than those. The financial advisory board makes recommendations to the finance department regarding budgetary matters to maintain intelligent fiscal management. The executive board meets to make decisions regarding the daily operations of the church and approve ministry events. At one point, we felt it was time to incorporate a church board of directors who would oversee the affairs of the church at all levels to ensure that all persons employed by the church were held accountable and that all decisions were in the best interest of the church. As pastor, I submit myself to the board of directors. Historically, final decisions were usually made by the senior pastor; however, I felt it was important to ensure that these final decisions are made as a united front rather than by an individual. I am able to share the vision and direction God has given me with this board, and the directors bring a great deal of experience and resources to the conversation. Their role is not to prevent God-given vision but to ensure that it manifests in the most efficient way possible. This team is made up of attorneys, insurance professionals, health-care professionals, blue-collar workers, and college students. It represents the demographic of our church.

I also put in place a pastoral advisory board that serves as an accountability board to the senior pastor. This board is made up of pastors across the country who are responsible for recommending disciplinary processes for ethical violations. The pastor is totally submitted to the recommendations of this board. In the event of the pastor's death, this board makes recommendations to the board of directors regarding the future of the church. They do not select the next pastor, but they advise the church during the difficult transition period on how to select the next leader.

These safeguards are necessary in the Mount Zion Baptist Church in order to maintain integrity as we shift to our destiny. You must recognize that your lack of integrity will have consequences that affect more than you. It's like the game of football. If one player is penalized, he is not the only one who suffers. The entire team is penalized. Because one player was offside, the entire team gets pushed back. The people in the stands cheering for that team get pushed back. The people watching on television or listening on the radio get pushed back. Dwight D. Eisenhower said, "The supreme quality for leadership is unquestionably integrity. Without it, no real success is possible, no matter whether it is on a section gang, a football field, in an army, or in an office."[2]

MATURITY

The next thing that is necessary for every leader to demonstrate is maturity. The fact that Joseph matured was indicative of the experiences he had gone through. Often, life is the greatest teacher and brings us best toward maturity. The lessons we learn often grow us up quicker. Based on the decisions Joseph will have to make and his response to his brothers, it is clear that he has matured beyond self-serving agendas to a more divinely purposed life. When you mature, you see life differently. You aren't as naive to things as you once were. I remember when this happened to me. I remember something igniting in my life and my tolerance level for ignorance and incompetence hitting the bottom. The level of integrity and focus required to navigate at the next level of leadership requires maturity.

Joseph's reply to his brothers was a powerful statement of maturity. It represented him being in a different place emotionally and spiritually. Mature people don't go tit for tat with folks over issues in the past. Maturity moves forward. So many people become paralyzed by the pain in their past that they are unable to move forward and be productive in the season God has them in. **Joseph refused to be bitter and chose to be better.** When you come to the place of destiny, you have to shift beyond pettiness and focus on what you are called to do. I once heard the story of how the cat caught the bird. There was a bird in the mouth of a cat, and someone asked how this could be. The bird has wings and has the ability to fly higher than the cat could ever jump. The story is told that the cat stared the bird down, hypnotizing it through distraction. While the bird was locked in the antics of the cat, it did not realize that the cat was inching closer to it in the tree. After a few minutes of staring and distracting, the cat apprehended the bird and brought it down from the tree to the ground. Now the bird was permanently on the cat's level. This is what happens to many of us. We allow things that never should distract us from purpose to bring us down to their level. When this happens, we succumb to things that could be devastating to our future.

Maturity does not sweat the little stuff. Maturity transcends and maintains itself in the midst of those who have hurt you. Psalm 27:6 declares, "And now shall mine head be lifted up above mine enemies round about me: therefore will I offer in his tabernacle sacrifices of joy; I will sing, yea, I will sing praises unto the LORD." This is a powerful example of maturity. It's the ability to be who you are regardless of the actions of those around you. Joseph did not waver in his integrity because of his maturity. You will be tested on numerous occasions to reveal your level of maturity.

I'm often tested to gauge where I am in my life. Once, a critic attempted to bait me into responding to an issue that I felt was unnecessary to respond to. When you mature, you understand that some things don't deserve a response because your response brings credibility to it. I was so upset that I felt the need to give the critic a piece of my mind. I wanted to lash out, like Peter did in the Garden of Gethsemane. As humorous as this may sound, it is clear that all of us demonstrate immaturity in some areas while staying mature in others. When Jesus asked the disciples to pray one hour, they fell asleep. Peter's immaturity continued to come to the forefront when he took out a sword and engaged in warfare in the garden. This was not God's intent. Peter's immaturity was about to get Jesus killed in a brawl in the Garden of Gethsemane rather than come to His glory on Calvary. Immature responses can interrupt the plans of God over your life. Jesus rebukes Peter. Immaturity will have you responding in ways that are inconsistent with your godly values. The Devil will use your immaturity to prevent the plans of God from manifesting in your life.

CHOOSING THE PATH OF WISDOM

Joseph was not only mature in his response; he also chose the path of wisdom. Wisdom is a powerful attribute for every leader. Proverbs 4:7 says, "Wisdom is the principal thing; therefore get wisdom: and with all thy getting get understanding." If you are going to be successful as a leader, you have to walk in wisdom. My prayer each day I wake up is for wisdom. Solomon was the wisest man in the world because he did not ask God for riches and fame; he asked for wisdom. God granted his request and gave him the other things as well. Solomon understood that without wisdom, any person would squander opportunities. Joseph's statement to his brothers was a statement of wisdom, because he recognized that what they did to him was a part of God's will for his life. Although it was painful, it had purpose.

Wisdom pauses before it acts. It thinks and considers the options first. Nelson Mandela said, "A good head and a good heart are always a formidable combination."[3] This is clearly the manifestation of wisdom. Joseph had a good head and a good heart, and it caused him to respond wisely in pivotal moments. Many leaders discover that wisdom cannot be taught but rather is gained through experience. Regardless of your pedigree academically, wisdom is one of the most important qualities a leader can have.

Wisdom forces a leader to focus on those things that are essential rather than interesting. I talked about this earlier. Essential Christian leadership comes from those who are called to be in the same way with Him. Following is being in the same way with Him who calls us to Him.

When we as leaders walk in wisdom, we wake up every day determined to focus on those things that are essential to the manifestation of our destiny and not those things that contribute to our demise. Howard Thurman speaks to this coupling of wisdom and determination to see our life's dreams through: "No experience, no event at any particular moment in time exhausts the meaning and the 'intent' of life as reflected in a way life lives itself out. This is why so very often men are unwilling to scale down the horizon of their hopes, dreams, and yearnings to the level of the events of their lives."[4] Every decision, interaction, connection, and response has specific consequences and must demonstrate wisdom in our lives.

SIGNIFICANT LEADERSHIP

Joseph's response also indicated that he had become significant as a leader. This is a powerful place to be, because it suggests you as a leader are interested in leadership that matters. We often strive for success, and there is nothing wrong with that. Actually, the Bible tells us that God's desire is to give us good success. Joshua 1:8 says, "This book of the law shall not depart out of thy mouth; but thou shalt meditate therein day and night, that thou mayest observe to do according to all that is written therein: for then thou shalt make thy way prosperous, and then thou shalt have good success." It is clear that God does not have a problem with leaders being successful. The problems occur when the definition of success gets minimized to those things that feed the ego rather than glorify God. So many young leaders get caught up in the trappings of success that they lose sight of the true purpose to which God called them. I've seen many young leaders covet the tangible blessings of other leaders and measure their success by achieving the same. They have no idea what those things cost those leaders to acquire. They have no understanding of the historical context that gave rise to those things in their lives. If the young leaders knew the toil and pain that those blessed leaders have been through, they might not covet them as much.

As a young leader, I was also seduced by what I believed was true success. I wanted the reptile shoes, custom suits, and expensive jewelry. There is nothing wrong with those things, but I thought having those things made me successful. I was certain I had arrived when I could wear certain things and go certain places. **God does not mind us having nice things; He just doesn't want those things to have us.** There was a point in my life where things had me. The only way a leader can get beyond the pull of this false sense of success is to embrace what it means to be significant.

Joseph was not just a successful leader; he was also significant. When you are significant, your contributions to the world have an impact far beyond you. We are benefiting from Joseph's vision today. Thousands of years later, we are investing money and saving for a rainy day because Joseph implemented a plan and cemented his legacy in history as significant. There have been a lot of successful people who have not left a footprint in history like those who are significant have. What your desire should be is to leave on record something so profound that it forces generations to come to recognize that you have passed this way. Steve Jobs was not just successful; he was significant. His vision changed the way we communicate on the phone and tablet. The smartphone will owe a tremendous debt to his legacy for generations to come.

When you are a significant leader, you move from being a noun to a verb. Xerox Corporation was one of the first companies in the photocopying business. Xerox had a corner on the market so profound and innovative that it moved from being a noun to a verb. Today, we don't just "copy" something; we "Xerox" it. Several years later, other companies got into the photocopying business. Kinko's corporation was one. Because Xerox became so significant a company, we can actually go into Kinko's asking to Xerox a copy. Xerox moved from a noun to a verb.

Here's another example. Michael Jordan had such a profound impact on the game of basketball that he not only was successful but also shifted to being significant. His trademark moves and amazing buzzer-beater shots were so powerful that they had an impact on this generation and those to come. There are people on the basketball court making extraordinary shots, and their response after making them is, "That's a Jordan." Michael Jordan's legacy is one of significance.

What will be written about you? What will people remember about your leadership? It has to be more than what you accomplished for you. It has to be something beyond you that affects the world in a way that is profound. There is something in you that can change a generation, shift culture, and transform thinking. There is something in you, like that in Joseph, that moves you from being a noun to a verb. You must strive for significance. Joseph's statement to his brothers was a statement that reaffirmed his desire for significance. What happened might have hurt, but it ultimately helped. It propelled you to a place of significance whereby your children's children will be the benefactors of your obedience to the will of God.

Significant leadership is not narcissistic. It is not self-centered. Significant leadership is concerned with elevating God's agenda so that others are influenced in a positive way. Joseph wanted his brothers to be affected positively. When you are significant as a leader, your enemies will have to acknowledge it. Success can come and go based on the world's standard, but significance remains regardless of the seasons of life. As you move forward in the manifestation of God's will for your life, strive diligently for significance.

REFLECTION

Joseph's statement to his brothers also demonstrates reflection. Every leader must spend time reflecting on the journey. How did you get where you are? What events transpired to propel you to the place you are in? Why did you go through what you went through? These are just a few questions you should reflect upon so you can remain faithful and grateful in your leadership. I'm often reminded of the words God speaks to His people in Deuteronomy 8:1-18:

All the commandments which I command thee this day shall ye observe to do, that ye may live, and multiply, and go in and possess the land which the LORD sware unto your fathers. And thou shalt remember all the way which the LORD thy God led thee these forty years in the wilderness, to humble thee, and to prove thee, to know what was in thine heart, whether thou wouldest keep his commandments, or no. And he humbled thee, and suffered thee to hunger, and fed thee with manna, which thou knewest not, neither did thy fathers know; that he might make thee know that man doth not live by bread only, but by every word that proceedeth out of the mouth of the LORD doth man live. Thy raiment waxed not old upon thee, neither did thy foot swell, these forty years. Thou shalt also consider in thine heart, that, as a man chasteneth his son, so the LORD thy God chasteneth thee. Therefore thou shalt keep the commandments of the LORD thy God, to walk in his ways, and to fear him. For the LORD thy God bringeth thee into a good land, a land of brooks of water, of fountains and depths that spring out of valleys and hills; A land of wheat, and barley, and vines, and fig trees, and pomegranates; a land of oil olive, and honey; A land wherein thou shalt eat bread without scarceness, thou shalt not lack any thing in it; a land whose stones are iron, and out of whose hills thou mayest dig brass. When thou hast eaten and art full, then thou shalt bless the LORD thy God for the good land which he hath given thee. Beware that thou forget not the LORD thy God, in not keeping his commandments, and his judgments, and his statutes, which I command thee this day: Lest when thou hast eaten and art full, and hast built goodly houses, and dwelt therein; And when thy herds and thy flocks multiply, and thy silver and thy gold is multiplied, and all that thou hast is multiplied; Then thine heart be lifted up, and thou forget the LORD thy God, which brought thee forth out of the land of Egypt, from the house of bondage; Who led thee through that great and terrible wilderness, wherein were fiery serpents, and scorpions, and drought, where there was no water; who brought thee forth water out of the rock of flint; Who fed thee in the wilderness with manna, which thy fathers knew not, that he might humble thee, and that he might prove thee, to do thee good at thy latter end; And thou say in thine heart, My power and the might of mine hand hath gotten me this wealth. But thou shalt remember the LORD thy God: for it is he that giveth thee power to get wealth, that he may establish his covenant which he sware unto thy fathers, as it is this day.

It was God's desire that those whom He had elevated never develop amnesia. I've seen so many leaders who forget the journey. Reflection is important because it reminds you of the powerful hand of God that allowed you to be where you are. When you reflect, you take nothing for granted. You realize how blessed you are. Joseph was so appreciative to be where he was that he would do nothing to jeopardize what God was doing in his life.

I often have moments of reflection that bring things into greater perspective for me. I think about being raised in a house with my sisters and brothers in a modest neighborhood and having parents who imparted values in me that made me the man I am today. I remember sleeping in bunk beds with my brother and knowing that there was something different about me. I think about being a little nappy-headed boy on Cheatham Street in Shreveport, Louisiana, who had so much energy it was misinterpreted as a behavioral disorder. God took the snotty-nose son of Joseph and Rosa Walker and raised him up for such a time as this. God took a little boy like me in His hands and allowed me to reach millions of people each week. I'm humbled when I reflect over the things that could have prevented my destiny from coming to pass. I didn't hang out with the right people all the time, yet God protected me. I didn't always go to the right places, but God kept a hedge of protection around me. I made my share of mistakes, but God didn't allow my falls to be fatal. God has been good to me. I'm not what I should be, but I thank God I'm not what I used to be. Whenever I am challenged or feel like I can't go on, I reflect and draw strength from what God has done in my past. I can say like Joseph, regarding everything that has happened in my past, that it was all for my good.

When you reflect, you see the providential work of God in every shift of your life. You are becoming the leader God desires every day. Your story is unique, and regardless of where God takes you, never stop telling your story. Your story is your testimony, and it is essential to where you are today. God has taken your mess and turned it into a powerful testimony. Often, people see your glory but have no idea of your story. I assure you there were people who saw where Joseph was and envied him still. I'm certain there were those in Egypt who wondered why he got the position and they didn't. The truth is in the story. When you reflect, you commit to bringing your story to the platform that God gives you.

Don't despise what you have experienced or be ashamed of it. Every jealous brother, every pit, every accusation, every prison, every palace, every problem and problem solved has led to your promotion. When you reflect, you declare with the songwriters Charles "Rusty" Goodman and Jimmie Davis, "I wouldn't take nothing for my journey now."

CONCLUSION

All leaders who desire to see God's will manifest in their lives must go through LeaderShifts. These shifts are necessary to propel you toward your destiny. Often, whatever happens is necessary to you becoming who God has ordained you to become. This work in you was begun before the foundations of the world. Before Joseph got the coat from his father, he was chosen in heaven for this assignment. I pray as you have read this book and reflect on your life that you will embrace the fact that you are the chosen one. You are the one ordained to change the world. Your assignment will transition organizations and create environments for transformation and empowerment. The innovative systems and strategies that are within you are purposed by God to change a generation. When you reflect, you will discover that nothing just happened in your life. Everything happened with intentionality and divine assistance to usher you into the place you are headed.

Only God can take a person through the extremes Joseph experienced and bring him out on top to help his people. Only God can take all that you've been through and package it in such a way that it is about to change the world. I pray that you walk in obedience and confidence and not in fear. There is something awesome ahead of you, and everything that has been has been the wind to push you toward it. Your history is a significant part of your destiny. Embrace it. Own it. Move forward with a willingness to do God's will at any cost. The greater the weight of your story, the greater the weight of your glory. You are a transformative leader who embraces the shifts of leadership. You are destined to solve problems that nobody else can solve.

This is your season, and I pray that this book has inspired you to get up and do something about it. Remember that you are not alone in your journey. I must walk out my journey, and you must walk out yours. All of our assignments have challenges, but we are inspired by what Paul says in 2 Corinthians 4:1-2: "Therefore seeing we have this ministry, as we have received mercy, we faint not; But have renounced the hidden things of dishonesty, not walking in craftiness, nor handling the word of God deceitfully; but by manifestation of the truth commending ourselves to every man's conscience in the sight of God."

It is not about us. True LeaderShift is about Him!

NOTES

1. FROM CHOSEN TO CONSECRATED

1. Parker Palmer, *Let Your Life Speak* (San Francisco: Jossey-Bass, 2000), 3.

2. James Baldwin, "The Black Boy Looks at the White Boy," in *The Price of the Ticket: Collected Nonfiction 1948-1985* (New York: St. Martin's Press, 1985), 302.

3. Saul Alinsky, Brainy Quote, last accessed August 26, 2013, www.brainyquote.com/quotes/quotes/s/saulalinsk138507 .html.

4. Palmer, *Let Your Life Speak,* 32.

5. John Whitmore, "Coaching for Performance," in *Coaching for Performance: Growing Human Potential and Purpose* (Boston: Nicholas Brealey Publishing, 2009), 186.

2. FROM NEARSIGHTED TO FARSIGHTED

1. Kirk Byron Jones, *Holy Play* (San Francisco: Jossey-Bass, 2007).

2. C. J. Mahaney, *Humility: True Greatness* (Sisters, OR: Multnomah Books, 2005).

3. Zora Neale Hurston, *Moses, Man of the Mountain* (New York: HarperPerennial, 1939).

4. Raymond Rasberry, "Only What You Do for Christ Will Last," on Music-Lyrics-Gospel.com, last accessed August 26, 2013, http://www.music-lyrics-gospel.com/gospel_music_lyrics/only_what_you_do_for_christ_will_last_1056.asp.

3. FROM OPPOSITION TO OPPORTUNITY

1. Rollo May, *The Courage to Create* (New York: W. W. Norton, 1975).

2. Ronald Heifetz, *Leadership without Easy Answers* (Cambridge, MA: The Belknap Press of Harvard University Press, 1994), 23.

3. Robert Greene, *The Concise Art of Seduction* (London: Profile Books LTD, 2003), xii–xiii.

4. Carter G. Woodson, *The Mis-Education of the Negro* (n.p.: Seven Treasures Publications, 2010).

5. Heifetz, *Leadership without Easy Answers,* 196.

6. Edgar A. Guest, "See It Through," from Poetry Foundation, last accessed August 26, 2013, http://www.poetryfoundation.org/poem/173583.

4. FROM THREAT TO PROMISE

1. Howard Thurman, *The Search for Common Ground* (Richmond, VA: Friends United Press, 1971), 2.

2. Ibid., 3.

3. Ronald Heifetz, *Leadership without Easy Answers* (Cambridge, MA: The Belknap Press of Harvard University Press, 1994), 191.

4. Anthony Pinn, *Understanding & Transforming the Black Church* (Eugene, OR: Cascade Books, 2010), 44.

5. FROM SERVANT TO STEWARD

1. Ronald Heifetz, *Leadership without Easy Answers* (Cambridge, MA: The Belknap Press of Harvard University Press, 1994), 275.

2. C. Gene Wilkes, *Jesus on Leadership* (Nashville: Tyndale, 1998).

3. Marshall Goldsmith, *What Got You Here Won't Get You There* (New York: Hyperion, 2007), 16.

4. Goodreads, "Barack Obama quotes," last modified April 16, 2013, accessed July 30, 2013, http://www.goodreads.com/author/quotes/6356.Barack_Obama.

6. FROM ACCUSED TO RIGHTEOUS

1. Robert Greene, *The 48 Laws of Power* (New York: Penguin Books, 1998), 148.

2. Robert Greene, *The Concise Art of Seduction* (London: Profile Books LTD, 2003), 162.

3. Gustavo Gutierrez, *On Job: God-Talk and the Suffering of the Innocent* (New York: Orbis Books, 1987), xvii.

4. Ibid., 11.

5. Barbara Kellerman and Deborah L. Rhode, W*omen and Leadership: The State of Play and Strategies for Change* (San Francisco: Jossey-Bass, 2007), 21.

6. Brian P. Hall, "Preventing Corporate Dis-Integrity: How Values Can Dramatically Improve Company Performance,"

last modified February 6, 2003, accessed July 30, 2013, http://www.valuestech.com/gui/dis-integrity.pdf.

7. Martin Luther King, Jr., *The Essential Writings and Speeches of Martin Luther King, Jr.,* ed. James M. Washington (New York: HarperOne, 1986), 52.

8. Kirk Byron Jones, *Rest in the Storm: Self-Care Strategies for Clergy and Other Caregivers* (Valley Forge, PA: Judson Press, 2001).

7. FROM CHAINED TO UNLEASHED

1. Marshall Goldsmith, *What Got You Here Won't Get You There* (New York: Hyperion, 2007), 17.

2. Martin Luther King, Jr., *The Essential Writings and Speeches of Martin Luther King, Jr.,* ed. James M. Washington (New York: HarperOne, 1986), 296.

3. John Whitmore, "Coaching for Performance," in *Coaching for Performance: Growing Human Potential and Purpose* (Boston: Nicholas Brealey Publishing, 2009), 155.

8. FROM CONCEDING TO SOLVING

1. Kirk Byron Jones, *Holy Play* (San Francisco: Jossey-Bass, 2007), 141.

2. John Calvin, *Institutes of the Christian Religion* (Peabody, MA: Publisher's Marketing, 2008).

3. C. J. Mahaney, *Humility: True Greatness* (Sisters, OR: Multnomah Books, 2005).

4. Jones, *Holy Play,* 141.

9. FROM DIMINISHED TO RESTORED

1. Parker Palmer, *Let Your Life Speak* (San Francisco: Jossey-Bass, 2000), 16.

2. Martin Luther King, Jr., *The Essential Writings and Speeches of Martin Luther King, Jr.*, ed. James M. Washington (New York: HarperOne, 1986), 51.

3. Ibid., 633.

4. Ronald Heifetz, *Leadership without Easy Answers* (Cambridge, MA: The Belknap Press of Harvard University Press, 1994), 273.

10. WHAT YOU MEANT FOR MY BAD, GOD MEANT FOR MY GOOD

1. Clayton M. Christensen, *How Will You Measure Your Life?* (New York: HarperCollins, 2012), 191.

2. Dwight D. Eisenhower, Brainy Quote, last accessed August 26, 2013, www.brainyquote.com/quotes/quotes/d/dwightdei109026.html.

3. Goodreads, "Nelson Mandela Quotes," last modified April 11, 2013, accessed September 9, 2013, http://www.goodreads.com/quotes/9960-a-good-head-and-good-heart-are-always-a-formidable.

4. Howard Thurman, *The Search for Common Ground* (Richmond, VA: Friends United Press, 1971), 45.

BIBLIOGRAPHY

Alinsky, Saul. Brainy Quote. Last accessed August 26, 2013. www.brainyquote.com/quotes/quotes/s/saulalinsk 138507.html.

Baldwin, James. "The Black Boy Looks at the White Boy." *The Price of the Ticket: Collected Nonfiction 1948-1985*. New York: St. Martin's Press, 1985.

Calvin, John. *Institutes of the Christian Religion*. Peabody, MA: Publisher's Marketing, 2008.

Christensen, Clayton M. *How Will You Measure Your Life?* New York: HarperCollins, 2012.

Eisenhower, Dwight D. Brainy Quote. Last accessed August 26, 2013. www.brainyquote.com/quotes/quotes/d/dwightdei109026.html

Goldsmith, Marshall. *What Got You Here Won't Get You There*. New York: Hyperion, 2007.

Goodreads. "Barack Obama quotes." Accessed July 30, 2013. Last modified April 16, 2013. http://www.goodreads.com/author/quotes/6356.Barack_Obama.

———. "Nelson Mandela Quotes." Accessed September 9, 2013. Last modified April 11, 2013. http://www.goodreads.com/quote/9960-a-good-head-and-good-heart-are-always-a-formidable.

Greene, Robert. T*he Concise Art of Seduction.* London: Profile Books LTD, 2003.

———. *The 48 Laws of Power.* New York: Penguin Books, 1998.

Guest, Edgar A. "See It Through." From Poetry Foundation. Last accessed August 26, 2013. http://www.poetryfoun dation.org/poem/173583.

Gutierrez, Gustavo. *On Job: God-Talk and the Suffering of the Innocent.* New York: Orbis Books, 1987.

Hall, Brian P. "Preventing Corporate Dis-Integrity: How Values Can Dramatically Improve Company Performance." Last Modified February 6, 2003. Accessed July 30, 2013. http://www.valuestech.com/gui/dis-integrity.pdf

Heifetz, Ronald. *Leadership without Easy Answers.* Cambridge, MA: The Belknap Press of Harvard University Press, 1994.

Hurston, Zora Neale. *Moses, Man of the Mountain.* New York: HarperPerennial, 1939.

Jones, Kirk Byron. *Holy Play.* San Francisco: Jossey-Bass, 2007.

———. *Rest in the Storm: Self-Care Strategies for Clergy and Other Caregivers.* Valley Forge, PA: Judson Press, 2001.

Kellerman, Barbara, and Deborah L. Rhode. W*omen and Leadership: The State of Play and Strategies for Change.* San Francisco: Jossey-Bass, 2007.

King, Martin Luther, Jr. T*he Essential Writings and Speeches of Martin Luther King, Jr.* Edited by James M. Washington. New York: HarperOne, 1986.

Mahaney, C. J. *Humility: True Greatness.* Sisters, OR: Multnomah Books, 2005.

May, Rollo. *The Courage to Create.* New York: W. W. Norton, 1975.

Palmer, Parker. *Let Your Life Speak.* San Francisco: Jossey-Bass, 2000.

Pinn, Anthony. *Understanding & Transforming the Black Church.* Eugene, OR: Cascade Books, 2010.

Rasberry, Raymond. "Only What You Do for Christ Will Last." On Music-Lyrics-Gospel.com. Last accessed August 26, 2013. http://www.music-lyrics-gospel.com/gospel_music_lyrics/only_what_you_do_for_christ_will_last_1056.asp.

Thurman, Howard. *The Search for Common Ground.* Richmond, VA: Friends United Press, 1971.

Whitmore, John. "Coaching for Performance." In *Coaching for Performance: Growing Human Potential and Purpose.* Boston: Nicholas Brealey Publishing, 2009.

Wilkes, C. Gene. *Jesus on Leadership.* Nashville: Tyndale, 1998.

Woodson, Carter G. *The Mis-Education of the Negro.* N.p.: Seven Treasures Publications, 2010.

For anyone who has ever grappled seriously with their privilege or come face to face with their own shortcomings, this book is a safe place to land.

And for anyone who's ever wondered if it's even possible to raise a happy family in difficult or unusual circumstances *[Worlds Apart]* offers hope and, what's better, guidance.

But these stories are also a sober reminder to parents that no matter how much love and security we lavish upon our children, we cannot protect them from the sorrows and difficulties of this life – nor is it our job.

Marilyn's book is a gem for all these reasons, and it is also a joy to read. The language is beautiful, and each story is seasoned with profound truths about life and faith. Somehow as we read, we are able to swallow the bitter along with the sweet. That is what grace is all about, and that is what this book is all about.

~Elizabeth Trotter, writer and editor at A Life Overseas *and co-author of*
A-41: Essays on life and ministry abroad,

Worlds Apart
A Third Culture Kid's Journey

Marilyn R. Gardner

Doorlight Publications
www.doorlightpublications.com

Copyright ©2018 Marilyn R. Gardner

Significant portions of this book previously published by Doorlight Publications in 2017 under the title Passages Through Pakistan

First published 2018 by Doorlight Publications.

ISBN 0-9982233-2-8
ISBN13 978-0-9982233-2-2

Design & Production by Ruth Anne Burke

To my brothers

who have loved me well,

in Pakistan and beyond.

The train rounds a bend.
The rest of the cars appear
one by one,
all tied to one another
far into the distance
It comes as a surprise
to be tied to things so far back

Nazım Hikmet
Human Landscapes from My Country

Contents

Foreword

I brought my children to the Horn of Africa in 2003. That move turned them into third culture kids, a term I barely understood at the time. Did I ruin them by making that move? Did I ruin them again when we made the decision for boarding school? And will I ruin them again, by sending them back to their passport country for university?

I met Marilyn while in the thick of wrestling with this question. My twins had just started boarding school. I struggled to live with the collision of their delight at the opportunity and my grief over this family decision. Marilyn stepped off the internet and into my life like a shepherd, wise and compassionate. She knows how to hold two conflicting realities. Delight and grief. Sorrow and contentment. Tragedy and forgiveness. Loneliness and belonging. Vulnerability and strength. Home and not home.

Marilyn showed me that I am not alone. My TCKs are not alone. Our questions, struggles, and joys have been forged through this international life and, though we are sometimes physically worlds apart from people like us, worlds apart from our passport country, and often worlds apart from our host country, we are part of a global community.

Worlds Apart, imbued with the sights and scents of Pakistan, invites the reader into that diverse and growing community. It tells the story of how Marilyn developed this wisdom. The story in these pages answers that, no, I did not ruin my children. Marilyn, a third culture kid herself, was not ruined by her parents' move to Pakistan, nor by going to boarding school. But at the same time, *Worlds Apart* answers my question with a resounding yes.

I have ruined my children in the same way Marilyn was ruined and in the same way Third Culture Kids around the planet are ruined. They are ruined for the ordinary, for complacency, for conformity. This is a book that shows the complications of a challenging childhood, the healing power of a faithful life, and the precious gifts third culture kids are to the world.

When people ask what it is like to live abroad, or to send my children to boarding school, or to face eventual repatriation to the US, I tell them to read this book.

Rachel Pieh Jones

INTRODUCTION

THE TERM 'third culture kid' was first developed in the 1960s by Dr. Ruth Useem. Dr. Useem was a sociologist and an anthropologist who coined the term after observing common characteristics of children who spent a significant amount of time growing up in a culture outside of their ancestral culture due to their parents' careers.

For children who grow up between worlds, identity formation does not work in expected ways. Instead, we move back and forth as our identity is forged and shaped between two often conflicting cultures. "A British child taking toddling steps on foreign soil or speaking his or her first words in Chinese with an amah (nanny) has no idea of what it means to be human yet, let alone 'British.' He or she simply responds to what is happening in the moment" (Pollock and Van Reken, 2001).

Sometimes we fit into both worlds easily; other times fitting into one or the other is like wearing a pair of ill-fitting shoes that cause blisters and sores until we can't wait to take them off.

While I was growing up, the term 'third culture kid' was not used, and little was known about these children. I am grateful that this term is now part of the vocabulary of expatriates and that there is now a body of research devoted to the study of third culture kids.

The definition of the 'third culture kid' gave me a context and a reference point, a perspective that helped me understand myself better and, in so doing, helped me to better relate to others. Without this understanding, my story would be incomplete.

> A Third Culture Kid (TCK) is a person who has spent a significant part of his or her developmental years outside the parents' culture. The TCK frequently builds relationships to all of the cultures, while not having full ownership in any. Although elements from each culture may be assimilated into the TCK's life experience, the sense of belonging is in relationship to others of similar background (David Pollock, *Among Worlds*).

> There is a group of us who bear no identifying marks. We don't have the same accent, we don't pronounce or even necessarily spell words the same way. We can't tell one another at first glance. We don't wear the "home team" t-shirt. But when we meet, it's like we're from the same place. We greet each other, we carry on, we tell stories, and we laugh wholeheartedly. It doesn't matter the age difference, the nationality, the gender. We connect. (Robynn Bliss, *Expectations and Burnout*)

As we grow older, we expect that we will fit into both worlds equally well, when in actual fact we fit into neither perfectly. Instead, we develop relationships and connections to both.

❖

As WITH ANY major writing endeavor, there are so many people to thank. I am grateful to my editors, Dan Brown and Ruth Anne Burke, who kept me on track and took a meandering set of writings and turned it into an actual book; my parents whose choices gave me Pakistan; my brothers who shared so many of the same stories; and my extended family at Murree Christian School. As in any extended family, I have my favorites. Any of them could write their own book, and while some things would be similar, each of us have our unique memories that shaped who we have become. Special thanks to my aunties and uncles from various mission organizations. Some are no longer alive, but others continue to amaze me with their sheer joy and faithfulness in living. Special thanks to Auntie Betty, who has encouraged my writing from the start. Some Pakistanis may never know I wrote this book – Arbab, Martha Domji, Jamila – yet I think about them almost daily and I am so grateful for their impact on my life. A huge thank you to Ambassador Jonathan Addleton, someone I am proud to call my friend, for reading and commenting on the manuscript.

All my love and thanks goes to my husband Cliff. Not a day goes by without him encouraging me to write, write, and write some more. He is my soulmate and encourager and I could not be more grateful.

Lastly to Pakistan, Land of the Pure, thank you for your never-ending hospitality, your beauty, and your love. May God protect you, and may you know peace.

Pakistan Zindabad.
(Long live Pakistan)

PROLOGUE

My Country
I don't have any caps left made back home
Nor any shoes that trod your roads
I've worn out your last shirt quite long ago
It was of Şile cloth
Now you only remain in the whiteness of my hair
Intact in my heart
Now you only remain in the whiteness of my hair
In the lines of my forehead
My country

Nazım Hikmet
Human Landscapes from My Country

In October of 2010 I went to Pakistan to work with people internally displaced by floods that had devastated much of the country. I had grown up in Pakistan, was nurtured on her soil, took my first steps and said my first words there. Pakistan was a land that knew me before I had a recollection of 'being', before I knew I was human. To return was a gift. My sister-in-law and I arrived in Karachi in the wee hours of the morning, exhausted by over twenty hours of travel. But I knew I was home. Every bone in my body felt it.

The two weeks that followed were full, hard, and glorious. We dispensed medicine out of the trunk of a van, drank *chai* made with unpasteurized buffalo milk, cried with the wounded, laughed at language mistakes, stopped to pick up fresh *pakoras* in the bazaar, and ate meals of hot, spicy curry while reminiscing with friends. Every day brought incredible joy. I was home.

On the last day of the trip, I made plans to visit an old friend. I had known Arbab in high school, and I loved her deeply, even as I acknowledged a monumental gulf between our worlds.

I waited at the front of the hospital compound, my hair held back in a short ponytail, a sky blue, light cotton *dupatta* over my head. The guard at the front gate left to fetch a motorized rickshaw to take us to Arbab's house. My heart beat fast, my foot tapped impatiently. As I waited, I stood with a doctor, a gifted surgeon. She was new to Pakistan and struggling with the cultural disconnect that so often comes when West meets East.

"I remember running around the foundation of these buildings when I was a girl," I smiled as I remembered.

She looked at me, measuring her words. "A compound like this must have made life as a child in Pakistan at least somewhat bearable" she said.

I stood still and stared at her in shock. Bearable? Bearable? I repeated the word to myself. I said it aloud. "Bearable? It was more than bearable. My childhood was extraordinary."

In that moment my life made sense. I could see my childhood in Pakistan, years of disconnect in the United States, life as an adult back in Pakistan and then in Egypt, and finally my return to the United States as a stranger, an alien who had to learn to live, learn to belong.

In that moment, like Thornton Wilder's Emily, I was poised above the earth looking down at myself, my life in full. Suspended above the earth looking down at the scene, it all fit. The puzzle was complete. Like Emily, I got to go back:

> I didn't realize. So all that was going on in life and we never noticed! Take me back–up the hill . . . But first: Wait! One more look! Good-bye! Good-bye, world! . . . Oh, earth, you're too wonderful for anybody to realize you. Do any human beings ever realize life while they live it?—every, every minute? (Thornton Wilder, *Our Town*)

This was my story, a story written by the master storyteller, the author of life. Suddenly it all made sense. All the pain, all the joy, all the tears, and all the laughter–all of it. It all had meaning like I had never imagined. God himself orchestrated the journey I had traveled since birth. I was in awe and wordlessly gave thanks.

Chapter 1
Ocean Voyages

She watched the gap between ship and shore grow to a huge gulf. Perhaps this was a little like dying, the departed no longer visible to the others, yet both still existed,
Only in different worlds

Susan Wiggs, *The Charm School*

❖

I was conceived, I am told, on the Queen Mary. That once-majestic ship is now retired, forever docked in the blue-green waters of the Pacific near Los Angeles. In May of 1959 my parents were aboard the Queen Mary with their three older children—all boys. The four-week journey from Karachi to New York had its share of adventures. From my present vantage point, my conception is the most notable of them. I began in a tiny compartment, on a massive ship that rocked on the ocean waves.

Prior to World War II, the Queen Mary was known for her elegance. Originally labelled Job #534, she "captured hearts on both sides of the Atlantic." On her maiden voyage in 1936 she sailed from Southampton to Cherbourg and then across the Atlantic to the New York Harbor. She was massive, with dining halls, ballrooms, swimming pools, and even a squash court. The Queen proudly took the wealthy back and forth between countries and continents.

Then war came. During World War II the Queen Mary was put to utilitarian use as a troop transport. Stripped of the opulence that had made her so popular and painted a camouflage grey, she was fast and stealthy. A postwar rehabilitation brought the Queen back to the seas as a commercial ocean liner, and for over twenty years she continued her journeys back and forth across the seas. Along with the wealthy, she now took missionaries to their destinations far from the comfort of their homes in the Western Hemisphere.

When I was seven years old, the Queen Mary made her final voyage, docking in Long Beach. A ten-year-old photograph shows my three oldest children in Southern California with the great liner in the background. My husband sent the photo to my parents with a note. "If it hadn't been for you, these three wouldn't be here."

My family had begun the journey at Karachi Harbor, embarking on a much-needed furlough. Pakistan had become their adopted home seven years before, and during that time they had only been back to the United States once. Until the mid 1960s, my parents always traveled by ship. Air travel was expensive, reserved for the wealthy; sea travel was more economical. There was something wonderful about those six-week journeys, Mom once remarked, wistfully. They provided time and space to acclimate oneself, to adapt while slowly moving away from one country and, equally slowly, entering another. It was a floating world between two worlds, without expectation from or connection to either. Long days and nights alternated in slow rhythm, allowing my parents to rest and rejuvenate before arriving at the bustling harbor in Ellis Island.

My parents traveled during the golden years of the Queen Mary. They offered, I imagine, a stark contrast to their fellow passengers. Mom began her first book, *Jars of Clay*, with an anecdote from their first voyage to Pakistan in 1954. Listening to their shortwave radio one evening, they heard a familiar voice: "I take missionaries out and bring monkeys back, and I don't know which is worse!" It was the captain of the ship. As missionaries with a growing family, they were worlds apart from this captain and from the luxury passengers who later traveled with them on the Queen Mary. Everyone knew it.

My passage through Pakistan began here, in an elegant boat on a vast ocean, with long days at sea, and nights spread with stars in an expansive sky. I wish I could travel in time to witness the journey. During those long days and nights at sea, life happened. I happened. And somehow that was no accident.

❖

ALTHOUGH I WAS conceived on a queen of the seas, I entered the world in a more ordinary place and time, in January, when Massachusetts is bitter cold, and snow falls heavy on the bare maples and oaks. A New England January is barren and bleak. The only warmth is inside beside a fire. I still hate the cold.

I was born in Winchendon, a factory town in North-Central Massachusetts. A giant rocking horse, painted white and red, sits on Winchendon's town common, a reminder of days when the town was a bustling toy-making hub. The original rocking horse, Clyde, created by one of the owners of the Converse Toy & Woodenware Company, is the town's icon.

Three baby girls were born that last week of January in the small town hospital. I was one of them. Those who may wish to make pilgrimage to the scene of such an important event are out of luck. The hospital did not survive past the seventies when it was overtaken by larger, more sophisticated medical centers in nearby cities. As the first baby girl in a family with three lively boys, I was, without doubt, the Princess. My place in this family was unassailable, and throughout my childhood I knew it.

Winchendon was Mom's hometown. My maternal grandparents, Stanley and Cyrena Ruth Kolodinski, had four children: Pauline, my mom; twins, Bill and Charlotte; and Jean, a blonde, blue-eyed beauty with a personality to match. My grandmother, known affectionately as "Grandma K" to most everyone, was a gentle, unassuming woman. She had survived a broken heart after my grandfather died of a heart attack when he was 50 years old. She grieved with grace. "They say that time heals these wounds," Grandma K said to me one day, "but I miss your Grandpa Stanley more now than I did the day after he died." It was a powerful, unforgettable lesson on grief.

Mom was smart. Few children from Winchendon went to college but she was determined that she would. Her Polish-Lithuanian father, who had come through Ellis Island as a child, was dismissive. "What do girls need with college?" he said. She was undeterred. At mom's college graduation, her dad was the proudest man in the room.

But a more decisive change had already happened many years earlier. A tall gentleman with a deep Swedish accent came to Winchendon's small Baptist church when Mom was a child. He spoke about mission work in India, and Mom's heart was stirred. That night she decided to do everything she could to become a missionary.

Dad's family was also from Western Massachusetts. Ralph Edward Brown was the fourth child and only son of Annie and Edward Utley Brown, my paternal grandparents. His mother, Annie, struggled to nurse him; he seemed unable to take either breast milk or regular formula and he failed to thrive. The milkman, aware of the problem, suggested sweetened condensed milk. Having nothing to lose, Annie diluted this in a bottle, and to everyone's astonishment, Ralph not only survived but thrived. To this day, he blames his love for sweet things on his early diet.

Tragedy struck when Dad was four. His father died during a hospitalization for a broken leg. Annie, left alone with five children and an empty space in her home and heart, raised the family with grit and grace during an era when life was not kind to a widow and her children. Dad recalls a community of friends and relatives, many from Morningside Baptist Church in Pittsfield, who walked alongside the family during this time.

Dad grew into a young man with a personality and character as large as his smile. After graduation he entered the Air Force, but to his disappointment instead of flying planes and braving enemy combatants, he spent his military career processing paperwork and filling out tedious forms in triplicate. Two years later, thanks to the GI bill, he enrolled at Gordon College on Boston's Fenway where he met his life-long love. Pauline evidently stole his heart after one or two "Joyces" and perhaps a "Ruthanne." He has never been completely clear on this. Undoubtedly, one of the things that attracted them to each other was their mutual desire to go overseas as foreign missionaries.

They were married in 1951, surrounded by mountain laurel and a host of family and friends attending and wishing them well. Almost immediately, they began planning their future overseas.

Mom and Dad welcomed their firstborn, my oldest brother, Edward Ralph, on March 16th, 1953, two years after they were married. A year-and-a-half later their lives dramatically changed when they boarded the Steel Recorder in New York Harbor to begin their voyage to Karachi.

A 50-year-old photograph shows Mom, wearing white gloves and pearl earrings, holding a baby in her arms. She is standing on the deck of a ship, a slight smile on her face, beautiful and shyly sophisticated, worlds away from the country where she would make her home for over 35 years. The photograph gives few clues of her resiliency, or the ability she would show to redirect her Yankee independence to fit cultural norms without ever losing a bit of spirit.

Dad became as accustomed to sitting cross-legged on the floor in a Marwari tribal village and relishing onion curry as he was preaching from the pulpit at Morningside Baptist and enjoying a potluck church supper. Mom learned to parse Sindhi verbs and decipher the nuances of language and culture. Veiled women became dear friends. Curry, and *chapatis,* became a staple. They learned to live, love, and make a home in desert towns extraordinarily different from Winchendon or Pittsfield where they were raised. When I was born, Mom and Dad had already established a life on both sides of the globe. They had a foot in both countries, and had learned to negotiate this space between two worlds.

Soon after my birth, my parents left from New York Harbor to begin the six-week ocean voyage back to Pakistan. Along with the still-lively three boys, they had a newborn in tow. This was my first full journey overseas. I am the baby in the faded black-and-white photograph. In my imagination, I see a young, vulnerable family on a huge ship in an ocean so vast they would go for days without seeing land. How did they do it? How did they nurture us and keep their hope and love alive? The answer is without doubt in their faith, a faith that had begun so many years before and continued to direct their decisions, both big and small

Our ship docked in the harbor at Karachi, Pakistan's busy port city. Karachi served as a useful stop prior to making the long rail journey to Ratodero, a small city where my parents made their home.

Karachi was a city of *gymkhanas,* large, palm-tree bordered roads, and sprawling villas. Along with that, the poor arrived daily from villages throughout Pakistan, and large slums emerged in various parts of the city. The distinct disparity between rich and poor was a reality that I was not aware of in childhood. I saw Karachi as a magical city – my favorite place to shop and vacation.

Our favorite grocery shopping area was the famed Empress Market, built during the British occupation. The market provided a number of shops where Mom could stock up on store-bought butter, meat, sugar, flour, and yeast to last the family at least three months. Travel was infrequent and not easy, so trips to Empress Market were important.

My memories of these early years are sometimes clouded, other times as vivid as the bright colors painted onto Pakistani trucks and buses. When I first arrived in Karachi the country was still young, born only 13 years earlier in 1947. In 1954 when my parents first arrived, Pakistan was raw with fresh memories of the violence and struggle of a difficult and precarious independence. Yet during my childhood, I would only partially grasp the challenging history of this country. My world was safe, cocooned by my parents' love and a sheltering community. I belonged. Pakistan was home. Anything outside of Pakistan was 'other.' I would not form memories of my country of birth and citizenship until much later.

MY EARLIEST MEMORY is from Ratodero, a small city located around 30 kilometers from Larkana. In the memory I am small, a preschooler, sitting on a bed on a rooftop, smiling beneath gauzy mosquito netting. A faded photograph confirms the image in my mind. I look at the camera. My older brother, Tommy, sitting on his bed beside mine, looks at me. We woke early on that rooftop, responding to the morning light and sounds of early morning – roosters, the call to prayer, oxen carrying heavy loads – that still evoke the joy of my childhood.

We were the only foreigners in the city, and we had the only car. Our house, where Bibles abounded and daily prayer was as important as daily bread, was surrounded on four sides by mosques. The call to prayer not only woke us in the morning, it was our melody at lunch, our call to afternoon tea, and the mournful, melancholy music of our evening hours. The high walls of the house guarded three courtyards at three different levels, giving us space to play and privacy from the many eyes curious to observe this white, foreign family. A trough that had at one time been used to water animals became our swimming pool in the hot months. We lived peaceful, noisy lives in this place.

This house, with its high ceilings and arched doors, was my first home. With it come memories of my dolls, my brothers, mosquito netting, early morning whispering –and a prized doctor set, perhaps my earliest achievement. I was a thumb sucker. Mom desperately wanted me to stop sucking my thumb so that parasites would stop entering my body. Determined to achieve this goal, she told me that if I could go a month without sucking my thumb she would give me a doctor set; a real, live, plastic doctor set. It would be white, with a red cross on the front. Inside would be plastic syringes, a thermometer, a stethoscope, along with fake bandages and eye patches. I had seen one of these before and I dreamed of having my own. The task was a difficult one, but I was stubborn. I wanted that doctor set.

Every day for thirty days I asked Mom about the set. I imagined giving my dolls shots and wound care. I wrapped make-believe bandages tightly across arms, legs, and naked torsos. I anticipated establishing a doll hospital, complete with injured dolls and beds made of boxes and old cloth. Mom, in her mercy, had determined that if I sucked my thumb at night it would not count. But every night, as she popped her head around my door to look at my tousled pixie hair rumpled on a pillow, she saw my thumb, just inches from my mouth, but never in.

On day thirty, I was declared the winner. I got my doctor set, and my imaginary play rose to new heights. It also foreshadowed the future. I went on to become a nurse with real bandages, stethoscopes, and syringes, and my patients would no longer be a motley set of dolls, but real people who hurt, bled, and sometimes died. Mom still tells this story with admiration and amazement in her eyes.

Why do some memories stay while others fade? Is it because the memory is so important to those close to us that they continually remind us, perhaps realizing that if it is not passed on then one of their memories, a family narrative, will die? Did Mom tell me this to pass on family history, or was it more than that? We are marked by stories from our childhood, our personalities linked and shaped by the narratives we are told. These memories of others become our stories and stay with us, even when they are old and faded. As life grows more complicated, we return to these stories to remember, to remind ourselves who we are. Remembering builds strength and resilience. The story established itself in my memory because it was bigger than a strong-willed little girl determined to get her prize. It told me who I was.

Research shows that a determining factor in the emotional health and resilience in a child is the knowledge that she is part of a bigger story. My stories and memories from Ratodero are gleaned from tattered pictures and from Mom and Dad. I was too young to remember most of them. But these small narratives place me within a larger family narrative, a narrative written on both sides of the globe with thousands of stories contributing to the whole. The story stubbornly continues through the years, determined to go on, like a four-year-old who stops sucking her thumb, single-minded and intent on a prize, determined to get the doctor set with its bright red cross emblazoned on the white exterior.

ONE OF THE most powerful and poignent stories in our family's narrative comes from a Christmas when I was three years old, living in Ratodero. The city, with its dusty streets, flat-roofed houses with courtyards, and donkeys and ox carts that brayed and roamed outside, resembled ancient Bethlehem more than anywhere Mom or Dad had ever been.

Despite the biblical setting, adjusting to Christmas in Pakistan was a challenge. Loneliness and homesickness tended to descend on my parents like thick clouds during the holidays, made more difficult by their desire to create magic for their children. They were acutely aware of the absence of grandparents and other extended family members back in the United States. During one particular Christmas Mom felt that it was more than she could bear. She felt more than ever like we were "deprived" of a "real" Christmas.

A few days before Christmas, after we were put to bed, Mom went up on the roof top. As she looked out over the city of Ratodero, the tears she had been holding back for our sake began to fall. She was a world removed from the Christmases of her past. There was no extended family, no white-steepled church, no lights on Main Street. As she watched the bright stars, millions of light years away, she heard singing just as the shepherds heard singing on that night so long ago. Could it be angels? It was a moment of wonder and awe that the God whom she loved so deeply would provide angels to bring comfort and a reminder that she was not alone.

There were no heavenly angels, but "earth angels" had arrived in the form of our dear friends, the Addletons and the Johnsons, two missionary families with seven kids between them. Out of love for our family they had traveled along a bumpy, dusty road, remembering that we were alone in this city. Once there they stood in the street outside our front door singing "Joy to the World, the Lord is Come. Let Earth receive Her King!" They celebrated with cups of hot cocoa and frosted sugar cookies before heading back into the night. Through the years we have told the story of these "angels from the rooftops" over and over, one more story in the larger family narrative.

LIFE IN SINDH seemed far from the broader national politics of Pakistan. Sindh was in the south and, though much of it was desert, fertile ground by the Indus River allowed for farming. In the 1900s barrages and canals were built that allowed better farming for Sindhis. Punjabis in the north occupied the corridors of power. Sindhis, a minority group both in population and geography, were often marginalized. And Sindh was hot. People who lived there bore the marks of a heat that wears down the body. They often exhibited a striking patience and acceptance of all of life, an acceptance that I also learned. Sitting on *charpais* (rope beds) in the hot sun makes you sanguine and not easily disturbed. Flies landed and lounged on our heads, aiming for the eyes and the lips if we did not fan them away. We learned to sit for hours on *charpais*, in sweltering church services, and in hot cars. Sindhis had a humor and good will that extended to those of us who were their guests. My gregarious father fit in perfectly. A photographer in Shikarpur once captured his photo, enlarged it, and prominently displayed it in his shop at the entrance of the Shikarpur bazaar so the entire community could see. Dad was "Brown Sahib" of the white hair and smile as big as his heart. His picture gazed on all who entered the area, ever looking out on a land and people that he had come to love.

We moved from town to town during my childhood, but I was unfazed. My constants were my boarding school, based in a solid stone building in Murree, and my parents, who, though flesh and blood, seemed equally solid and immoveable. Pakistan was home. She adopted me, a foreigner, and took me in. I belonged. I belonged in the family and in the community into which I was born. I belonged in the country where I took my first steps. Legal documents might say otherwise, but they were unimportant to the reality of my experience.

I learned early on of the beauty and hospitality of Pakistan. My eyes captured landscapes that the best photographers in the world could not capture, and the music and colors are etched on my mind. I was welcomed into homes and churches, played in courtyards and on canal banks.

In my childhood, the Pakistan I knew was a place of color and life: bright oranges, reds, yellows, and greens of spices and fabrics. I knew the ready invitations to come for tea that brought smiles to my face and delight to my heart. I knew the best food in the world – mouthwatering and piping hot *pakoras*; kebabs purchased in the middle of the bazaar in the afternoon; spicy, red-orange, charred chicken *tikka* with *naan* and fresh lemon; the cold tang of lemon squash; and chicken *masala*'s thick, onion-filled sauce that made my nose run through an entire meal. The tastes and spices lingered long after the meal was over. I knew Pakistan as a place of food, music, colors, and laughter.

This was my home, the setting of my earliest memories, my first steps, my first kiss, my first love. I literally cut my first teeth in this land. Pakistan was a place of life and faith. I was surrounded by Pakistanis who loved me and put up with the immaturity of my childhood. This was where my physical and faith journey began. Would I ever love another place so much? I didn't think so.

Later, I would come to know the complexity and contradiction that defined this homeland that had adopted me, but in early years I knew only the good. I would later discover more of her history. I would learn of a Pakistan birthed in violence and tragedy, a land that continues to face crisis after crisis – some at the hands of other governments, and some of its own making. I would learn of the difficulty of a country that struggled to find her identity apart from the larger Indian subcontinent. I would see the struggles in my friends around marriage and family and learn of the massive disparities between the wealthy and the poor. Later, I would learn that in addition to the beauty of friendship and hospitality there was also the horror of violent fundamentalism. I would be introduced to and angered by the one-dimensional Pakistan of Western perception and media. I would understand that alongside stunning landscapes of high mountains and clear lakes was the dirt and raw sewage of cities. I would later face disease, high infant morbidity and mortality, inescapable poverty, and the light hair and big bellies of malnutrition. I would grow to see many dimensions of this beautiful, complex land.

But the Pakistan of early childhood was a beautiful home, and I loved that home.

My earliest memories are in Ratodero, but Jacobabad is the place I associate most strongly with my earliest years. Jacobabad was founded in the 1800s by a British general, General John Jacob. General Jacob was known for doing a great deal to help the city, and while many other cities bearing the names of British elite were renamed, the residents of

Jacobabad refused to change the name. General Jacob was buried in the city and left a large Victorian clock tower in the center that stands to this day. Jacobabad consistently recorded some of the hottest temperatures in the subcontinent. With summer temperatures soaring to 48 degrees Celsius and beyond, it is easy to see why people are relaxed. Jacobabad is so hot that it's difficult to get excited or angry about anything.

We moved to Jacobabad when I was five, and at our house there I remember Mom's first attempts at gardening. Her native Massachusetts was full of vibrant colors that characterized the four seasons. The climate of Sindh – the heat, the lack of foliage, the desert plants, the unknown seasons – none of it was familiar. Mom was desperate for some color in the clay that surrounded our house. While bougainvillea and desert plants survived and brought with them flashes of color, there was nothing that compared to the variety and vibrancy of the plant life of her Massachusetts home. After failed attempts at planting flowers, she finally gave up and placed some fake flowers in flowerbeds surrounding the house. We were all delighted with the outcome. Bright spots of yellow, purple, fuchsia, blue, and green radiated against the mud-colored brick of our home. From far away they looked real. That was good enough for us.

Others around us were equally pleased. Only hours after they were planted, the flowers disappeared. We were deeply disappointed, angry that someone would steal our flowers. This was our home, our yard, our haven, and a thief had violated our space. I don't remember Mom's reaction. I can guess that she was disappointed and angry, perhaps tearful. Mom missed her home more than she could possibly articulate, especially to her children who would not understand the loneliness of living in an alien land until they were older. But that is her story. My story is one of childish indignation and hurt. It was my earliest experience of betrayal. Who would do this to us? I thought we were loved. When you're loved, people don't steal your flowers.

I was a headstrong little girl, stubborn and sassy. I suffered for my independence in various ways – at five a broken bone, at six my mouth washed out with soap for talking back to Mom and Dad, at seven a spanking for sticking out my tongue at Pakistani friends. The broken bone was the most traumatic; sticking out my tongue would provide the best life lesson.

The afternoon that I broke my leg, I had been sent to the top of my bunk bed as punishment for some now-forgotten offense. After granting me the allotted time to reflect on my actions, Mom called me to the kitchen, and I threw myself off my bed in anger at the perceived injustice. My anger immediately dissolved into tears of pain, and I was immediately sorry for my naughtiness. From my howls of pain and inability to walk, my parents knew this was more than a small sprain. But Jacobabad was a three-hour drive from a mission hospital in the city of Sukkur. The trip would have to wait for the morning.

That night I woke up intermittently to deep pain and to the sound of Mom's beautiful voice reading from Patricia St. John's *Rainbow Garden*. She read about a bratty young protagonist, Elaine, who broke her leg and ended up spending the night with a criminal. Hearing the story of Elaine, how she survived her trauma, and how she came out on the other side, at peace with both God and the people around her, made my accident seem like it would yield something worthy. Even at five, I identified with characters in books, and the story seemed uncanny in resemblance to my situation.

We left for Sukkur the next morning. I saw the doctor and ended up with a thigh-high cast. Along with providing a canvas for autographs and artistic endeavors, it was also my passport to empathy, a respite from the regular good-hearted teasing of my brothers.

Other events in Jacobabad show how dependent we were on each other and on friends from afar. At one point, Dad was traveling while Mom stayed at home with my little brother Dan and me. My older brothers were away at boarding school, and we were the only foreigners in the city. All three of us spiked high fevers. Mom tried desperately to cope, but grew increasingly anxious about her ability to look after two little ones while being so sick herself. There were no telephones, and we didn't travel without a great deal of planning. If we needed help quickly, we used telegrams. Finally, realizing she could no longer carry on alone, Mom sent a telegram to friends in Shikarpur. "Ralph traveling. Stop. Kids and I very sick. Stop. Need help. Stop."

That same night, Auntie Betty and Uncle Ben Ralston arrived from Shikarpur, where they lived with their three boys. They had left as soon as they received the telegram asking for help. Wrapping us tightly in quilts, they put all three of us into their car and drove into the night toward the safety of community. Auntie Betty held me on her lap, tight and secure. I knew in that moment that more than anything I wanted to be held. The safety and security that were absent when we were alone, bodies broken by fever, had now arrived, and I never wanted to be let go. I remember thinking that I needed to scratch my nose, but if I wiggled free to scratch my nose, Auntie Betty might think I didn't want to be held. I couldn't risk it. So I remained still as Auntie Betty continued to hold me, oblivious to the internal struggle and my deep, human need for security. We drove through the dark night toward Shikarpur and the safe community of missionary aunties, uncles, and friends who would care for us.

Our community in Jacobabad was a small, struggling Christian church and school. Sunday mornings and evenings, the Christian community gathered, strong voices singing Punjabi hymns with enthusiasm. Events and hospitality were constant, whether it was tea with two or three, or large programs with hundreds of children. Sometimes Mom stayed at home with my little brother while Dad perched me on the bar of his bicycle to ride to the services. One Sunday I caught my foot in the spokes of the wheel. I screamed with pain as I looked down at torn skin and blood. Pakistanis immediately came to my aid, carrying me off the bike and holding me, speaking gentle phrases in Sindhi to comfort my tears as my father resituated himself. They were kind and considerate, deeply concerned for my welfare. Dad took me home, where my ankle received the attention of salve and bandages, the security and safety of love. Safety and love became the solid foundation for my childhood, always appearing when I needed them. Bad things might happen, but help would come, whether from Auntie Betty or Pakistani strangers. I would be cared for.

My attitude toward Pakistanis was not always noble, particularly in my early childhood. The hardest spanking I ever received was for sticking my tongue out at two Pakistani teenagers after church one day. My brothers and I were waiting in our car for our parents and, without parental supervision, I was enduring the teasing that only a girl growing up in a family of boys could imagine. Onlookers in the church yard found this understandably amusing, so I turned the wrath that meant nothing to my brothers onto the closest onlookers. Looking at them, I stuck out my tongue and put my fingers into my ears, waving my hands. It's a face that has been used by children through the centuries, but I immediately regretted my lapse in judgment. "We're telling!" shouted one or two of my brothers, and I dreaded what would come. The spanking I received that day was a lesson I never forgot. My parents might not always understand their host culture, they might have their own frustrations with some of the cultural differences they daily encountered, but they always knew that they were guests. To have one of their children act so obnoxiously would not be tolerated. The spanking was a lesson in humility and respect, and I bore the sting of it for a long time. The lesson was unforgettable.

My childhood life was a blur of movement and change. We lived all over the Sindh desert – in Ratodero, Jacobabad, Larkana, Hyderabad, and Shikarpur. At four-year intervals we travelled to the United States, and every summer we packed our bags and moved our household to Murree.

Murree, where cool breezes blew through pine trees, and the ghosts of a past British military presence seem to swirl around the rafters of old churches and graveyards, is a resort town 7,000 feet above sea level. The town is located in the foothills of the Himalayan mountain region. On clear days you can see some of the highest, most spectacular mountains in the world. Murree's history as a mountain resort goes back to the 1800s. Until 1864, Murree was the summer capital of the Punjab Province of British India. When the hot weather became too much to bear, and all one could do was sit under high ceilings with fans blowing hot air around the room, people with means would escape to Murree. The town had some noted visitors and residents. A British novelist, Berta Ruck, was born there and grew up to write several short stories and over 90 romance novels. Had I known that a British novelist lived in such close proximity to me, I would likely have dreamed of appearing as a character in one of her books, preferably a beautiful young woman with a dramatic and unrequited love.

The town's main mall area stretched from the post office perched on top of a hill, past the Holy Trinity Church, on down to St. Margaret's Church and gardens. Holy Trinity, built in 1857, marked the center of town and was the place of worship for British army officers in colonial days and for missionaries following Pakistan's independence. On sunny days, flower *wallahs* would sell beautiful blue irises and long-stemmed white lilies to Pakistani and foreign women alike. Small shops that sold bolts of bright-colored cloth, fragile bangles, and other goods lined the wide street. This was where I ate my first ice cream cone, had my first kiss, and discovered marijuana growing in the church yard of Holy Trinity. Murree was special.

Some of my early memories of our home in Murree are of blackened windows and early lights out. Until ten years ago, I had no idea why. I was in kindergarten and, although children are excellent recorders of events, they are often poor interpreters. My mind recorded the event, but I remembered only the impact on our lives. The 'why' was unimportant. Recently my husband, an excellent historian, became curious about what war had us in the grip of those precautions in 1965. It was the war was between India and Pakistan over the disputed Kashmir territory, which was just north of us. Pakistan sent military forces into Kashmir to challenge Indian occupation and enforce its claims. India responded with a full-scale attack on all of West Pakistan. The war lasted 17 days, ending with a cease-fire negotiated by the Soviet Union and the United States.

As a five-year-old child, I was blissfully ignorant of the turmoil that raged around us. What mattered was that we had cocoa and stories in Mom and Dad's bed during mandatory blackouts. The BBC radio with its catchy theme tune was on night and day as Mom and Dad anxiously listened for any news. Blackouts ended soon after the cease-fire, but the books and cocoa with the soundtrack of the BBC World Service were continuing features in our lives. Six years later, in 1971, when India and Pakistan went to war again, and East Pakistan became Bangladesh, the BBC was still a part of our family routine. I would not realize until much later the atrocities on both sides of this bloody, violent conflict, but the clipped accents of the BBC newscasters entered my psyche as familiar sounds of home and belonging. I would desperately miss these voices after I left home.

To my adult perspective, it is remarkable that in the midst of these events I was never afraid. Only my immediate world was important. Warplanes might fly overhead, and newscasters proclaim dire warnings, but my world was safe. Such is the beauty of a secure childhood.

FOR THE MISSIONARY family, 'furlough' had distinctive connotations quite unknown to Merriam-Webster, which defines a furlough as time away for soldiers, employees, or prisoners. For missionary families, furloughs involved reunion with family, a grueling schedule of church events, and the shock of how much we had changed while away from our passport countries. During the "furlough" year, we adopted a "normal" American life. We walked to day school, we packed school lunches, we participated in after-school events, and we attended church youth groups.

My parents' life in Pakistan came at a cost and that cost had names – Grandma K; Aunt Jean and Uncle Jim; their children; our cousins whose names all began with a first initial of J; Aunt Charlotte who would give us treat bags to last an entire sea voyage across the Atlantic Ocean; and my father's sisters – Aunt Lois, Aunt Edna, Aunt Ruth, and Aunt Gracia. Scattered from Tacoma, Washington, to Winchendon, Massachusetts, were many relatives with many names. There were also childhood friends and college soulmates. There was Mom's friend Joanne who had also given birth at the same hospital during the same cold January that I entered the world, and Dad's friend Doc Murdoch who regaled us with tales of Dad as a college student. All of these names became real to us during furlough years as Mom and Dad reconnected, introducing us to the world they had left.

Grandma K was one of the constants during our furlough years. It was during this time that she introduced her five 'foreign' grandchildren to the wonders of baseball, candlepin bowling, and Ritz crackers with peanut butter. While my parents would head off to churches, we would sit in Grandma K's small living room watching Red Sox games on her little black-and-white television. I like to believe it would delight her that I, her most unlikely granddaughter who grew up across the ocean, now live within walking distance of the great Fenway Park and avidly follow the Red Sox . Grandma K knew how to create a safe place for us during our furlough years.

Furloughs also meant church visits. Every four years I was reminded of the good folk who supported our family through tithing and more. Our family's financial livelihood depended on churches believing in what my parents were doing. My thoughts about these churches were not always gracious. I fashioned myself as superior, boasting greater knowledge of the world and more stamps in my passport than they had ever seen before. While in Pakistan, I was secure in family and community, but that identity was threatened in the strange new environment of furlough. I protected myself with an air of superiority, desperately trying to hold on to a sense of self. The result was arrogance.

That air of superiority was bolstered by minor celebrity status that included features in *The Worcester Telegram* or *The Winchendon Courier*, and supporting roles on stage at church missions conferences. In predominantly Roman Catholic New England, my parents were a novelty. Mom's hometown was perhaps grudgingly proud that one of their own had made it far beyond Winchendon to a land known only through a couple of paragraphs in social studies textbooks.

There was also pure magic in those early furloughs, especially at Christmas. Pakistani Christmases were wonderful expressions of a life between worlds. We draped lights and tinsel on desert shrubs, served hundreds of cups of tea to Pakistani guests who came to wish us a *Bara Din mubarak* (Blessed Big Day,) participated in long and dramatic Christmas pageants, and woke to early-morning stockings. Christmases in America were completely different. Our New England white Christmases meant sledding in my cousins' back yard, "real" Christmas trees with sparkling lights, presents, and family and friends pouring into our lives with gifts and love. Of course these Christmases were magical.

On my first American Christmas, we lived in Aunt Jean and Uncle Jim's Hyde Park Street home in Winchendon. Grandma K had vacated her living quarters in the front of the house, making room for our family for the year. Behind the house Uncle Jim's land stretched back to 'Big Hill', a small hillock to those who were big, but a place of adventure – perfect for sledding, perfect for picnics – to us who were little. I was four that Christmas, and on Christmas morning I could barely contain my excitement. After the traditional stocking in Mom and Dad's bed, Dad and my Uncle Jim shut the door of the living room where we would open gifts together. "Is it time yet? Can we go in?" I remember none of the gifts, but I will never forget the magic of the wait.

Earlier in the season, Mom and I secretly decorated my grandmother's small apartment on Central Street with a tree and Christmas ornaments. We left before Grandma K returned home. Later I smiled a wide, gap-toothed smile as I stood on a chair listening on the telephone to Grandma's exclamations of delight and surprise. I understand now the emotions Mom must have felt at such times. These visits home to the place of her childhood, where white, fluffy snow dressed the sidewalks in winter and wildflowers grew in the summer, provided precious, fleeting opportunities to be with her mom and to introduce her children to her family and heritage. As a child, I could not know that the meaning of home would be different for me. Mom's roots would always be in Massachusetts, but Pakistan would become the place of my earliest memories, relationships, and faith formation. For my parents, furloughs were a respite and connection – a return home – that I could only later understand.

I FIND IT hard to look back on the faith of my childhood without making it more complicated than it actually was. Adult feelings and my adult journey overwhelm my childhood self. But faith was not complicated. Faith just was. From my infant dedication in a baptist church in Massachusetts, faith was a part of my life, intertwined with my personhood and my sense of self. Faith was all around me. It was in my parent's decision to leave their home country. It was in the daily prayers we said in our home. Faith was in the church services we attended, in the people who became a part of our lives. And faith was not only present in Christians. An equally-strong faith surrounded us. The call to prayer clocked our comings and our goings, mosques were around every corner, greetings included the name of God, responses to invitations invoked the name of God. Faith was ever-present. It guided our lives and the lives of those around us.

Faith was "asking Jesus into my heart" when I was five years old. My younger brother Dan had tonsillitis. Mom, Dan, and I had traveled to Quetta, where he would have his tonsils taken out by a British surgeon. We stayed with missionary friends from New Zealand. I was in bed, tucked in tight after bedtime stories, songs, and prayer. But I couldn't sleep. First I was hungry, so Mom patiently brought me a small, sweet banana. Sleep eluded me.

When I disturbed Mom again, it wasn't about physical hunger. I told her I wanted to ask Jesus into my heart. We prayed a short prayer – a simple prayer that many have called the "salvation" prayer. I didn't know what it was called, but in my childish understanding, and as one who was already secure and beloved, sleep came quickly as my five-year old self rested in that prayer and in Jesus. I have no doubt that something happened that night. In my limited understanding of life and faith, I prayed a child's prayer, completely trusting and uncomplicated. That child's prayer set a foundation that would continue to grow in clarity – and in complexity.

Inseparable from this first concrete memory of faith formation is the memory of my mother, repeatedly returning to my room long after I should have been asleep. Perhaps this too – the patience of a mother in a child's spiritual journey – paved the way for a strong future faith that began so simply in childlike prayer.

CHAPTER 2
RAIL JOURNEYS

Railway termini are our gates to the glorious and the unknown. Through them we pass out into adventure and sunshine, to them, alas! we return.

E. M. Forster, *Howards End*

TRAIN TRAVEL IN Pakistan began on the 13th of May, 1861, when a 105-mile rail line joined Karachi to Kotri. Almost a century later, trains were part of the fabric of our lives; the Awami Express, the Bolan Mail, Karachi Express, and the Khyber Mail became household words. We spent hours on trains, hours waiting at stations, and hours traveling bumpy roads to and from the stations. Pakistan's railway system was central to the nation's commercial, educational, and social networks, and it still is. But trains were not always associated with progress. During the bloody partition of India, trains carrying mutilated bodies from both sides of the conflict steamed into Amritsar and Lahore, playing a gruesome role in the strife-filled beginning of the Land of the Pure.

Pakistani train stations are busy places, alive with *chai-wallahs* (tea vendors), vendors of hard-boiled eggs, stands selling hot *puris* (deep-fried flat bread) and *halwa* (a sweet, dense pudding), and hawkers of small paper cones filled with *channa dal* (lentil curry). Thousands of travelers make their way through train stations across the country, luggage and *bisters* (large canvas carriers stuffed with bedding) piled high around them as they wait. Families traveled together, the wealthy in first or air-conditioned class, the poor in cramped and crowded third class compartments. We experienced both, straddling the worlds of rich and poor.

Because we traveled the 800 miles to our boarding school by train, the train station became an emotion-laden place: a place of nervous dread and anticipation as I awaited the arrival of our train; a place of silent tears as I waved goodbye, through dirt-smudged windows; a place of relief and joy as I stepped out of the train that returned me to the waiting arms and hearts of my parents. The backdrop to all of these emotions was the sheer exhaustion of long days and nights of travel. The rhythmic sounds of the train, the smell of dust on fake leather seats, the noise and chaos of train stations, the high-pitched sounds of street vendors, and the smell of hot *puris* and *halwa* were all a part of childhood, sounds and smells seared into the memory.

Each journey's routine was the same. We waited on a crowded platform, surrounded by every imaginable size of bag, attracting a crowd of curious onlookers. Pale skin and strange speech immediately marked us as foreign. When the train finally pulled in, waiting gave way to a frantic flurry of people and luggage as we rushed to load our bags before the train pulled away from the station. Once the train arrived, it was almost impossible to say a proper goodbye; yet it was equally impossible to say goodbye before that. We were stuck in limbo, filled with a desire to speak, but tongue-tied until it was too late. Once aboard, the rhythm of the train overtook us, moving from ears and body to soul, poetic and lyrical, taking us farther, farther, and farther even as it brought us closer, closer, closer.

ONLY THREE YEARS ago, Mom made the startling observation that between ages six and eighteen I had never slept in the same bed for more than three months. I was astonished. My internal restlessness and the impulse to rearrange furniture several times each year seemed to make better sense, validating what I had seen as a deficit. Mom's simple, matter-of-fact observation, like the rhythm of trains, evokes a recurring theme in my story.

Throughout my early years, I had been prepared for the day when I would leave for boarding school. I knew I would be leaving for the largely unknown – but exciting – world of boarding school. I knew that as soon as I was school age, I would join brothers and friends on the journey away from the Sindh desert to the lush pine trees and snow-capped peaks of Murree. I would pack my *bister* and watch as my mother sewed nametags onto every item of clothing, just as she had for my brothers. The fact that most children in my passport country did not experience this until 18 years old did not occur to any of us. This was normal life. We would never have thought to question it. What I didn't realize is that with this rite of passage, the comforts of home and shelter of unconditional love would end.

The best education for missionaries in Pakistan was Murree Christian School, situated in the beautiful foothills of the Himalayas. The school was a cooperative effort of several mission groups established in Pakistan, and it became a unique opportunity to put aside theological differences and focus on the shared need to educate the children of missionaries. The school made it possible for parents to stay in Pakistan with the assurance that their children would be prepared for higher education in their countries of citizenship.

I was seven when I joined my first Train Party. My imagination had gone wild with delight. What could be better than a party? I had dreamt of the day I would join other children heading off to school on this legendary and festive-sounding journey that marked the beginning and end of each school semester.

The day came, and I suddenly awoke from the dream. As we packed our luggage into the car, the reality hit me. This was goodbye. I was leaving home and leaving the security of home. I would no longer awaken in the security of my bedroom to the sight of my sleeping younger brother. Mom would no longer read me bedtime stories, or sing to me when I couldn't sleep.

I cried through the hour-long drive to the station. I cried because I had forgotten a doll at home, and I cried because I had just turned seven years old and 800 miles to home was as distant as the moon. I cried heavy sobs that racked my child body as I clutched my black stuffed lamb, sure that the world was coming to an end. At the station, eyes blinded by tears, I clung to Mom, crying in my heart, "Don't make me go. I can't leave you. You can't leave me!" The separation had happened too quickly. I was not ready.

Five minutes after the train pulled away, I was sitting with my friends, engaged in talk and play. I knew my mom had not died, I knew instinctively that I would see her again, but I also knew that her physical presence was no longer a reality in my world. So I did what most kids would do: I settled into my immediate surroundings, finding comfort where I could. I knew I had lost something, but I wasn't sure what it was. The loss was ambiguous. Mom was physically absent but present in my mind. I knew she would reappear, but I had lost her all the same.

We arrived in Rawalpindi 18 hours later, our bodies grimy with dust, our food gone, and our journey almost complete. The bus ride up the mountain was bumpy and exciting. As difficult as it was to leave home, I was seeing friends who I had not seen for three months. A lot had happened in three months, and we talked and laughed, whispering secrets to each other, excited to be together once again. On arrival, house parents greeted us. We washed up and unpacked, claiming beds and dressers, trying to put our personal stamp onto institutional living.

For the next three months I shared a bedroom with seven roommates, supervised by a housemother struggling to meet the needs of 20 to 30 little children, children who needed to eat, brush their teeth, bathe, dress, study, and sleep. Along with the practical needs were the emotional and spiritual needs. These were the unseen needs that satisfy the deepest of human longings, namely love and belonging. It was a seemingly impossible task, but we would not know how impossible until much later in our lives.

The first night I was exhausted and sleep came quickly. I woke disoriented, unsure of where I was. When I remembered, the blur and taste of hot, salty tears clouded my vision and lingered on my tongue. I dared not show my tears; it was not safe. We were all small, all facing separation and loss, all experiencing the first of many times of homesickness. We were surrounded by others as young as we were, by others with the same tears and fears, the same deep sense of loss. The scene would repeat itself each time I entered boarding school from the time I was six until the day I graduated. And each time, a cold, metal-framed bunk bed and the living God were my only witnesses. The one captured my tears, the other comforted them. With these two witnesses, I knew I could go on.

My memories of boarding school are happy and sad, much like anyone's childhood memories. Although separated from my parents so early, I knew that we were precious to them. It was more than intuition. My parents showed us that we were a priority. They surprised us with unexpected visits, listened to our school stories, and sent us letters and packages. And never in my memory did they utter the words, "We are sending you to boarding school so that we can do the work that God called us to." In the future, I would learn that other children were not so fortunate. I don't remember ever hearing the word "call." That word would enter my vocabulary later, and I would always have an uneasiness when hearing or using it. But at the time, I never felt inferior to their work. I knew boarding school was about me, about my education and friends, not about giving Mom and Dad more time for the work that they did. I knew beyond doubt that if

I ever needed my parents they would be on the next plane, train, or bus. They would move heaven and the Pakistani transportation system so that they could be by my side. There was never a question as to their top priorities.

Nevertheless, after that first train party and each time I left on the train, as Mom's face grew more distant with each chug of the train's engine, I felt an acute loss. I strained my head as far out the window as I could for as long as I could until her face disappeared in a final cloud of dust, and I knew that home had been left behind. My early years of security and belonging had given way to constant movement and divided loyalties.

Murree Christian School, known to us as MCS, was housed in an old stone church built by the British to serve colonial officers and their families. The school took over the building in 1956, and gradually added additional classrooms, a dormitory with a large dining hall, kitchens, an infirmary, and studio apartments for house parents. The setting was idyllic. Murree was warm and green in the early summer, golden in the autumn months, white with snow on evergreens in the winter, and vivid with color and daisies in the springtime. Even the torrential rains and fog that swept in with the August monsoons were dramatically beautiful.

Our dormitory rooms varied in size and configuration with louvered windows along one end. I was often in a large room with four bunk beds. We shared dressers, drawers, and loft space, but our beds were our own. Each of us brought pieces of home – knick-knacks, a jewelry box, a family picture that would decorate our dressers. Our belongings were sparse, but we had plenty of space on the school grounds – a basketball court, monkey bars, and a front court that provided an excellent place for teenaged couples to sit, talking quietly, holding hands, and keeping each other's gaze until the bell rang, signaling the end of break. The *chai* shop across the street was a grungy, dilapidated building where *chai* poured from steaming kettles into tea glasses. This *chai* shop was off limits until we reached junior high school, but when we were finally allowed to cross the street and sit down at the worn tables, we would savor the hot sweet *chai*, warming us from the outside in. Along with this, we occasionally feasted on spicy omelets accompanied by delicious, *ghee*-filled *parathas*.

This school and its surroundings are etched on my memory. These were the places where my body grew and faith was formed. As I grew, these became my sacred places, places of beauty and belonging.

MURREE WAS IN close proximity to the disputed territory of Kashmir. From its beginnings, Pakistan's relationship with India was precarious, and Kashmir was the center of this conflict. We always seemed on the brink of war. Hence our evacuation suitcases. Each suitcase held clothing, water, and food with a shelf life of ten years or more. That meant Spam, beans, crackers, and tinned cheese.

The evacuation suitcases were meant for dire emergencies, but to a child they served a more immediate and practical function. As our normal supplies of special food from home dwindled, we raided the suitcases one by one, dividing up the Spam, the cheese, and the crackers. We left the beans. None of us cared much for those. But the other foods satisfied our growling tummies during evenings long after our house parents believed us to be asleep. Had we needed to escape through the mountains like the Von Trapps, we might not have survived for long. Fortunately, miraculously, we never needed the suitcases.

Emergency food was not all that disappeared. In preparation for our departure, Mom painstakingly and lovingly sewed little white tags bearing our names – Edward Brown, Stanley Brown, Thomas Brown, Marilyn Brown, Daniel Brown – onto every shirt, sock, piece of underwear, and pair of pants. How Mom must have grieved as she sewed tiny stitches around the small white tags to ensure they would not come off during harsh washings in old-fashioned ringer washing machines. Despite the tags that marked them as ours, most of the socks and half of the underwear were missing at the end of three months.

Evacuation suitcases and nametags were among the rituals and symbols of our curious subculture. Other cultural markers included midnight feasts, Spring Sports Day, the Summer Carnival, tea time at four each afternoon, and study hall at seven each evening.

Midnight feasts were special times, organized by us, and sometimes, but not always, sanctioned by our house parents. We would gather food from wherever we could. Sometimes it was goodies from home, other times we bought sweets and savories in shops in the town of Murree, still other times we would beg the kitchen staff to sneak us cookies and homemade rolls. Stashing our food supplies under our beds, we excitedly set our alarms for midnight. At midnight, we would wake each other up and sneak to a pre-set location to eat, giggle, and talk. These feasts were amazing fixtures of our boarding school childhood. When we got older, the feasts sometimes included boys who walked a mile at midnight to sneak into our dorms. Nothing suspicious ever happened that I am aware of, but what teenager wouldn't want to be in a place where their crush would sneak into their lounge at midnight? Safety never entered the conversation, though it surely kept some of our house parents awake at night.

Spring sports days and summer carnivals were also part of our shared experience. Both were school-wide events with activities for every age level. Sports day divided the entire school into three teams: Red, Blue, and Yellow. We were divided according to the alphabet, and it was the luck of the draw as to which team had the most talent each year. I was on the Red Team, and our team usually lost. I like to think that we were all far more talented in the arts. The carnival was an equally exciting event and the whole school would come together to eat special food, participate in games, and make money for the Junior class.

Along with the events, homesickness and furloughs were part of the common vocabulary of our experience. We knew that our lives were significantly different from our peers in our home countries. But we only faced this directly every four or five years. When we did, isolation, loneliness, and a questioning of who we were shook our security and shaped our faith.

Our sub-culture also had its legendary figures. Auntie Doris was my house parent from age six to seven, and she might have walked out of an Enid Blyton boarding school story. Auntie Doris was mean. According to rumor, she was placed at the school because she lacked the language skills or psychological resilience to handle life in more remote areas of Pakistan. At MCS she could speak English, and interaction with Pakistanis was less demanding. But a call from God was a call from God. Who could dispute that? This was 1966, and missionaries did not feel the luxury to quibble about such things. So Auntie Doris was given charge of the most vulnerable of children, little girls.

Auntie Doris stories became wide-spread and terrifying. She inspected rooms with a white glove, meting out collective punishment when she found dust; she spanked little girls with a hairbrush enhanced with a nail; she forced a fourth grader to put her hand into an un-flushed toilet to retrieve candy wrappers. Whether the stories are true or false, they worked; most of us were terrified of Auntie Doris. She was a large, stern woman unequal to the task of caring for twenty-four little girls. After lights were out, only the most foolhardy of us would whisper to our roommates. Gathered for devotions in her room, we listened, for hours it seemed, as Auntie Doris read to us from a large Old Testament. We dared not yawn for fear of her wrath.

While I was under the care of Auntie Doris, my brother Stan broke his arm. It was late November of my first year in boarding. Autumn's golden leaves had fallen, and cold had spread through the old stone buildings and dormitories. I remember fear spreading through me when I heard rumor, then the truth, then truth laced with rumor. Stan and his roommates had been playing superheroes, jumping off the top of their triple bunk beds onto a floor covered with mattresses. When he jumped, my brother's arm hit a space between two mattresses and badly fractured. The struggle of trying to make sense of this accident while in the care of an emotionally-absent houseparent was too much for me. I felt an agonizing confusion and acute emptiness. My brothers were my heroes. I didn't know what would happen to Stan. I desperately needed the reassurance of a parental figure to calm my fears and answer my questions. Would he be all right? Who would care for him? Would the arm heal? Oh, how I missed Mom.

A few days later she came. Mom was goodness and light and safety all wrapped into one. I understood Psalm 23 in a new way that moment. "*Yay! Though I walk through the valley of the shadow of death I will not fear, for Mama will be with me.*" I slept better that night than I had all semester. The message went soul-deep. If I needed my parents, they would be there. It didn't matter where I was, where they were, what had happened, whether I was at fault. They would come. They would walk me through the shadows. This assurance set down deep roots in my heart. I would know, eventually, that my God was like that too, and indeed that my parents were imitating Him.

I learned much later that after Mom left my room she went directly to the principal's house, in tears, to demand action on Auntie Doris. "It may be cold in Murree," she told him, "But it's icy in that little girls' dormitory!" Her concern was not with physical temperature; the frigid emotional climate made the physical cold seem balmy. Mom stayed just long enough to make everything better. She left Stan safe and comfortable with a cast on his fractured arm. She checked in with my brothers Ed and Tom and their respective house parents. And she did her best with Auntie Doris. More than all of this, she did something that erased guilt and left a deep spiritual mark.

A Danish evangelist spoke at school chapel while Mom was with us. He had come before, and each time he spoke his eloquence and passion rocked our chapel. He closed with the hymn, "Just as I am, without one plea / But that thy blood, was shed for me / And that thou bidst me come to thee / O Lamb of God I come, I come." By verse three, the weeping could be heard across the chapel. The child's prayer that I had prayed three years before in the city of Quetta was challenged each time the Danish evangelist came. At each altar call, I went forward. It didn't matter that the prayer uttered in Quetta was real, it didn't matter that I had already asked Jesus to forgive my sins and enter my little heart. What mattered was the deep sorrow I felt that I had grieved God and needed to repent and ask him into my heart again, and again, and again.

This time, because of my brother's broken arm, Mom was there. Once again my tears flowed. Once again I was about to go forward, to repent, to receive Jesus, again. Instead, I don't know how, I ended up sobbing in the arms of my mom. As I sobbed, she gently assured me that I didn't have to ask Jesus into my heart over and over and over again. Her gentle explanations and sound theology did their job; this was the end of my altar call journey. I never again went forward during a plea for repentance and salvation, and "Just as I Am" would never again manipulate me into doubting my salvation. I belonged to God, and to Mom, and no one could take that away.

Remarkably, my strongest memory of that year with Auntie Doris is a sweet memory. Midway through each semester, we had a school break for a "long weekend" of four or five days to allow most children to travel home to visit parents. Some of us lived too far away. Friends sometimes invited us to their homes, but this semester I was not so lucky. Along with three or four other girls, I was sentenced to spend the long weekend in boarding with Auntie Doris. To our astonishment, this long-weekend version of Auntie Doris was an altered Auntie Doris. She made us popcorn, took us for trips to town, read us special bedtime stories, and offered us delicious foods.

The biggest surprise of all came one bedtime. As I dozed off after a day of activity, snuggled in my bottom bunk with my stuffed lamb, I felt someone kneeling beside me. As I opened sleepy eyes, Auntie Doris reached over and kissed the top of my head. "Goodnight, Marilyn!" she whispered softly. Shock jolted me awake. Did it really happen? Auntie Doris, mean, terrible Auntie Doris, had kissed me!

Most of my memories of that year have faded. But that kiss from Auntie Doris, that contrast between what I had seen and experienced most of the year and what I experienced on one long weekend, showed me the complexity of human character. It also taught me the power of grace to shape and redeem memory. That bedtime kiss is my most durable memory of a year that might have left permanent scars. This would be a repeated theme of my boarding school experience. Poignant hard times and overwhelming happy times made their mark with indelible ink on the story of my life, and my faith was shaped, not shattered, by these memories. Through those years, and many that followed, I have come to know God as the "Memory Keeper."

At the end of my first year an angel arrived. She was tall and pretty, she had a God-given love for "her little girls," and her voice confirmed her celestial credentials. Auntie Eunice came to Pakistan on a college internship, and she fell in love. But the object of her devotion was not a man; it was the students at Murree Christian School. When she returned to Canada at the end of her internship, she evidently said to God that if she could work with kids at Murree the rest of her life, she would not care about marriage or a family. God granted this request, and she entered into life at MCS as the little girls' housemother. Auntie Eunice read us stories, curled our hair, and made us fudge. She welcomed us to her small studio apartment, which she decorated with color and flair. She dressed with the same flair. She was beautiful, she was smart, she sang, and she listened. The contrast with Auntie Doris was startling, and wonderful. Wounds slowly healed and we happily settled into this new normal.

In the spring of second grade, I suffered a new wound that would leave an enduring scar. I was often ill in those first years in boarding school. One day I was kept after school. Everyone knew I was faking, my teacher told me. I was to stop it. Just stop. Who was "everyone"? I didn't know, but I was quite sure that all of the boarding and teaching staff were talking about me. The words hit me the way they were intended. I would not be sick again. I felt completely misunderstood. I remember walking slowly out of the classroom, my face burning with shame. What would I tell my friends? The only secrets we had were those that were cried into our pillows at night. Would I cry this secret into my pillow, or would I share it?

My friends were waiting. "What happened?" Five little girls crowded around me at our afternoon tea-time. "She thinks I'm faking." There. I had put my shame into words. Maybe it wouldn't have so much power over me. But it did. I was not sick again during that semester. But the damage was severe, and it multiplied in strength; each time the memory awoke, I cringed with embarrassment and accusation. I internalized the accusation, and secretly branded myself an impostor, a scarlet letter emblazoned on my heart.

In June, at the close of the spring semester, Mom arrived to collect me. I learned much later that a houseparent pulled mom aside to tell her of the concern that I was fabricating illness and the staff didn't quite know what to do with me. Mom was beside herself with worry and fear. Did she have a daughter who was so damaged that she was feigning illness? Dad was still far away in Sindh, unreachable by telephone, and she was single parenting five children who ranged from a preschooler to a teenager. With nowhere else to turn, she approached a doctor and close family friend who was working in the summer missionary clinic.

Dr. John Bavington lived with his wife Mary and their children in the city of Peshawar where he practiced both physical medicine and psychiatry. He was a unique practitioner in a country where care for diseases of the mind was rare. As John checked me over, he puzzled over my symptoms, finally concluding, "I think she has amoeba. Let's get stool samples and try to isolate the parasites." It took him a long time to identify the amoeba, invisible rascals that these parasites are, but he finally isolated them and put me on a course of treatment. Mom's relief was intense. Her child was not damaged, and she was vindicated.

Sometimes the parts of the story we don't remember are the most important. I did not remember the chapter of the story in which I was the victim of a parasite that was feeding off my body. I only recalled the chapter in which I was told to stop faking. I remembered the version in which I stood, face down, burning with the heat of shame. I remembered the version in which I wanted to cry foul and explain myself, the part where I felt misunderstood and alone. I only remembered the accusation, not the vindication.

During the summer, I ate fresh vegetables and fruits and rested at home. When fall came, I went into boarding again. I would not be sick again for a significant amount of time, until my sixth grade year, when I learned how to put the thermometer just close enough to a light bulb to watch it rise to a perfect low-grade fever of 99.4 degrees. Anything more might have been suspect, but 99.4 guaranteed that I would be left in the dorm while classmates went on to school, giving me the opportunity to be by myself and get some much needed time alone. Ironically, I was never caught, nor was I ever again accused of faking illness.

IN THE SPRING of third grade, Lizzy Hover's dad died. A year younger than me and the third of four children, Lizzy was curly-haired and vibrant. She was full of personality, with a sense of humor that resonated with mine. I loved Lizzy. She was fun and honest, and even as a young girl she didn't care what people thought of her. One year, Lizzy wrote a book report on a book that she had made up. Unfortunately, she wrote it so poorly that the teacher asked her to go fetch the book from the library in order to help her improve on the assignment. Unlike the rest of us, Lizzy was able to emerge from this unscathed. That was Lizzy Hover.

I heard Lizzy sobbing early one Sunday morning, and my heart filled with dread. Lizzy Hover didn't cry. As my roommates and I waited silently in our beds, we knew something was terribly wrong. From my top bunk with a clear view out the door, I saw Lizzy walking down the hall with Auntie Eunice, and I was filled with fear. A short while later Auntie Eunice gathered us together in her apartment to relay the tragic news. The school had received a telegram. Peter Hover, Lizzy's father and a beloved British doctor, had died in a road accident.

Peter and his wife Carol, also a doctor, served in the Caravan Christian Hospital. They transported an entire mobile hospital to remote areas of the Sindh region to offer health care clinics and surgeries to people without any access to medical care. When the accident happened, the Hovers were heading to Murree, where their three older children, David, Meg and Lizzy, were in boarding school. Their youngest child, Janet, was with them. Peter and Carol were each driving a different vehicle, when a sudden storm of dust, created by busses, surrounded their vehicles. Peter's vehicle collided head-on with an oncoming bus.

My parents, miles away in Hyderabad, were among the first to learn of the accident. In *Jars of Clay*, Mom recalled those days so long ago:

> In the searing heat of the day, not a breath of breeze blew across the landscape. Whenever a car passed or went off onto the shoulder, a cloud of dust

hung in the still air, blocking visibility. About 200 miles north of Hyderabad, Carol realized she could no longer see Peter behind her. Several new buses, traveling south together to Karachi had passed them throwing up that monstrous cloud of dust. Stopping at the edge of the narrow highway, she saw people running toward the road. "There must have been an accident," she said, "and Peter has stopped to help."

But Peter would not be helping. He had been seriously injured. Perhaps he had lost his bearings in the cloud of dust; perhaps the bus that hit him head on had strayed to the wrong side of the road. Peter Hover died there beside the highway, his badly injured head cradled in his wife's arms. (*Pauline A Brown*, Jars of Clay)

Carol, Janet, and a young nurse Cecelia arrived to our home in Hyderabad with Peter's body. It was after midnight, and there was no undertaker to call, no funeral home to help with arrangements. Dad and Dr. Carol bathed the body and prepared it for burial. They then laid him in our guest room surrounded by ice, a ceiling fan blowing air from high above.

Peter Hover's death had a huge impact on my parents, and on me. The Hovers were dear friends, around my mom and dad's age, and fellow workers in Sindh. We saw the Hover family frequently. The loss was acute. We all knew the Hover children, and we all knew their parents. We were a small community and our tragedies were shared. So we grieved for Lizzy, Meg, and David. And we grieved for ourselves. If it could happen to their father, what would stop it from happening to my father? None of us were safe. This was the first time I had experienced death. Each time I experienced another tragedy, the memory resurfaced and reopened the wound of Peter Hover's death.

After a leave in the UK, Carol Hover returned to Pakistan with her children and resumed practicing as a physician at Shikarpur Christian Hospital, the women's and children's hospital set up by my parents' mission. The hospital had been at a crisis point, and my parents' mission was wondering if it could stay open. Doctors and nurses were tired and more staff were desperately needed. The untimely death of Peter Hover was a tragedy; that Dr. Carol would not hesitate to return to Pakistan and use her skills as a physician in Shikarpur was a gift to hundreds of people and one of the great mysteries of life. Cynics might call this mystery a cruel turn of fate, while believers see it as God's grace despite the tragedy of a broken world. I grew up with people who believed it was grace.

In the following years, while on school vacations, I would often see Carol Hover by the bedside of a patient, praying. When we visited Shikarpur, I would run through the hospital corridors with Meg and Lizzy, briefly forgetful of the tragedy.

One winter visit when I was twelve, when the Hover family was living in a ward of the hospital, Meg introduced me to Ian Fleming's James Bond novels. I was frightened, and excited, by their raciness. But James Bond still faced stiff competition for my attention from Enid Blyton's boarding school stories. After small doses of the adult world, we tired of it, always returning to the familiar and relatable. I read and pretended for hours with the Hover kids in a small room that would later serve as a medication room after the hospital became fully functional.

Carol Hover became one of many women who modeled life for me. She had strength and fortitude. She knew grace. She wore character, humor, and dignity along with her white doctor's coat and stethoscope. As a girl I watched her and would silently marvel. It was like watching a stage-play in which the actors face extraordinary challenges but refuse to abandon the script or walk off stage. Was this faith? I was beginning to see it as such.

Tragedies were a background to our lives. We saw deformities and disability; illness claimed the lives of babies, children, and adults; tragic accidents were common. I don't remember feeling squeamish or morbid about this. Perhaps early on we learned that life could be extinguished in the briefest second. The words in Urdu, *Insha'Allah*, if God wills, were part of our vocabulary, spoken by Muslims, echoed by Christians. God was author of life. God was author of death. There seemed little any of us could do; we were participants in the story, not its author.

Because we were not shielded from these tragedies, early on I would create in my mind an album of the unexplainable. This album began with Peter Hover's death, and it has filled through the years. A permanent fixture in my mind, it will never be lost or left behind. I knew early on that some things would never, ever make sense. So my album began with Lizzy Hover's early-morning tears and the news of her father's death.

PETER HOVER DIED in the spring, and that summer our family left for a year-long furlough. We moved to Fitchburg, Massachusetts, to Klondike Avenue, just a short distance from Highland Baptist, my parents' home church. If there was any time when our lives reflected the normal experience of other American children, this was it.

Klondike Avenue was perfect. We rented a New England home perched on an incline with a large lawn stretching down to the street. I loved this house with its den, patio, and large eat-in kitchen. There were four bedrooms and a large, finished attic that functioned as a game room. There was always a Risk game spread out on the floor, my older brothers competing to conquer the world. Best of all, the house came with instant friendships. We rented from Rodney and Lucy Pierce, members of Highland Baptist, and several members of the extended Pierce family lived on our street and opened their homes and their hearts to us. The Russ Pierces had a pool where we swam on summer afternoons; the Rodney Pierces had a huge back field, perfect for softball on spring evenings; and each week I walked to the A-frame at the end of the street for piano lessons with Sandy Waaramaa. Carin Waaramaa, Sandy's daughter, came to our door the day we moved in to introduce herself in a shaky voice. We became best friends, and I can't imagine what 4th grade would have been without Carin.

Into a world that I did not understand, the Waaramaa family brought not just piano lessons, but security and love. A few years ago when I heard the news of Carin's death, my heart hurt. She died young, leaving behind a son in elementary school and a young daughter. Carin's death severed a fragile bond to a memorable year in my life.

Our "normal" year flew by. We enrolled in day school, where we drank white milk from small cardboard cartons. We attended church and Sunday school. I went to Pioneer girls; my brothers attended youth group. We did what Christian American families did, and we did it well. But when the year ended, we were not reluctant to leave. Pakistan beckoned us. Throughout the year, friends had written to us on aerogrammes, keeping us apprised of life back home. In Fitchburg we were novelties, our status elevated in our 'missionary' role, and the novelty could only be sustained for so long. In fact, it was already growing thin. It was time to get back to the places and people where we kids were most comfortable.

But this time we would be leaving my brother Ed behind, returning to Pakistan as a family of six rather than seven. I was ten years old, as egocentric as is possible. Yet even I wondered how we were going to do this. How could we break apart this family of ours? But I was incapable of imagining how wrenching this decision was for my parents and my brother. They had talked it out together. Ed would stay with Uncle Jim and Aunt Jean in Winchendon. He would finish high school at Murdock High School. Ed was mature. He had mastered the role of oldest child. But he would never be a full part of our family in the same way. He would grow up quickly, faced with a pregnant classmate, drug-using peers, and a struggling youth group. I would be back in Pakistan, hearing only sound bites, and living with all the egocentric gusto of youth at the brink of puberty. It was three years before I saw Ed again. When I did, he was engaged to be married. While I was still a child, he became a man.

A year later, I sat beside Mom at what would have been my brother's high school graduation. Insensitive to the grief she was experiencing, I was petulant and self-centered, impatient to leave the auditorium for punch and cake, while Mom, through her tears, frantically wrote notes to the graduates. These were Ed's classmates. This was his time. He should have been there celebrating, with his classmates and my parents, this milestone in his life. Instead, he was oceans away in a small town in New England. This was the cost of a life overseas. Mom had committed to this life, having no idea what would be required. She was living out the requirements, the sacrifice, in front of me and I had no idea.

Years before, when Ed was six years old, he had nearly drowned in the waters of a canal. At that time, Mom had been struggling with the idea of sending a child to boarding school. The pain of sending such a young child away seemed like far too much to ask of her. Then on a warm day soon before Ed turned six, Mom went on a picnic with our friends, the Addletons, to a canal nearby. Dad was traveling, and Mom was watching over Stan, and Tom, both active toddlers. Ed played happily with a toy boat near the canal. Mom turned her head away, and when she looked back Ed was nowhere to be seen. Quickly they realized that he had fallen into the canal. Hu Addleton dove into the canal, but came up twice empty handed. The third time, he brought up the lifeless, muddy body of my brother. Pulling mud and debris from my brother's mouth, Mom began to pray. She started chest compressions and basic CPR. Miraculously, my brother lived.

Something changed in Mom the day that Ed was rescued. The miracle was so profound that it became the hallmark of God's care for her children. I was not even a thought in my parents' mind at the time, but I grew up with this family story. It was our own family miracle. The night of graduation I believe might have been almost as difficult as the day that she thought she had lost him. As the auditorium emptied of people, Mom did the same thing she had done twelve years earlier – she gave my brother to God. But I was oblivious as I sat beside her, blind to the emotions that stirred in her.

FOR THE THREE months a year that the whole family lived in Murree we lived two distinct lives, home life and boarding school life. The one common link was school; everything else was different. Home life was rustic. During monsoon rains our floors were dotted with buckets and pans to catch the leaks, and the walls and floors were perpetually damp and dingy. Our toilet was a wooden commode with a portable tin pot that had to be emptied twice a day. We were a short step up from camping. Year to year we moved from house to house. We rented from Presbyterians, Methodists, or Evangelical Alliance missionaries, and all the houses had names: Park House, Rosenheim, Kuldana Cottage, Forest Dell. A romantic may have called them cottages, but the reality was quite different. They were small, and squeezing in a family of seven was a challenge. Mom hung thin curtains across a rope to offer some privacy to whichever family member was entering puberty at the time. As the only girl, I gloried in having a room of my own from the time I was ten years old through the remainder of my time at home. Though we never owned these houses, their walls held the memories and the secrets of our childhood and adolescence.

In Murree, Mom moved and dressed with greater freedom. Women could wear western-style clothes and walk freely on the hillside paths. She worked hard to create a sense of home. Despite meager household supplies, we enjoyed delicious homemade meals, fresh-baked bread, and we often arrived home to large bowls of fresh plums and apricots. During the school day, Mom made jams to last through the year, pickles to enjoy with our sandwiches, and kept up with the massive chore of feeding and caring for a large family with no short cuts and no ready-made foods. This could not have been easy, and it was another display of Mom's resilience. She walked miles to get together with the moms of my friends, taught Sunday School, and struggled to offer stability to her five children. Mom would later write that this was the time of the year that felt most familiar, most 'normal' to her.

Coming home from school daily instead of heading back to a dormitory room was a welcome change. We entered the front door to the smell of homemade brownies and to the sight of large bowls of fruit on the table. Mom worked to give us a healthier diet than we were accustomed to at the school. We took homemade lunches to school daily, bringing extra treats for less fortunate schoolmates whose parents were unable to come to Murree during the summer.

During these summers, Mom participated in our lives in the ways she always wanted to. She waited to greet us after school, to ask about our day. We talked, did homework, ate dinner together, and functioned as a family. This was the kind of parenting that had been modeled for her in her own childhood. But it was only for a few months during the summer. My father did not have even this luxury. He was alone in the heat of Sindh with no air conditioner and the expectation that he would continue functioning in the work of the mission. Mom and Dad missed each other tremendously during these times, particularly in the years where some of their children tried their patience through experimentation with anything that wasn't allowed.

On summer Sunday nights we walked along the Mall in the town of Murree to services at Holy Trinity Church. For me the attraction was social, never spiritual. My friends were often there, and as we grew older, we pleaded with our parents to allow us to sit together. We would sit as far back in the church as possible, tiptoeing out, two-by-two, to buy soft-serve ice cream from a nearby shop. During closing hymns, we tiptoed back, imagining the adults in our lives to be none the wiser. I loved those times, and I remember them with little guilt and a great deal of pleasure.

In the summer of first grade I began a life-long love affair with Julie Andrews and *The Sound of Music*. A diplomat from the Canadian Embassy in Islamabad was able to obtain the film, and the school administration granted permission to show it to the entire school during school hours. To the "innocent minds" of Murree Christian School, this was a momentous event. For a school that catered to a wide spectrum of beliefs and wide variations in tolerance for what was and wasn't appropriate for kids – my dad hated playing cards, another father disapproved of any physical touch between couples – showing a "mainstream" movie like *The Sound of Music* was risky. Evidently, those in high power previewed the film and deemed it suitable for the young minds of missionary children ages six to eighteen. The school actually cancelled classes so that the entire student body could watch it.

The day of the movie we left Park House for school as usual. By the end of the day, I was changed forever. The first note of "The Hills are Alive" captured me. I became Maria – Maria of the dirndl and guitar, singing with confident joy on her beautiful hills, Maria the young nun misunderstood by the others, Maria the young beauty in love with the Austrian naval officer. But my six-year-old self was not just enraptured by the beautiful music and dramatic retelling of the Von Trapp family story. In the midst of all the singing, the beauty, the love story, I saw that men had the ability to make choices: choices that were good and choices that were evil. It was the precursor to what I would learn later: in the midst of all that was lovely and beautiful in Murree, all that I loved, there was dysfunction, there was bad, sometimes there was evil.

In movies, I could handle the paradox of good and evil. Good always triumphed. But as I grew in both body and faith in our real world, good did not always triumph. There would always be an album of the unexplainable. In Murree, as we travelled the seasons from fresh air and spring daisies, to crisp fall apples and the smell of wood fires in late October, we grew older and gradually lost innocence, sometimes through our own actions and sometimes through the actions of others. The *Sound of Music* captured the innocence of my childhood even as it introduced me to a more complex world.

AMONG THE MANY lovely things that Murree had to offer, perhaps the finest was the perfect afternoon tea. Tea had been a part of my life since I graduated from mother's milk. Whether English tea or Pakistani *chai*, tea soothed and calmed, brought perspective and healing, and turned bad days into good. *High tea* took all the best in tea and added a dose of elegance. And the most delightful place for high tea was Lintotts on the Mall in Murree. Lintotts was a little girl's dream. Its wide veranda overlooked the Mall, a vestige of days when sipping afternoon tea on a veranda was a primary occupation of British army wives.

Tea service at Lintotts was an art. Tiny china pots of strong tea were complemented by little pitchers of warm milk and sugar bowls covered with bead-edged netting to guard against flies. Three-tiered floral china plates were filled with pastries, some chocolate, some vanilla, and all creamy. Lintotts elderly, turbaned waiters were attentive to every need, and would surely have drawn Jane Austen's attention, had she ever been fortunate enough to have tea at Lintotts. In fact, this was a high tea that would have fit perfectly into Jane Austen's world of light humor and delightful, entertaining company who were never morose or depressing.

Lintotts was a special outing for Mom and me. My brothers were never part of it. I don't remember much conversation. Talk was unnecessary. Just being there, being together, was the delight. High tea transported me into a make-believe grown-up world. Problems, worries, and frustrations faded in the quiet noise of spoons against china cups and muted conversation. Then, finally, after the last sip of tea, and after the last clink of silver spoons on china cups, we began the long walk home, up and down the hills of Murree, rested and sure of one thing: life needed times reserved for tea, uninterrupted and fully at peace. I have never forgotten that lesson.

There was a darker side to high tea I would only confront much later. This pleasure that so delighted me as a little girl was a survival of Pakistan's colonial past. The British Raj, the era of British rule, lasted for almost 100 years. It included the entire Indian subcontinent. Pakistan was born in 1948, and my parents arrived only five years later. I was completely blind to my privilege as a little, white, English-speaking girl. I cringe now at what I took for granted. Those who were white and English-speaking went to the head of the line. Those who were white and English-speaking could casually criticize Pakistanis without thought. We traveled where we pleased, we went first class or third class on trains – it was our choice. We were educated and would have a world of opportunity. I thank God for parents that had the conscience and determination to discipline me and teach me in various ways that I was not better than those around me. Still, with a strong personality and ego to match, those lessons sometimes fell on ears unwilling to listen and a heart that would need continual reminders that privilege is not something I earned or deserved.

My memories of boarding are kept alive through an album of letters, written in a child's uneven script and carefully preserved by my mother. The letters span my childhood from age six to eighteen. The early letters are brief, in neat penmanship.

Many years have passed since I painstakingly composed letters into words, words into sentences, and sentences into paragraphs, finally handing the letter to a hawk-eyed teacher who would judge it worthy to be sent to parents. Parents, I might add, who missed us so much that they could not possibly have cared about penmanship or grammar. The irony is profound.

My earliest letters reflect a deep, sisterly concern for my youngest brother, Danny, still at home with my parents. With run-on sentences and widely divergent thoughts I ask about a sweater my mother was knitting, thank my parents for a family picture, and end the letter with greetings and love for Danny and Daddy. I talk about trying to help house parents and not being homesick because "I get to come home soon." Each letter begins with the date on the left corner, a greeting of "Dear Family" and a sentence or two specifically about Danny, the importance of Danny. I was zealous for his welfare: *How is Danny? Is Danny lonesome? Does Danny miss me? Is Danny having fun with the kitty? Say 'hi' to Danny. I miss Danny.* In later letters my concern for siblings extends to my older brothers: *Eddy is sick. Stanley bought me peanut butter. Tommy asked Nancy Kennedy to the banquet. Don't tell him that I told you.*

I was slightly in awe of Ed. He was seven years older than me, teased me least, and I adored him. I talked about him for hours to my friends after he left home. Stanley was the life of our family with a quick wit and a fast tongue. I was most like him. Both of us could raise our parents' wrath more quickly than our siblings could. We did not fear conflict; we often looked for it. Tom was the brilliant middle child. It wasn't until I was in the U.S. for my first year of high school that I learned how cute he was. I became popular to girls who imagined I was the doorway to his heart. How wrong they were.

It was Tom who tutored me so that I would pass my Physics final in junior year, Tom who helped to push me up a mountain when I was ready to give up, and Tom who would phone me during my college years to make sure I was eating right. I was sitting in our school infirmary when I heard news that Tom had broken his leg. I remember looking at the messengers and wanting to kill them. They spoke with such confidence that he would be okay. *How did they know?* I thought with anger. He was *my* brother. They weren't related to him. I cared about Tom far more than they did. Soon after, I ran to my dorm room and threw myself on my bed, bursting into tears. Alone on my bed, I sobbed and I sobbed. In the meantime, Tom was being rushed to a hospital to have his leg put into a cast. I would not see him until later, when he was surrounded by sympathetic friends and had become a hero of sorts. I watched shyly from the sidelines, a sibling who felt like a stranger. My heart was still hurting but his presence confirmed that the messengers had been right – he was okay.

Danny, my youngest brother, was wise beyond his years. One of the first pictures of the two of us shows me on tiptoe, scowling over his crib. I must have instinctively known that this little baby was competition for Mom and Dad's attention, and I would have none of it. But then, in a completely uncharacteristic act of kindness, I gave him a doll.

After my older brothers were launched from the family nest, and only Dan and I were left at boarding school, I began to appreciate him more, and deeply wanted his admiration. He had mine because of his intelligence and wisdom; I needed his as well.

Sibling relationships are strange. We grow up together, eat at the same dinner table, are loved and nurtured, disciplined and scolded by the same parents. We sit together around Christmas trees or *Eid* feasts, go together to churches, mosques, or synagogues. Our siblings have similar features, characteristics, and memories. But sibling relationships are complex and perplexing. Boarding school undoubtedly adds another layer to that complexity. Should I acknowledge siblings when at boarding school? Some of us did, some didn't. Should I look to them for guidance and comfort? Or will I allow them to grow distant even as I see them every day, like the faces of my parents at the train station?

The distance that grows between many siblings as they grow older threatened to separate us early, before we were ready. Older siblings became teenagers, and peer pressure and other concerns diverted their interest from younger brothers and sisters. We who were younger were left wondering what had happened. When did the ease with which we had communicated, laughed, and fought turn into difficulty trying to figure out what to say to each other? When did a solid relationship turn sketchy and strained? When did I become an embarrassment to my older brothers? Was it when I gained weight? Was it when I was punished, and gossip spread through school's well-oiled rumor mill?

The embarrassment ended, though I don't know when. Blood runs thick in our family, and ties are strong, carrying with them an innate recognition of the importance of being siblings. In life's journey, we knew that siblings mattered; sometimes they were all we had.

IN THIRD GRADE our class staged a play on the theme of gossip. Esmeralda, the lead character, was a little girl, like us, in boarding school. We all memorized the theme song. "*Gossip, gossip, gossip, evil a thing,*" we sang in unison. "*Much unhappiness it brings,*" we continued, completely ignoring the warning, and the advice that followed: *"If you can't say something nice, Don't talk at all is my advice."*

We lived in close quarters, usually six or eight to a room. Bunk beds lined the walls. We shared dresser space, bathroom space, three-inch baths twice a week, and secrets. We had best friends and bitter enemies. We knew what it was to be mean, and for others to be mean to us. Survival as a six-year-old in boarding school depended on savvy and on learning to negotiate the social challenges of a six-year-old world. Survival was sometimes about gossiping or listening to gossip. Survival was also about sharing, crying, fighting, and hiding our indescribable homesickness. The odd thing is that most of us wouldn't trade it. Boarding school was like life – a paradox. We would just learn that lesson earlier than most of our peers in our passport countries.

As we grew older, gossip became more insidious, more destructive. Our school was small. Everyone knew everyone's business. I would grow to deeply miss this tight community after I left, but while I was there, I suffered, as did others, from secret telling and sharing, from meanness and gossip. When I became the subject of gossip, life was intolerable. But I still had to go on. I ate, studied, slept, and played with the same people. There was nowhere to escape. I had to bear the discomfort until the winds changed, and another person was the victim. It's what we did. We survived. This survival was just life. I never thought about it. I did what I had to. I tried to please those who were popular. I was mean to those who weren't. And I had my soul-friends that I could trust, who bring a smile to my face as I remember them.

We didn't put spiritual language on gossip, although our house parents did. But the fact that it occurred within an insular community and Christian context made it worse, and

I still hate gossip even as I am still drawn into it like a small child in boarding school.

OUR LARGE AUDITORIUM was the center of the school building. It also functioned as our main meeting place. All of the classrooms were located off the auditorium, and so at break, lunch times, or the end of the day, we would spill out into the auditorium, a sea of children from twelve through eighteen. Every day around noon the mail arrived. Mail delivery was a highlight of our day. In elementary school, our house parents collected the mail and called our names one by one. In junior high and high school, we gathered at the school office where mail was sorted into little boxes.

We would exit our classrooms quickly and head toward the area at the front of the building where the main office and the principal's office were located. Whether it was a plain envelope or a blue aerogramme, mail was exciting. It signified connections with the world outside, connection with parents, with friends who had left Pakistan, with relatives from the United Kingdom or the United States, Sweden or Germany.

Three times a term Mom and Dad sent packages, always shoebox size, wrapped in brown paper and tied with string, sometimes sealed with wax. I rushed to find a private space amidst a crowd to open this treasure. I knew even before I opened the package what it would hold: eight brownies, separated into two layers; thick, tangy, lemon squares wrapped in wax paper, reinforced with thick aluminum foil; homemade cookies; and fudge. Often mom sent a small jar containing homemade jelly or marshmallow fluff carefully wrapped in paper to keep the glass from shattering on the long, bumpy ride from the Sindh desert to our school's pine-forested mountains. Mom always included a note.

As much as I wanted to keep the package to myself, at least for a few minutes, the unspoken rules were clear. The popular kids took a share. Of course, I shared with Nancy, my best friend. And then, well, some kids never got packages from home and empathy demanded that I give them a bite or two. And before I knew it, the package was gone, disappearing as quickly as Mom's face through the train window or as Dad's voice echoing from the train platform.

Those brown paper packages were a reminder that I was special, tangible proof that I had parents, and that from 800 miles away they cared about me. Though I sometimes felt lost in boarding school, at home I had parents who prayed for me, thought of me, baked for me.

Packages told an unwritten story of a mom who baked in the heat to make sure she had our favorite goodies to send, a mom who laid everything out on the table, wrapping, and packing, making sure that all was equally distributed. Packages told of a dad who went about his daily work with a stop at the post office, chatting with the postman about politics, the weather, and the price of onions, a dad who made sure that these well-wrapped treasures made it via an inefficient postal system from the desert of Sindh to the green mountains of Murree. Packages were concrete proof of family and home, of belonging and love.

My world of packages and boarding school is long gone. The packages I now receive are generally from a bookseller, delivering books to our apartment, the packages lying on the ground until someone gets home to dust them off and take them inside. But recently there was a package, wrapped carefully, first in a white envelope, then in brown paper. It was a gift from someone I had never met. My heart leapt, just like it used to when I was a little girl opening up that package with brownies and lemon squares. Some things never grow old—and "brown paper packages tied up with string" must be one of them.

Nothing is simple, and when it comes to boarding school and attitudes to boarding school, I learned early on to be capable of complexity. Just as packages, for all their delight, came with their challenges, so it is with boarding school. Even now when people find out that I went to boarding school, they pause. They don't know how to begin the conversation, but eventually it comes out. The conversation is awkward and at some point, they have to spit it out: "How did your mom do that? That must have been so hard!"

It's always a matter-of-fact statement, and I deeply appreciate that the person is trying to communicate, to move into my world, to understand it. But nothing is ever that simple. Yes, it was hard. My experience certainly included bone-chilling sadness and unstoppable aches. And it was also wonderful. It was full of stomach-aching laughter and tears of joy.

Many of us find it hard to reconcile the good with the bad. For years, I thought it would be disloyal to my parents if I talked about the hard. I have come to realize that most of the things that I found hard, they too found difficult. Reducing boarding school to a single experience or story fails to do it justice. It's far more complex than a single story.

Boarding school, like any childhood life-experience, was paradoxical. It was marked by tears at train stations, goodbyes that left a pit in my stomach, early morning wake up on the first day of boarding, confused and disoriented, and the evil of gossip. Boarding was homesickness and misunderstanding, wishing Mom would be there, only to feel unable to communicate once she arrived. Boarding school with its rules and institutional living wasn't easy. From bunk beds to dressers, all of our living space was shared. We bathed once a week in three inches of water, and washed our hair once a week unless we melted snow. Boarding school separated us from our families, even when we saw our siblings. We learned to relate to family in a completely new way. We had to learn crowd control and learn who could make our lives miserable, or comfortable. It was community living – at its worst, but also at its best.

We made life-long friends and relished deep conversation. We experienced the excitement of train parties and sipped hot chai at train stations. We loved story time at night, performing plays after school, midnight feasts, and picnics at a large rock we called Big Rock located in the woods that surrounded our hostel. We played Kick the Can and Flashlight Beckon until we were called in for bed. We shared secrets and friendship, boyfriends and deep discussions. We went on camping trips, drank late-night chai around rickety tables with friends, held hands with boys on Sunday night walks, and sang for hours to an old guitar. We discovered who we were and struggled to understand what we believed in conversations that I remember to this day.

For many moms, sending a child to boarding school is probably a bit like giving them up for adoption. You are entrusting another to care for that child whom you birthed, whom you love, who holds your heart. Your heart has to expand and let others speak into your child's daily life. My parents faced criticism from well-meaning folks, and when we visited the United States Mom often had to bite her tongue in the face of self-righteous comments and barely veiled criticism: "You may be able to send your kids to boarding school, but I could never do that."

I knew beyond doubt that Mom and Dad loved me. They understood that they were never the primary authors of their children's story. That authorship belonged to God, and they were the writing instruments. So they wrote on our lives and allowed others to write as well. Some of my boarding parents wrote words of wisdom, laughter, joy, and discipline. Others weren't sure what to write. And some, in their human frailty, wrote carelessly or cruelly.

Auntie Eunice wrote music and joy into my childhood world. From the time I met her at age seven, her angelic voice rang through the halls of our dormitory. I always knew when she was coming. Sometimes I would say I was homesick just so I could have Auntie Eunice to myself. She mothered us well, yet always gave us up without a grudge when our real moms came to reclaim us. We were always her kids.

Deb wrote chapters into my life when I was a teenager, when boys and belief were complicated and I was learning to work out my faith with fear and trembling. Deb's small studio apartment had room for my cooking, my laughter, and my tears – sometimes falling so fast it was hard to keep up. Deb loved me when I was unlovable and kept in touch with me when I faced the daunting task of returning to my passport country for college. She was more friend than housemother.

Deb and Eunice taught me to love well, without holding too tight. They taught me about sacrifice and perseverance. They taught me about laughter and the long journey. As I grew, they became my friends – friends I could pray with, cry with, and laugh with until the wee morning hours.

But the unseen woman in the story is Mom, offstage but always instrumental. She gave me to God and prayed for those who could walk beside me when she wasn't there. It could have easily gone another way. I know adults whose boarding school journey was so painful that it is a closed chapter in their lives. I know others who are bitter and desperately look for answers and healing. This could easily have been me. I have learned to trust God as the memory keeper, and recognize that there was grace in the space between.

Boarding school brought with it joys and losses that cannot be dissected until later in life. Boarding school was the good and the terrible, the happy and the sad, the laughter and the tears. I learned that grace covers memories, and magic can happen in unlikely places; that one bad houseparent doesn't define your life; and that forgiveness is a necessary ingredient of life. Boarding school crammed most of life's lessons into twelve years.

STAGED EACH YEAR before the winter holidays, the Christmas pageant was symbolic of the end of term and our return home. We loved acting, and we frequently staged shows in our lounge, even without an audience. The pageant offered a larger stage and an audience of adults. We sometimes performed at the annual dinner that was designed to show appreciation to the national staff at the school. It was an important event, a time to show gratitude to the Pakistanis who worked tirelessly and often quite anonymously. As self-centered children, caught up in our own games, we often forgot their names.

I was never Mary; always a wiseman, never a Mary. I desperately wanted to be Mary, with her blue robe and glowing perfection. But I had a short, pixie haircut and I was on the stocky side. Stocky, short-haired Mary wouldn't do. The honor went instead to my pretty best friend, Nancy.

With olive skin, long dark hair, and deep brown eyes, Nancy was a natural for Mary.

But my desire never changed. I knew that some parts are better than others. Like the Sunday School teacher in *The Best Christmas Pageant Ever*, teachers may say over and over that there are no small parts, just small actors and that every part is just as important as every other part. But kids are smarter than that. We knew that Mary was the most important. And we also knew that the part required long, beautiful black hair and dark eyes, not a short pixie cut and a stocky body. That for sure would move you into the lesser role of shepherd or wiseman. But as long as there was a pageant, I wanted to be Mary. Disguised as a wiseman in purple robe, bearing beautiful brass from the bazaar, internally I was Mary.

At Murree, there were other 'Mary' parts—solos at school concerts, awards at ceremonies, prizes for Scripture memorization or perfect attendance. As a child I longed for those parts, longed to be Mary, but in the elementary years, I found myself playing the wiseman, come from afar. I looked on in envy, and only slowly grew to value the role of the wiseman. Contentment is a process that can come and go, depending on our willingness to accept the roles that life brings. Boarding school both helps and hurts that process. It helps because in many ways we were forced to grow up quickly. In other ways, we learned to fight inside what we saw as unfair. But no one ever saw my internal fight. It festered until I realized, much later, that the burden of resentment was heavy and had filled up my backpack. It was no longer worth carrying the weight, and I had to release it.

In rare moments of insight, I willingly and gratefully accepted my role as a wiseman. I would think about wisemen in the grand scheme of life and realize they were uniquely prepared for their role. But then the moments passed, and

I would long, just once, to be Mary. My big break finally came when I was thirty-five and living in Cairo, Egypt, but it came far too late. The live Christmas pageant needed baby Jesus, and my three-month old son Jonathan won the 'who gets to be Baby Jesus' lottery. And so I became Mary, but in a supporting role. Perhaps the way it was always meant to be played.

WHEN I BEGAN to relay stories of my boarding school days to my children, the beginning was always the same. *"Once upon a time there was a little girl who lived far, far away in a country called Pakistan..."* It was a little girl, a far-away land, a 'once upon a time.' The plot would change from that point, launching on a journey that included trains, boats, horse-drawn *tongas*, motor rickshaws, Saturday night movies, roommates, and mean teachers. These bedtime stories were truth told through a memory that had rewritten them through the years. The stories included the important ingredients of midnight feasts, fudge, condensed milk, and Ovaltine. They included camping trips and cats that ran away, evacuation suitcases and train trips. The reality that was mine became a story for my children and later on, for others. I communicated memories of this world through a narrative, so that this world wouldn't die.

Bedtime stories often help a parent make peace with both the past and the present. Lying beside your child on a bed, soft pillows under both heads and the favorite stuffed toy held tightly in their arms as both of you slip into a land where you never grow up, is a perfect recipe for peace and contentment.

In bedtime stories, I could rewrite endings, and by telling these stories, I began to see my own passage through childhood with new eyes. What had seemed at the time to be difficult now faded into the background and the 'laced with grace' memories surfaced, all of them bringing a smile and slight nostalgia. Best of all, as my children would doze off, I was left with my silent thoughts and thankfulness that I had grown up enough to see and hear the story through adult eyes and ears.

Like the bedtime stories I told my own children, bedtimes at boarding school were unique times of growing up and growing faith. My earliest memories of boarding school bedtimes are of painfully long devotions with no stories, but Auntie Eunice changed that. Each night she read a bedtime story, told us a Bible story, and prayed with us. We prayed for teachers and the house parents, for our parents who lived far away and did important work, and every night we would pray for Esther Cutherell. I had never met Esther Cutherell, but I knew that we prayed for Esther because she had a hole in her heart. As a little girl, I couldn't imagine this. A hole in her heart? How is she living? How can she walk around? She was three years younger than me. I didn't understand it, but in my child-heart, I prayed.

Then one day the news came. Esther was better. The hole in her heart was gone. She had surgery and she was alive and well, and one day we would all meet her. There was great rejoicing in our little girl's dorm. Our prayers had worked. A little girl was now well, the hole in her heart was healed. I knew that it was doctors who had helped with the miracle, but that didn't make it any less a miracle in my mind.

After prayer time, we would shuffle off to our rooms in floppy slippers and bathrobes, and climb into bed. Auntie Eunice came bed to bed, tucking us in and kissing us goodnight. I don't know how she managed to give so much love to so many girls, but she did.

This could be why my earliest sense of God being close, of God caring for me as an individual, comes from a bunk bed. Our institutional style dormitory rooms had two, three, or four sets of bunk beds, depending on the size. Sometimes I was on the top bunk, other times I was on the bottom. Our only privacy was found in our bunk beds after lights out. In an unspoken rule of boarding school, the only space we could really claim was our bed. And so I did. I claimed it. My bunk bed held secrets that no one else, not even my best friend, would know. Bunk beds never told secrets. They stored them and kept them safe. There in the dark I could be honest with myself, and tears, joy, or anger could flow.

I was in a bunk bed on the bleak, cold November night when Mom arrived unexpectedly after Stan broke his arm. Years later, when I went through my first heartbreak over a blonde-haired, blue-eyed boy named Jeff Taylor, I cried myself to sleep in a bunk bed. When friends were not talking to me and I miserably laid down my head, willing myself to be somewhere else, I was in a bunk bed. If it was a good day, my thoughts right before sleep were like the sunshine and daisies that filled the summer before monsoon season. If it was a difficult day, my thoughts were as dark as the sky right before the heavens burst and monsoon rains flooded the ground. In that bunk bed, I could finally admit that boarding school life was not easy, that there were times of sorrow and struggle.

And I found God in a bunk bed. In that tiny, private space, my first fervent prayers for comfort went up to an unseen God in a Heaven that seemed far away, and I experienced his comfort and presence. It was in a bunk bed that this unseen God responded, an invisible hand reaching out to comfort a little girl who held fast to a stuffed lamb. There were many ways and places where I believe my faith grew, where I met the big and hard questions of life. One of those places was surely a bunk bed, an icon of sorts, witness to a faith that was written on my heart by God's hand.

CHAPTER 3
TONGA RIDES

Once upon a time, these carriages carried lovely ladies and the wealthy. Now . . . they carry only trash and heavy goods.

Kamat's Potpourri, Carts of India

TONGAS WERE A quintessential part of our world in Sindh, and the clip-clop clip-clop of horses' hooves on asphalt echoes through my memory, arousing longing. At age sixteen I wrote to a friend in America: "Three days a week I go and volunteer at a hospital. I go in the morning and a horse-drawn carriage takes me...." A flair for the dramatic and a vivid imagination allowed me to picture myself as a young girl in a Victorian novel being taken through the streets of Shikarpur. In reality, a *tonga* is a simple horse-drawn cart with two large, sturdy wheels that bump along rough, unpaved, dusty streets with large potholes. Before automobiles became common, *tongas* were ubiquitous throughout the subcontinent, and they continue in use in many places. A seat in the front allows a driver to steer the horse; a rear-facing seat holds passengers. A large canopy covers both. Baggage, or hay for the horses, or a combination of baggage and hay, can be stowed under the seat. At home, during school vacations, we travelled by *tonga* daily, observing and being observed by the world around us from our perch on the back seat.

The comforting clip-clop of a *tonga* was the signature sound of school vacations when life slowed to a measured pace. Winter vacation came just when I needed it most. Like hiking a high mountain, imagining I could not go a step farther, boarding school reached a point where I felt I couldn't spend one more day, hour, minute in this place. I had lived with roommates and classmates for three solid months with only the occasional weekend for a break. A bitter December cold had taken the place of crisp fall, and we shivered beside kerosene heaters to try to warm up as best we could. Then, like the miracle of suddenly realizing that you had finally reached the summit, school was over and vacation had begun. I could see the end and knew I could make it.

We packed trunks and *bisters*, tossing dirty clothes in with the clean. The count of underwear, socks, and sweaters was lower than a few months earlier, and everything was more worn and frayed. Soon we would board the sturdy school bus to ride two hours down the mountain to the Rawalpindi train station. I could hardly wait. For this journey, we had no special food packed with a mother's love and tears. We ate bone-dry sandwiches, filled with small traces of peanut butter and jelly or cheddar cheese, and the bread stuck to the roofs of our mouths. Once on board we yelled out the train windows to summon eager vendors of *puris* and *halwa*, hot *chai* and hard-boiled eggs. To our taste-starved palates, the station platform offered a heavenly buffet, and we quickly tossed our sandwiches out the window, oblivious to the malnourished children we passed each day.

The journey home was subdued – we were tired – and it was long. Those of us who lived in Sindh had the longest route, travelling for eighteen to twenty-four hours. We waved goodbye to classmates at station after station as the train threaded its way through the Punjab. Not many of us were left as we entered the flat, dry landscape of Sindh. With the change of landscape, I realized that our arrival was imminent, and nervous tension filled my stomach. I was so excited but so nervous – nervous to see parents who, but for letters and packages, had been absent for three months, and nervous to interact with siblings who had become strangers.

The train chugged into the station. Tired, smelly bodies jumped out; heavy trunks and stuffed *bisters* were piled onto the station platform. We shyly reunited as a family after three months of separation. Dirty, tired, slightly overwhelmed, we fell into the open arms of our parents. The looks on their faces spoke of pure love and perhaps nervousness as well. We were almost home.

Mom welcomed us with guest towels, china, and favorite meals. We slept in as long as we liked. But Mom never tolerated laziness; after a week, life returned to routine. Five days a week we were up by six-thirty or seven for breakfast – steaming hot bowls of *suji* or *dahlia* with fresh cream and molasses syrup, or eggs and toast made with homemade bread. Mom's cooking was a delectable change from boarding school food.

We each had chores. We all washed clothes, threading them through the old wringer washing machine, fearful lest a finger should slip between the rollers and be crushed. I was the ironing specialist. To this day, I love the transformation of wrinkled to smooth. I labored the longest over my father's white, square, cotton handkerchiefs. Dad seemed to have hundreds of them. I carefully ironed smooth each corner, then, using a spray bottle for steam, I pressed the center of the handkerchief, folded it up in a square, and applied a final touch of the iron to make sure it was perfect. Finally, I placed them on the edge of the ironing board, stacked neat, waiting for my father. It was a methodical task, one that I could easily perform while daydreaming of book characters – Elaine in *Rainbow Garden*, Sarah in *The Little Princess*, Contrary Mary in *The Secret Garden*. So I ironed and dreamed, taking the wrinkled, making it smooth. Ironing dad's handkerchiefs would become a metaphor for the wrinkled problems of life, and for the firm hand of the problem solver whose touch makes wrinkles smooth.

Two afternoons a week, I went visiting with Mom. One of my brothers called for a *tonga* and off we would lurch, carefully draped in *dupattas*, eyes downward – or not. Sometimes I delighted in looking up, looking around me, defiantly, at the sea of men, cars, horses, oxcarts, vendors, machinists, and tire shops that surrounded our home. In adolescence, I enjoyed the attention, imagining myself a mysterious foreigner whom everyone we passed wanted to meet. In reality, I was awkward, a chubby adolescent who nevertheless believed I was beautiful even at my most graceless stages.

We were welcomed with great hospitality to the homes of friends, and into their inner courtyards and tea times. The inner sanctum of the courtyard was a women's world, a world where *burqas* were put aside and *dupattas* taken from heads and secured around necks. This was where real life happened, where women talked about babies, birth control, husbands, scandal, neighbor gossip, food, and relatives. Conversation was in Urdu or Sindhi, and I followed along, periodically interrupting Mom to ask for clarification or remind her to tell her friends something that I wanted them to know. As I grew older, the daughters of Mom's friends became my friends, and our conversations became deeper and more honest.

Our friends came from every socioeconomic level, and their homes and habitats reflected their material status. Sometimes our visits took place in Christian slums where one-room mud houses sat side by side with round, brown cow manure patties on the outside walls, drying to provide the family with fuel to cook over open fires. Other times we would be ushered through small side doors into large courtyards surrounded by rooms with opulent furniture covered in plastic. Still other times we would be visiting in middle class homes in the center of the city. We would sit on plastic-clad sofas, pictures hung high above us along the walls.

There was equal diversity in religions. We would visit in Hindu homes, Muslim homes, and Christian homes. As foreigners, we had an advantage in being seen as "other" – an advantage that allowed us much freedom in communicating across religion and culture. We were aligned with no one, and it allowed us to form friendships with many different women.

It was the inner courtyards of Muslim women where I had the most fun, where my curiosity, empathy, and respect grew.

In this inner sanctum the oldest woman was usually in command, her word was law. Those inner courtyard moments offered a small window into some of the workings of Pakistani society. Courtyards were the domain of strong women, women who lived their lives under the shadows of minarets and husbands, women seen as oppressed by the outside world. I never saw the oppression. I saw color and life, spices and personality.

Though the homes and people were different, the visits followed the same routine. We would arrive and small talk would begin: the weather, the children, sometimes local events. The conversation then moved on into deeper topics. What was really going on with the children, who was pregnant, who couldn't get pregnant. "Could one of your doctors help?" was sometimes asked. Often the relationships had first been forged at the hospital during a moment of crisis.

That was certainly the case with my friend Jamila. She had ended up at the hospital unable to get pregnant and was diagnosed with pelvic inflammatory disease. The cause? Untreated sexually transmitted diseases, probably acquired from a husband's business trip to a large city. These sensitive areas were difficult to navigate. In Jamila's case, there was a happy ending, at least in terms of pregnancy. She was treated with antibiotics and got pregnant soon afterwards. I would see her again several years later, and she would be shaking her head in despair, asking me how she could prevent another pregnancy. After her first child, she produced three more babies in three years. She was tired.

As we talked, we would drink steaming cups of tea and eat special savory and sweet treats. Hot, fresh *pakoras, samosa* with special chutney, and my favorites, *gulab jamuns,* a round, rust-colored, donut-like sweet, soaked in a sugar syrup. As the afternoon went on, my mom was sensitive to the chores of the household and would ask permission to leave. "So soon?" they would say. But we knew it was simply hospitality. There was a lot to do to prepare for the evening meal, and we'd best be on our way. We would leave as the late afternoon sun was setting, the silhouettes of palm trees outlined against a red-gold sky. As the *tonga* approached our door, echoes of the call to prayer would begin. We had left one world, and were entering into the world our family created within our four walls.

This women's world was extended into the *zenana* section of the bazaar. Every bazaar had an area that was for women only. The shopkeepers were men, but other men were excluded. Beyond the curtain of a shop, *burqas* could be thrown off and we would watch as bolts of bright-colored silks, satins, and cotton were strewn across counter tops. Chatter about weddings and events mingled with fierce bargaining for the best prices. I learned early to bargain. I have never become reconciled to paying a set price.

Sindh was conservative, and *purdah* was almost universally observed. *Purdah* segregated women from men who were not part of the family, and ensured that women's bodies were covered to protect from the eyes of men who were not in their family or community, and therefore not welcome. Each time I returned to Sindh, I stepped into this system and, with it, into a way of life. I dressed and acted like those around me, wearing the latest styles of *shalwar, chemise,* and *dupatta.*

I learned early how to buy cloth and drape a *dupatta*. While I might have looked the part, my skin was pale and my laugh was loud. When I went to the bazaar with girlfriends, they shushed me, embarrassed of the attention I drew. Religion ordered life, and modesty was part of that order. In my teen years, we covered ourselves with long Iranian *chadors*, half circles of patterned rayon that draped beautifully over our bodies. One of the biggest compliments of my adult years was when I once wore Pakistani clothes in Chicago and a young Pakistani man remarked that he could tell I was raised in Pakistan because I wore them with such ease.

Later I saw that I didn't learn as much as I could have, as much as I should have, during these times in the inner courtyard. Initially I was a child, queen of my own universe. Rather than listen closely to stories from Pakistanis, I would be restless and want them to know who I was, what was important to me. When I became a teenager, I was more aware, though still egocentric. During those years I began to ask more questions and see each woman as an individual with a story. I paid more attention and my curiosity turned into respect, later producing empathy. How I long to go back and relive those moments, to ask more questions, to understand better. It was only after leaving Pakistan that I really recognized what a privilege it was to spend time in the inner courtyards, to glimpse a life that those born and bred in the West would never experience.

LIKE THE INNER courtyards of our friends' homes, the Shikarpur Christian Hospital compound was a space where women ruled. The hospital was run by female doctors, midwives, nurses, and teachers, and served female patients. A gifted doctor, Dr. Maybel Bruce, realized early in her medical career in Pakistan that the medical needs of women in Sindh were too great for a mobile clinic. Out of her vision a hospital was born and grew into a sanctuary where dedicated doctors saved the lives of women who defied textbook theory and lived under circumstances and situations where they should have died. It became a secure place where healthy babies were born to proud mamas, where women's lives were saved when deliveries became complicated, and where women came to be treated for the pelvic inflammatory diseases they acquired after their husbands returned from the big city. Their bodies bore the cost of a husband's unfaithfulness.

Because of the work of the hospital, Shikarpur naturally became a central location for missionaries to live. Almost all of the missionary families in Shikarpur were somehow connected to the hospital. Doctors, nurses, pharmacists, and administrators all lived either on the hospital compound or in close proximity.

Periodically, someone would talk about the old days, days when Shikarpur was a beautiful city with gardens, roses, and large homes gracing the streets. It was a banking city, a financial capital strategically located because of its accessibility from Central and West Asia. History tells of a city with culture, trade, architecture, and green space. Shikarpur was described as the capital of "merchants, money changers, and bankers."

When Pakistan gained independence from India and established itself as a separate Muslim nation, hundreds of thousands of Hindus were displaced and journeyed to India to begin a new life. Just as Hindus left, Muslims entered and Shikarpur continued to grow.

I don't know when Shikarpur began to lose its beauty and former glory. Part of the change came with partition and strained relations with India, but well before that time of transition and war, the city was not what it had been in the 1800s when horse-drawn Victorian carriages carried the wealthy to the Shahi Bagh gardens, when bankers completed business deals in high-ceilinged villas, and when children visited a zoo that had cheetahs, lions, and wild boar.

This was a Shikarpur I never knew. While walking through the bazaar, if I looked up, I could see faint glimpses of the former glory in old, beautifully-crafted windows. But eventually my eyes would have to shift downward and take in the surroundings at eye level. Eye level brought me back to the present, and the glory of the past was no longer visible.

While I never saw the Shikarpur of that time, it was still a special place for me. Our family was always welcomed with great joy, and we kids saw it as a place of vacation and fun, a place where there were others who were like us, missionary families living between worlds.

FROM THE TIME I was four years old, playing with my hard-earned doctor set, I wanted to be a nurse. I wanted to work with people around healthcare needs. I wanted to sit with them in their illness, walk them through their pain. My desire strengthened as I observed the inner workings of Shikarpur Christian Hospital. In my final two years of high school I officially volunteered, learning how to work in a busy outpatient clinic, weighing and measuring moms and babies, helping give shots to children.

The hospital was known throughout the district as a place of *baraka*, of blessing. In the local Civil Hospital good care was difficult to find, and patients were treated according to income level. This hospital was different. "You care about us!" the women would say repeatedly. Any foreigner seen in those parts was immediately thought to belong to the hospital. We could walk in the bazaar and have a woman fully veiled in a *burqa* stop us, asking when the hospital was next open, asking if we would deliver her sister's baby. The hospital was a lifeline, a beacon of good practice and caring staff.

The hospital compound housed clinics, exam rooms, and patient wards. Toward the rear gate there were also large buildings with separate apartments for expatriate medical staff and a dormitory for single Pakistani nurses. As I grew older, the dormitory became a place of friendship and learning, as most of the nurses were only slightly older than me.

Because I saw and absorbed so much from the hospital and its core of devoted women and men, the nursing profession almost chose me. The hospital's inner workings were familiar to me. I knew the inpatient ward where *charpais* were placed in a straight row on both sides of a low wall. I knew the courtyard where family members would camp out, making meals and tea for their sick relatives. I knew the private rooms, where the wealthier of the area came for medical care. Before the hospital officially opened, I raced with friends and siblings up and down the chipped marble corridors, dodging adults who appeared out of nowhere to tell us to calm down.

On winter vacations in my junior and senior years of high school, the hospital became part of my weekly routine. Three days a week, I left our house after breakfast, wearing *chador* and *dupatta*, to volunteer at the outpatient clinic. In a small room off the outpatient waiting room I recorded the weights of moms and babies and of pregnant and postpartum women on paper cards in small, neat handwriting. I gave injections with glass syringes that had been pre-sterilized, along with rubber gloves and needles, in giant autoclaves. I grasped tongs, picked up the needle, and attached it to the glass syringe. I swabbed the container of fluid with a small, alcohol-soaked cotton ball, and inserted the needle, carefully extracting the required amount. This was my introduction to sterile technique. When I arrived in the United States to begin my nursing program, I would discover that these methods were primitive, and I was met by surprise and disbelief when I told my fellow students what I had learned.

These opportunities were a gift that I didn't fully appreciate until I embarked on my career. Two dedicated nurse midwives, Auntie Hannah and Auntie Phyllis, mentored me. Both had hearts that overflowed with love for the women and children of the Indus Valley. They were the finest nurses I have known. Outpatient clinic ended in early or mid-afternoon, depending on what emergencies came through the dusty roads and arrived at the gates of the hospital compound, and I would make my way home, tired but ready to grow my imagination through afternoon play.

The health needs in upper Sindh were overwhelming. Hospitals were often a last resort, and our doctors and nurses saw medical problems that were rare and almost unbelievable. Too often, families brought women in too late, only to die on arrival. This was where I first encountered a woman with a fistula, an opening between her bladder and vagina, a result of delayed delivery, a small pelvis, and poor obstetrical care. It is impossible to forget the overpowering smell of leaking urine, and the look of desperation and resignation on the face of a young woman, probably only a few years older than I, who was facing suffering and social isolation. I also encountered guilt. Why her not me? What had I done to deserve a life of privilege, a life where I was a prized only daughter, applauded and beloved? I faced anger at conditions that put a woman at such risk. Social justice was not a word that was used to gain political or spiritual points; it was a reality for those who worked in Pakistan, an outpouring of love of God extended towards those with needs of every sort.

Seen against the vast need, the hospital was like a band-aid on an oozing, massive wound. Later in life, my stories of Shikarpur Christian Hospital would be criticized by "enlightened" westerners with no use for missionary doctors and nurses and scornful of such band-aid approaches. But a band-aid makes a huge difference to the person suffering from the wounds. The staff at the hospital took the time to care, to clean, to treat, to protect. Any care given at this hospital was given in the name of Jesus, a name that all the staff – whether Pakistani, Canadian, Dutch, American, or Australian – believed to have authority and power. It was a name and person known by both Christians and Muslims, though different attributes were given to this name: to one the way to God, a Savior, to the other a great prophet, to both someone of great importance. So the band-aids were given in Jesus' name, and physical lives were saved, building a reputation that spread throughout the area. When I returned many years later to work on a flood-relief team based out of the hospital, its reputation had only grown. People continued to wait for hours to receive care within its walls, a sanctuary, and a refuge in a hurting world.

THE PAKISTANI, AMERICAN, British, and Australian women who shaped my life and faith each have a separate place in my memory. My own mom, through every developmental stage of my life, showed me patience, compassion, and unconditional love. She became my favorite feminist, a woman who was not content to know how to read herself, but taught other women to read around her worn kitchen table, somehow fitting it in amidst her skinning of chickens, paying of bills, boiling of milk, and yelling at *chowkidars,* the men who would guard our house and run errands to the bazaar. Mom was and is smart, strong, and articulate. She gave birth to five children, and she read aloud to them before they had finished breast-feeding. Mom raised me to believe women were amazing and could do anything, even in a male-dominated society where women were rarely seen outside the home.

Auntie Betty Addleton, mother of my best friend Nancy, could make a mud hut look like a mansion. As her friends struggled with peeling concrete walls and salts eating through paint leaving stained blotches, Betty covered the walls floor to ceiling with expertly-made drapes. Using paint, creativity, and ingenuity, Betty created magic in her home, shaping spaces of rest and escape, oases from the heat and chaos. After visiting Nancy, I always left filled with creative ideas, returning home to rearrange the furniture, make pillows for the bed, and create beauty. Betty taught me that beauty could be created in unimagineable spaces, and that such beauty was to be shared and celebrated.

Dr. Mary Wilder, a brilliant doctor, was as funny and quick-witted as she was compassionate. I was in awe of her brain, but so comfortable with her personality that I never feared her. Auntie Hannah Leutbecher, who ended sentences with "eh" in honor of her adopted Canadian home, became like an older sister to us. Every year she came on our family vacation to the beach in Karachi. Auntie Hannah was pretty and fun, always willing to play games and try things with us, and was one of Mom's best friends. Auntie Connie Johnson was petite and Swedish, mother to four sons, two of whom were my close friends. Auntie Connie dropped everything to welcome people into her home. She had a laugh that was bigger than she was, and a heart that honored all. Dr. Carol

Hover was strength personified, single-parenting her four children after the tragic death of her husband, and loving so many so well.

Martha Domji, daughter of an influential Marwari convert to Christianity, was my age, and her spirit and sense of humor were like mine. Despite language differences, we had no barriers in our communication. Martha became my soulmate, my *Anne of Green Gables* "kindred spirit." Angel, Elizabeth, and Soraya, all a few years older than me, extended generous offers of friendship. Though female and Christian in a land where both those things were strikes against them, both Angel and Elizabeth became doctors. This was a tribute to their brains and resilience. Sadly, Soraya died of breast cancer when she was barely in her thirties.

As I grew older, Muslim friends were also a part of my world. There was Jamila, married young and unable to get pregnant; Arbab, a gifted seamstress, sewing clothes so that all four of her children could go on to college, despite the fact that she had only attended a few grades of school; and Hajirah, Arbab's sister, unmarried and highly educated, a classy Sindhi woman who taught children at a school during the mornings and language to missionary women during the afternoons. There was another Arbab, a Brahui woman living on the grounds of the Holland Bungalow, soft-spoken and lovely, chiding me that I looked ugly every time my skin became brown from beach sun. I would laugh and tell her that I wanted to look like her. It was true. When I reached high school, I never thought I looked Pakistani enough and always wanted my skin to be browner. My only chance to work at this was at the beach every year. Soon after, I would head back to school in Murree where the tan quickly faded in the cool of the mountains. Although the same age as me physically, Arbab was years older in experience and wisdom.

She had birthed three babies by the time I turned 18. I was a petulant child; she was a woman of valor.

All of these women were amazing in their own right, modeling grace and wisdom as they lived out their faith as minorities, as woman, or as both. These were my models, strong women with hearts open to love God and the world. They did not preach or chastise, but they lived out loud a faith that worked its way into my heart and soul.

During some of our years of living in Larkana, home to the famous Bhutto family, there were no other foreigners in our town, just our family. Pakistani school schedules differed from ours, so our neighbors were in school while we were on vacation. On weekends, we went to church and visited church families. On slow weekday afternoons, Mom and I would go visiting. The rest of the time, we had our imaginations and our books.

We were never bored. After chores were completed each day I had books, games, and brothers bursting with creative ideas. A hot air balloon was one of these, a work of art, painstakingly pieced together from squares of tissue paper. The finished product was six feet by four feet. We attached wires to the bottom, joining them in the center to hold the flame that would send it soaring into the air. Construction took a long time, and every day I looked to see what progress had been made. I was not allowed to participate in the making of the balloon, but the truth is, being impatient with details, I would have quickly tired of the care with which it was being assembled.

Launch day finally came. We gathered excitedly as Stan lit the flame. We watched the balloon rise up, up, up into the cloudless blue sky of Sindh. Then, after climbing a couple of hundred meters, a gust of wind fanned the flame, the balloon wobbled, the tissue paper caught on fire, and we watched aghast as a flaming ball of fire hurtled straight toward the petrol station across from our house. Hearts beating fast, my brothers ran to find the remains while townspeople gathered, staring up at the sky in awe and, perhaps, terror. No one was hurt and nothing blew up, but clearly the hot air balloon needed a design check. Not easily defeated, my brothers began work on a second.

Our environment fostered imagination and Mom encouraged it. I lived in my books, taking on each character, acting them out in my head. In a single day, I was a Swiss girl in a boarding school in the Alps, a young woman in South Africa, or solving mysteries as Nancy Drew. Reading opened the world to me, and I would walk around, immersed in my inner dialogue. In my imagination, I could be anyone and anywhere.

Mom also read aloud to us in the evenings, on car trips, and on picnics beside the canal bank. She put planning and effort into those picnics. To make a picnic lunch in Sindh, Mom had to bake bread, make mayonnaise from scratch, hard boil eggs in time to cool, make cookies, buy fruit and wash it in iodine solution, and more. These were major events. Finally, with a basket packed full of homemade sandwiches, carrot sticks, hardboiled eggs, and a famous chocolate wacky cake (also known as "Depression Cake" because it was made with no eggs and no milk) we would head off in late afternoon, Mom dragging Dad away from work at his overloaded desk.

Picnics were time away from compounds, visiting, and the endless interruptions that were a part of everyday life. Sitting together on an old blanket spread over the dry brush of the canal bank, we were alone as a family. After eating and talking, Mom always brought out a book. She read us *The*

Chosen and *The Promise* by Chaim Potok, *The Chronicles of Narnia* by C.S. Lewis, and *The Glad Season* by Paula Elizabeth Sutts, about a boy growing up with his grandmother in the far north of Canada. The stories enriched our lives, and all five of us siblings are still avid readers.

Another outing that sparked our imaginations was to the ancient city of Mohenjo-Daro, whose name means "Mound of the Dead" in Sindhi. It is incredible that we picnicked amidst the ruins of one of the great urban centers of the Indus Valley Civilization, picking through artifacts as if it was a children's playground. In 1980, two years after I graduated from high school, Mohenjo-Daro was declared a UNESCO World Heritage Site, but as children, we had no idea how important it was to the world of archaeology. We laughed at the flocks of tourists that would come on buses with the latest cameras from Hong Kong over their shoulders. This was home. Why would anyone want to take so many pictures? Of course, we took our own pictures. That was different. That was to record a memory, to remind ourselves of our time together, our outing, our special place. It had nothing to do with the fame of the area.

Mohenjo-Daro's ancient bricks delineated areas where houses and thriving communities once stood, and my friends and I imagined we were transported back to that day, ancient, beautiful young women, long hair flowing, and the eyes of every ancient young man in the region on us, vying for our love. Mom had her own reasons for imagining. As we would walk through the ruins, I remember her rueful observation that this ancient city had closed sewers. In the twentieth century cities where we lived, raw sewage flowed in narrow, shallow, open trenches throughout the cities. I would not know the significance of this until later in my life, when I realized that many of the most common diseases in the area could have been avoided with closed sewers.

Kot Diji Fort was another favorite family outing. Kot Diji, built in the early seventeenth century, was 25 miles east of the Indus River and strategically built at the edge of the desert to give its occupants prior warning of approaching enemies. The fort was protected by a massive wall and huge iron gates. We knew almost every room, and would race through it as though it were nothing special. Just inside the gates, a deep well with an enormous unguarded opening left me with nightmares after our visits. My fear of falling in that well, though unspoken, was acute.

My sister-in-law once remarked that elementary school education is wasted on the young. These outings were like that, their significance lost in their normalcy and the frequency with which we visited. I did not care that Mohenjo-Daro or Kot Diji Fort were archaeological treasures. I was a child, and as a child these places were there for my pleasure, for our family outings. In later years these places increased in importance to me, but with a sad irony: as I appreciated their archeological importance, I was left with simply a photograph and a memory, unable to visit and without anyone who cared to hear my stories of a remarkable childhood that was so unremarkable to me.

So it was that at the end of a day of walking through the ruins of Mohenjo-Daro or Kot Diji, we made our way home under a dark, cloudless sky filled with stars. I would fall asleep, tired, but full and satisfied, dreaming of ancient things, lost civilizations, and the importance of closed sewers.

SUMMERS WE VACATIONED in the Swat and Kaghan Valleys. Both were astonishingly beautiful and untrammeled. We effortlessly traversed swinging footbridges swaying far above rushing rivers, glorying in our immortal youth, oblivious to the danger. Tall mountains towered over these river valleys, their heights covered with meringue-like peaks of snow. We sometimes camped, sometimes booked government rest houses. We hiked beside rivers, savored delicious kebabs roasted over open fires, and ended each night reading by the light of a hissing pressure lantern.

Each winter we spent our most significant family times at Hawke's Bay in Karachi. Bladen Wilmer Hawke, the ninth Baron Hawke of Towton, set up the first cottage on this beach in the 1930s. The beach was named for him, and Hawke's Bay became an affectionate household word that still brings a sigh of deep gratitude and unappeased yearning. Though only a week long, these vacations gave so much rest and joy that they seemed longer. Our family would sign up for a beach week in late January or early February when the weather had cast off the cool of winter and we could be certain of sunshine and warmth.

We left on the 300-mile, eight-hour trip before the sun came up, amidst the sounds of oxcarts and the early morning *muezzin,* lurching off in a Land Rover filled to the brim with kids, supplies, bedding, clothes, books, and Auntie Hannah. We reached Karachi in the afternoon, stopping in the city to load up on supplies, impatient for the ocean. Royal palm trees lined the road to Hawke's Bay, and we could smell the ocean long before it came into view. The week was filled with the best that vacation offers. For a family never shy of fighting, that week was always surprisingly harmonious. We played, rested, and read together. Maybe it was the magic of Auntie Hannah's presence, maybe it was the magic of the beach, maybe both and more.

Sometimes we watched the struggle of a mama green sea turtle lumbering up the beach in the moonlight. While for us the beach was full of people and fun, for this turtle it was a long, lonely walk. These turtles were massive, weighing hundreds of pounds, and the journey from sea to land was not only arduous because of their size, but also because she had traveled so many miles to get there.

Once on land, the turtle lumbered far up the beach, laboriously excavated a hole big enough to lay about 80 eggs, covered it with sand, and camouflaged it as if it had already been disturbed and nothing had been found, aiming to trick predators into believing there was nothing there. Finally, exhausted, she struggled her way back to the ocean, resting her heavy, weary body, allowing the ocean waves of the Arabian Sea to carry her away. She would never know that she was observed, watched by a family unknown to her, staying in a small hut nearby. She would never know the life lessons she taught, the quiet that would come upon a noisy bunch so that we wouldn't disturb her important work.

If we were lucky, we watched the baby green sea turtles hatch, struggling their way across the sand to the ocean. A lone dog might alert us of their arrival, sniffing at a pile of dirt, frantically digging. We ran, shouted, and waved the dog off, fiercely protective. These baby turtles were much as we were, vulnerable and small. They faced a big, dangerous world, and their struggle was overwhelming. Make it to the ocean. Survive. Grow. Thrive. Growing up in Pakistan was a bit like being a baby sea turtle. Pakistan and the small community we were a part of cocooned us for a while, and then we had to go; we had to make it in a world that could be hostile to who we were and what we believed. While in Pakistan, we had parents and a community that warned off those that might cause harm, but we too had to make our journey to and across the sea. And in many ways, we made it alone.

I never tired of watching baby turtles make their way to the sea, but I didn't understand their lesson until later. As children, gathered around, we were frantic to help. We did not yet understand that it was critically important for these turtles to struggle their way to the ocean without help; the lonely journey across the sand is a turtle's first step in gaining the strength to survive.

THAT MY PARENTS took the time to take us on picnics and outings critically shaped our sense of family and our sense of self in relation to the family. At every crossroad, two worlds intersected, the broader world of a mission community in Pakistan and the smaller world of us, the Browns. We were molded and shaped by both, parents who loved us first and Pakistan second, and parents who were called to a God who had entrusted them with five children. We watched some of our friends become lost in the shadows, lost to well-meaning parents with a calling. We were not. We were loved through reading and picnics, through outings to ancient sites and running through forts, through creative play, through dinnertime discussions.

We were also loved through pets. There was Frisky and then there were a series of 'Old Black Cats' (OBC we called them), and the stories and memories of our pets meld into one another. Stories of cats giving birth to tiny kittens, cats running away and being found, or not, and cats traveling throughout the country in a sturdy Land Rover. There was the time when our cat ran away – we were certain she heard our conversation the night before about leaving for America, and, knowing her beloved family was leaving, would have none of it. There was the time when she followed us on a hiking trip in the Kaghan Valley, the time when, frightened by a friend's dog, she jumped out of a window and ran into the night, only to be found in a place that housed sacred Hindu cows.

In recent years, our cat stories came into print form in Mom's book called *Cat Tales*. The book chronicles our cats and our family adventures with these cats. Mom loved our cats – all of them. She would go to remarkable lengths to make sure the cats were safe and well cared for. In my earliest letters from home, I ask a lot of questions about our cat: "How is Frisky?" I ask. "Tell Frisky 'hi' for me." "What has Frisky been up to?" The only thing I show more affection for is my younger brother, Danny.

When Mom wrote the book, I felt like I had a window into her experience as a mom in a way I never had before. The book about our cats felt as much about her as it did about our pets. Through the escapades of our cat I saw more of what it was for her to trust, to fear, to wonder if she and my dad were foolishly putting a family in danger, away from any relatives and thousands of miles from where she and Dad had grown up.

Mom and Dad weren't perfect, but somehow, by grace, they gave us what we needed to grow healthy and whole. We grew in faith and imagination, we grew in compassion and discipline, and we were never lost to a bigger mission. We were a vital part of both of these intersecting worlds. Family picnics, outings, and pets were an essential part of why we were never lost.

The Addletons were always part of my life. Betty was gracious and beautiful; Hu, personable and handsome. They were southerners, natives of Georgia, gifted in relationships and clear in their call. We each had a best friend in the

Addleton family: David and Stan; Jonathan and Tom; and beautiful, dark-haired, dark-eyed Nancy would surely have been my best friend forever, my BFF, if the term had been invented. We were partners in crime, confidantes about everything. Nancy was as close to a princess as any of my friends could be.

My memories of Nancy begin at age four. She was to spend the weekend at Mount Pleasant, our ironically-named house in Murree with its leaky roof, pungent commode, and well-worn furniture. A high fever cancelled our sleepover, but Nancy's clothes had already been delivered to my house. Oh how I loved her clothes. In my feverish state I imagined that by some act of God the clothes would be mine to keep, or that, in a fit of generosity, Nancy and Auntie Betty had given them to me. When I woke next morning, fever-free, the clothes were gone and my best friend was staying with someone else.

Nancy, with her cute black poodle, Dixie, her go-go boots, and her southern charm, was a constant in my early life. We talked about boys and made no-bake cookies. I marveled at her flair for decorating and her paint-splattered wastebaskets. We leafed through a book about the Beatles, shouting 'mine' every time we came to a picture of George Harrison. We shared boarding school joys and miseries, got mononucleosis at the same time, and had to leave boarding early, and oohed and aahed at her red velvet 9th grade banquet dress. We spent every winter vacation together in Sindh, and this meant time with the whole Addleton family. We stayed up so late that Auntie Betty had to reprimand us, and laughed so hard about silly things that we cried. We did all the things that best friends are supposed to do.

We dreamed of returning to the U.S. together to attend Emory University, where we would wear miniskirts in defiance of the Murree Christian School dress code. I left Pakistan to spend ninth grade in the United States. One year stretched to two. We wrote each other continuously, and it was a wonderful day when I came back from school to find a blue aerogram from Nancy, reassurance that somewhere in the world I was not a cultural misfit. I always had Nancy.

Until she was no longer there. When I returned to Pakistan, Nancy was gone.

Friendships formed in our small community were and are unique. We forged relationships with likely and unlikely people, and they occupied our hearts and souls. Together we faced birth, death, tragedy, sickness, political instability, separation from blood relatives, car accidents, boarding school, tension in relationships, food rations, and so much more.

These memories and events were woven together into an immense tapestry. But unless cared for, a tapestry gets loose threads, and those threads can unravel into holes – holes of too many goodbyes, unraveling of loss. We push the losses aside, dismiss the goodbyes as just part of life, part of being third culture kids. But buried losses don't stay buried. Like a submarine, they eventually surface, and we realize that they were never gone. So our griefs, our goodbyes, would surface later in life, like angry monsters demanding a redo of the goodbyes, demanding time to grieve the losses, demanding another chance. But we get only one chance at childhood. When that childhood is lived thousands of miles and oceans away from the place you live as an adult, you can't go back. When our childhood is good and filled with a sense of wonder, it outweighs the pain and grief that came along the way. We may long to recreate it, perhaps because in it we see something of what the world should be, what the world could be. But recreating it is an impossibility, and in our case, even revisiting the places and people was impossible.

EVERY VACATION FROM the time I was ten years old, Mom encouraged me to study Urdu. She tried to teach me herself, bought me children's books to learn the script, cajoled, pleaded, and threatened. It did no good. I had every opportunity to learn this rich language, and I squandered it. My regret has lasted a lifetime.

My brothers could naturally learn and practice Urdu in the bazaars. They had freedom to wander, to talk to shop keepers, to make friendships outside the walls of our home. My opportunities were more limited. Visits were not spontaneous but had to be pre-planned. A note had to be sent to friends. "Could we visit?" Mom would ask. The reply might come a day or two later. My brothers had none of these restrictions, and their language abilities reflect this.

Like so many things in childhood, I didn't know what I had until I lost it. I didn't recognize the importance of being bilingual until I was in high school. By that time, I had only two years left in school, and a busy social life in English, my language of friendship, love, and popularity. I squandered opportunities to learn, opting instead to flirt, gossip, and share in English. I was a teenager. It didn't matter where in the world I was, my highest priorities were popularity, friendships, talking, and boys – not always in that order. While I could have been conjugating verbs and learning more vocabulary, I was instead busy with a social life with friends, and a vivid imagination when alone. My Urdu became "fossilized" so that I would never get past a certain point and would repeatedly make the same mistakes. Even as I lament this, I understand it. As children we make decisions based on the immediate. It is the rare child that thinks ahead and realizes that they might grow to regret some of their decisions. I was not that rare child.

It was on vacations that I had the most contact with Pakistanis. During the school year I lived in a world of international expatriate friends: Margo from Canada, Carol from Australia, Jenny from New Zealand, Elizabeth from Scotland. Their names evoke a kaleidoscope of memories from my boarding school years. But during school vacation, our family participated in the local church made up of Punjabi Christians who had migrated their way to the Sindh area and formed small communities that lived and worshiped together. I was acutely aware of living between two worlds when I attended church services while on school vacations. When young, I was not always good at making friends with Pakistanis, feeling insecure in my language skills and growing more introverted as a result. This sometimes elicited bad behavior.

Like the incident when I stuck my tongue out at the two Pakistani teenagers after church, resulting in the hardest spanking I ever received, there were other times where I wore superiority and privilege like it was my right. I bow my head in shame at these memories. As much as I felt I belonged in Pakistan, I was a guest, and my parents would not tolerate rude behavior. Not deterred by my occasionally-bad behavior and immaturity, my parents continued to invite Pakistanis of every economic level to our home, sometimes serving several dozen cups of tea in a day. They modeled friendship and love through hospitality and cups of tea. In this way, I learned, friendships are made and discussion and disagreement go down easy, swallowed with the creamy chai made with buffalo milk and the crunchy goodness of Digestive Biscuits.

Daily devotions were the spiritual food that my parents relied on. It was bread and water to them. The first thing I saw when I peeked in my parents' room every morning was Dad on his knees beside an unmade bed, pouring his heart out to his Creator, his Redeemer, dare I say – his Friend. Mom and Dad were a window to a bigger picture, a picture of redemption and restoration.

Mom and Dad urged us to create our own patterns of communicating with God. Praying, reading the Bible, reflecting in a journal – all of this was encouraged. When I was young, that was fine. It was part of life. But as I grew older, I wearied of this expectation. I was not interested. I could think of far better and more captivating activities. Why pick up my boring Bible when right beside my bed was a Nancy Drew book in which I knew she would find the murderer and once again be the heroine of her own series? Why would I want to read stories about people with names like Enoch or Sampson or Nathaniel when I could read stories about Darrell Rivers and nasty, spiteful Gwendoline at a boarding school called *Mallory Towers* in Cornwall?

The books that captured my imagination seemed far more useful in my world than any Old Testament character could possibly be. In the Bible I found no boarding school stories with gossipy girls and a heroine who put them in their place. *Mallory Towers* seemed far more practical. I could not yet see that the remarkable stories of deeply flawed biblical characters told the great story of redemption. I had not yet learned that the phrase "But God..." anticipates a divine intervention in the broken mess of humanity. I had not yet experienced the great hope I found later in words of Scripture. Instead, I saw red-letter boring wrapped up in black binding.

Dad would pop his head into my bedroom and jovially say, "Good morning Marilyn! How are you? Having your devotions?" And so I learned to deceive. I picked up my *Mallory Towers*, wrapped it in my bedclothes, and read away to my heart's content, albeit with a prickly conscience. He would come and pose the question, and I, with a guilty smile, would nod even as I read about Gwendoline making Darrell cry and spreading vicious rumors throughout *Mallory Towers*.

I became adept at deceiving, brilliant at people pleasing. I skillfully delivered what I knew people wanted, regardless of its truth. This was, in part, a survival skill, learned and honed to perfection in boarding school. But discovering the long-term effects of this pattern was critical in my spiritual formation. I perfected my ability to deceive under the bedclothes during vacation. I repented of the same at many different points through my life.

Yet through these years, my faith grew deep roots from a father who modeled discipline and obedience, from a mother who modeled trust and love, from a community that, though desperately imperfect, knew forgiveness and second chances. I learned that deceit practiced under blankets with books can and is forgiven. I learned that, as amazing as *Mallory Towers*, *The Bobbsey Twins*, and *The Chosen* were, the stories woven through the Bible would form in me truth claims that would never die.

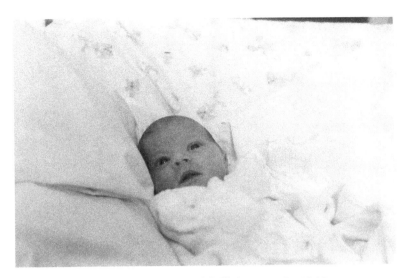

Marilyn, 1 week old, February 3, 1960

Held by Polly Brown on board the passenger liner Giulio
Cesare, May 17, 1960

Polly and Ralph Brown with Marilyn (held by Polly), Tom
(held by Ralph), and Stan (right, in the background) on
board the Giulio Cesare, May 17, 1960

With Ed, dressed for church, Summer 1961

Visiting a Christian family in the villiage of Garhi Yasin, 1962

Danny with Marilyn's doll, 1963

Swimming with Tom, Ratodero, 1964

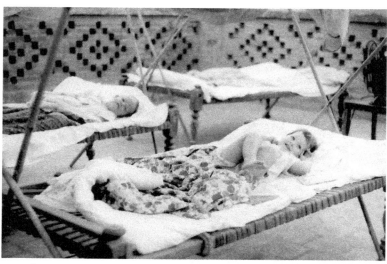

On the rooftop of the house in Ratodero with Tom,
Spring 1964

Walking in the park in Hyderabad.
From left: Moeet (friend of Ed and Stan), Ed, Stan,
Tom (just visible), Marilyn, Polly, and Dan

Vacation at Hawkes Bay, 1968
From left: Ed, Stan, Dan, Polly, Marilyn, and Tom

Ed and Sharon's graduation from Gordon College,
Wenham, Mass., 1975. From left: Ruth Kolodinski, Polly,
Marilyn, Sharon, Ed, Dan, Ralph, and Tom

Murree Christian School cheerleaders at an interschool
convention in Karachi, 1977

Murree Christian School high school banquet with
boyfriend Skip, 1977

Islamabad airport, leaving Pakistan after high school
graduation, Summer 1978

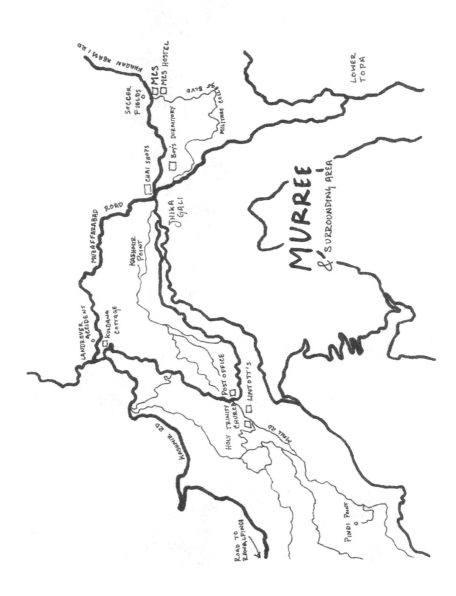

CHAPTER 4
BUS TRIPS

Life is similar to a bus ride. The journey begins when we board the bus. We meet people along our way of which some are strangers, some friends and some strangers yet to be friends. There are stops at intervals and people board in. At times some of these people make their presence felt, leave an impact through their grace and beauty on us fellow passengers while on other occasions they remain indifferent.

Chirag Tulsiani

THE SIGHT OF brightly painted buses crowded with double the people they can physically seat is as common to residents of Pakistan as it is shocking to visitors. Bright red, pink, orange, yellow, and blue flowers, paisley designs, yellow suns and moons, pictures of voluptuous women— all these find their artsy home on these buses. People hang out of doors, windows, and sit on the roofs as these buses barrel down dangerous roads. A road might have high walls of rock on one side, cliffs that plunge hundreds of feet down mountains on the other, but buses travel on, oblivious to the certain death an accident would bring.

The history of bus and truck art dates back to the British Raj. In the 1920's a bus company commissioned a group of artisans under the leadership of a man named Ustad Elahi Bakhsh to paint buses so that the company could attract more passengers.

Recently, the United States discovered this art form, and the Smithsonian Museum in Washington, D.C., now features a truck painted with the classic colors, symbols, and designs commonly seen in the Indian subcontinent.

Despite globalization and the occasional cultural erosion that comes with it, bus art has survived. Satellite dishes may be found on the roofs of remote village houses and cell phones far from cities, but bus art still brightens the landscape of the country.

My early adolescent years in Pakistan were like these busses. They are brilliant with colorful, passionate drawings depicting love and life on their bodies. But it was the plainest bus in the country that was an ever-present part of my passage through Pakistan, the Murree Christian School Bus. This army-green bus had *Murree Christian School* in bold lettering across both sides. The emblem was painted in solid white beside the letters. It was iconic, a symbol of our school and my upbringing.

to my own faith? If I acknowledged the painful pieces of childhood, could my faith withstand it? Or would I be left with a "where were you God?" echoing hollow in my heart?

A friend of many years, a counselor with a specialty in helping children in trauma, helped me understand the distorted theology that was controlling my memories. When I finally began to admit that all was not perfect, I felt a profound sense of freedom and relief. As I became more honest about my life, I realized the depths of God's care for me and his limitless grace in my journey.

Three events forced me out of the safety of childhood and into a world that was much more difficult to understand.

THE WINTER FOLLOWING the car accident, the year I turned twelve, my parents gave my brothers an air rifle for Christmas. My brothers loved this air rifle. They used it for target shooting, and they learned gun safety. Gun safety was paramount to my non-hunting, non-gun-toting parents. We went on vacation to the city of Shikarpur, and we brought the air rifle along. A friend of mine, just one year older than me, borrowed the gun. He was on the rooftop with a few other children, shooting at birds. Another friend came to the rooftop carrying the infant daughter of a Pakistani couple in her arms. She was chided for bringing the baby to the area. My friend asked her to take the baby down the stairs, off the roof, away from the gun. As he lowered it, the rifle went off. A pellet hit the baby in a soft spot directly behind the ear. She was killed instantly.

The tragedy made no sense at any level.

The following days felt like a terrible dream – a dream that you are unable to wake from, and so you go back to sleep only to relive the terrible dream again. Mom and Dad were two of the first adults that my friend saw after the gun went off. He stood in shock, shaking his head, asking how he would live with this, how he could move forward knowing the baby was dead, knowing a gun in his hands had extinguished a life. Mom's response was clear and authoritative with both challenge and comfort. "You can live with this because of grace. You can live with this because of forgiveness." I was in a back room watching the entire interaction. Her words echo in my memory.

The next day, I went with Mom to the modest two-room house of the baby's parents. Before we even reached the front door, we heard the loud wailing of relatives and friends gathered to express their grief. The baby's mom was not left alone to grieve; instead the community would grieve with her, bear witness to the pain of loss. They would walk her through the difficult days ahead. These things happened in Pakistan – accidents, illness, death – all of these were part of life. You didn't fight them; you walked through them, even as you wailed along the way. But you never walked through them alone. You were surrounded by family and community.

The responses I witnessed to these tragedies were foundational to my faith. The courage of those most affected was profound. No one remained locked in their grief forever. They didn't claim that their pain and suffering were unique or exclusive, though many could have.

The parents of the baby girl were the same. They continued to live. They never pressed charges. They grieved, they wailed, and they moved forward. My friend went on to become a fine physician, one who walked beside others during their grief and loss. We did not talk about the events of that winter for several years, but when we did, it was with mutual understanding of tragedy and loss.

By the following summer, I had stopped talking about this tragedy, although I would often think about it. I have no idea if the adults in our community talked about the death. To my knowledge, no one ever received counseling for this event. How did people cope? How did those most affected resolve their feelings and their grief? Those are some of the questions that emerged later in my life. At that time, I did not think of or ask those questions. Instead, it was one more chapter in the album of the unexplainable.

Later I would become friends with the mother of the baby girl through my work at the hospital. In my teen years, I would daily see the father during school vacations. Later I would grasp the impact of that day, and I would better understand the fear in the missionary community that there would be retaliation. I would learn of the responses of my parents. But in those days following the accident, I didn't know any of that. I just knew that a baby had tragically died, and that my friend had killed her. Neither of us would ever forget it.

THAT SUMMER *To Sir With Love* came to the cinema in Murree. Films like this were a rare event, and it was an enormous privilege to attend. Several of us were going including my best friend Nancy, some of my brothers and their friends, several I don't remember. We walked together as a large group to a theater located on Murree's long Mall road. The population of Murree tripled in the summer, bringing wealthy Pakistani families for long vacations and those not as wealthy for day trips, and Mall Road held all the main shops and restaurants of a seasonal tourist town.

At thirteen I was fairly well developed. My chest had sprouted breasts, and I had begun to show my inheritance of a curvy round body, the gift of generations of women before me. A young Pakistani man first challenged me with his eyes, and when I quickly looked away reached out his hand and grabbed my buttocks, squeezing as he did so. I felt a mixture of shame and horror. The thought of telling anyone never occurred to me. That's not what we did. We bore the inappropriate touch of men, whether Pakistani or foreign, because we were conditioned to bear it. We now call this sexual harassment, but we had no name for it. It was "no big deal." My innocence challenged, I sat through *To Sir With Love* which held themes of its own that both scared and confused me, themes I didn't understand and wouldn't until later in my teen years.

As girls growing into young women, no one ever talked about being grabbed or touched inappropriately. We all figured this sort of thing happened to everyone, that being touched or treated poorly was just a by-product of being raised as a female in Pakistan. This was not reflective of my life at home, where a father and four brothers were solicitous for my well-being. Nor was it reflective of the men I knew at the church we attended during our school vacations or the Muslim families we visited regularly. This was the behavior of strangers, men and boys who didn't know me and would never see me again, taking liberties that were completely inappropriate. Ironically, if it had been other men or boys touching the women in their families, they would have been justified in violently attacking the man who wronged their women. But I was not one of the women or girls in their family. I was fair game.

The idea that I would acknowledge, much less fight touch, would never have occurred to me. How does that affect a young girl who was becoming a woman? I speak only for myself when I say that it sets a dangerous precedent for suffering shame in silence, for believing I was 'less than,' my body an object instead of an integral part of me as a woman, as a person. In the tapestry that makes up my life, this was one of the pictures woven into the whole. It is a picture that was never discussed, and so I dismissed the feelings, put them aside, telling myself they were unimportant in the bigger tapestry.

There would be other incidents when I was subjected to unwarranted and unwanted looks and touch, where I averted my eyes quickly, my face burning in shame. That day, on the Mall Road in Murree, was the first and it set a pattern of bearing shame in silence. Had I told my mom, the shame and lies might not have penetrated so deeply. I believe we could have talked about it; that talking could have opened up a door into some of her own struggles. But I never mentioned it. I was silent.

I crossed a threshold that night. I entered a world I did not wish to enter and came of age in a way I did not choose. I adhered to the unspoken code of silence that dictated our lives when it came to being touched inappropriately. Through the years the memory would heal. I would learn that God's image is powerful, that though they would try over and over, mere men are no match for those who bear his mark, for those who are called "beloved." God, in his limitless creativity, would find ways to remind me who I was that far outweighed the message that I was an object. Like the story of *The Sound of Music,* wrong and evil may threaten to overpower that which was good, that which was beautiful, but it would never truly win.

❖

IN SOME COMING of age moments, we are spectators; in others, we play the lead role. In sixth grade I became the lead in a drama that threatened to define my entire boarding school experience.

My house parents, Uncle Bill and Aunt Ann, came to Murree with all the confidence of a young, newly-married American couple who knew everything. They were good-looking, confident, and conservative. We all wanted to be their favorites. They were just that kind of people. Like the popular girl in junior high. You may not trust her, but you want to be her favorite because she is cool and pretty and being her favorite will make you cool and pretty. That was Uncle Bill and Aunt Ann.

The semester had been a rocky one. The beauty of the fall in Murree accompanied by fresh apples of every variety and crisp sunny fall days had given way to a bone-chilling November. We struggled to stay warm in stone buildings that were barely heated with small and smelly kerosene stoves. With the cold came more and more tension in our dormitory. There were eight of us in a room, all pre-teen girls. We fought like feral cats, we gossiped endlessly, we hid our fears and cried into our pillowcases because we were all so miserable.

In November, a gang-like environment had emerged, and I was a gang leader. My rival was a dear friend, who was not dear to me right then. We led rival factions that fought over nothing that I can now remember except Jeff Taylor, the blond and blue-eyed, handsome and suave-as-a-sixth-grader-can-be love interest newly arrived from California by way of Bangladesh. In the summer and early fall he was mine. The unspoken laws of the pre-teen world gave me exclusive rights until I no longer wanted him. He was my boyfriend and I was his girlfriend until death or a pre-teen break-up did us part. But my friend broke the rule. She stole Jeff Taylor from under my nose while I was sick in the infirmary. We divided into rival groups. Susan and her cohort were arrayed against me and my allies, including the formidable Helen, a strong German girl with a mean streak that went deep.

To say Uncle Bill and Aunt Ann were unprepared for their assignment was a gross understatement. The way the children of missionaries were described in Western countries made them sound like mini gods – they may have sinned but not like the general population of children in our passport countries. The kids that Bill and Ann ended up caring for were anything but an angelic host. We were pre-teen girls. We loved the Beatles, mini-skirts, trying on make-up, and Jeff Taylor. We did not take our faith seriously and struggled to find our own place and figure out where we belonged through puberty, boarding school, and our identity as missionary kids who knew little of their passport countries. Our lives changed dramatically between boarding school and 'home' – those places where our parents worked which could be as far away as Sindh, or as close as the capital, a two-hour drive from our school.

We knew our lives were different from the lives of Pakistani young women our age, and we were beginning to be acutely aware of those differences. But we also knew we were different than those in our countries of origin, those countries deemed our places of citizenship through laws written on paper and upheld by governments. By contrast, Bill and Ann were American born and bred. Their first foray into cross-cultural living came in their first four months of marriage. Into this mix came an unrealistic expectation on their part and bad behavior on ours.

At some point Uncle Bill and Auntie Ann cracked. My friend-turned-rival became victim to the first beating. Word spread quickly that she had been beaten with a drumstick. The profound effect on her was apparent, and a level of fear mixed with the cold of that November had all of us wondering who would be next. Somehow, we knew there would be a 'next.'

Helen and I were next. Bill and Ann invited us in, just for a talk, on a Saturday afternoon. They asked us to explain our behavior and admonished us on the many wrongs of that behavior. Uncle Bill held a large Bible, and I'm sure many Bible verses were quoted. I don't remember any of them. I do remember that the phrase "direct disobedience" was used over and over again, and then the dreaded words, "I'm sorry to have to do this to you but if we don't you will never learn...."

I was told to bend over, feet apart. My whole body began to shake as I felt the sting of the twelve-inch drumstick on my backside. Though I knew it had been just a few seconds before, it felt like hours. The lashes kept coming and with them a litany of my sins – "This is for lying," swish, "This is for direct disobedience," swish. Twelve swishes in all. I would have loved to have been stoic, to hold in my tears as an act of ultimate defiance, but I had never felt so much physical pain purposely inflicted by another human being. My tears were for both the physical pain and the awful emotions that accompanied it.

"I'm sorry, please stop!" I kept imploring Bill, but the lashes kept coming. Helen looked on in dread knowing she would be next.

As we tearfully left the apartment, I began counting the hours when I could see Mom's face and be held in her arms. Only two-and-a-half weeks left until the 800-mile journey home. I could not wait.

I was bruised for weeks after the beating, and news of the event spread quickly across the community. It is safe to say that many felt Helen and I were brats and got what was well-deserved. With this, Uncle Bill solidified his place of power, and the punishment was never questioned. I had only one more semester to live under him, and I resolved that the drumstick would never again come down on my backside. Never.

The effect of the beating on our roommates reinforced the fear that already permeated our dorm room. Trust had already eroded. Now the little that was left among us was completely gone. Instead of comforting each other, there were those who used the beatings as threats. "If you don't do such and such, then I'm telling Uncle Bill" really meant "If you don't do whatever I want, then you're going to get the next beating." It was unbearable.

I don't know how Uncle Bill and Aunt Ann communicated to my parents, but I know that before I arrived home, Mom and Dad knew what had happened. Perhaps thinking there could be repercussions, Bill and Ann had penned an articulate, loving letter to my parents. Perhaps it was a boarding report. I don't know. My guess is that it was clothed in language that would absolve them of any guilt over the severity of the punishment, any regret over the way they responded. The "we did this because we love her" and some other carefully worded language would have been a part of this communication. They were able to wound far more with that communication than they had with the drumstick. In my mind, they had influenced my parents before I was able to say a word, before I was able to give my side of the story, as immature as it may have been.

I felt like the comfort that I longed for on that November day and had lived for during the final two weeks of the semester would never come, but, mercifully, the semester ended and I was safely on the train heading home. Vacation had come, the most welcome of any I had ever experienced. With the beating, I had crossed a threshold, I had come of age.

Until that time, I had experienced deep love at times of punishment. I rarely questioned whether I deserved the punishment because there was an undeniable trust of those who punished me. The actions of these boarding parents were actions of an immature couple who had never parented and were in a place where they took their authority too seriously. They saw our normal adolescent behavior, if not stopped, as evidence of rebellion in the future that would have eternal consequences. Intuitively I knew that the punishment did not fit the offense. I knew that the punishment was too severe, that they had overstepped a boundary that should not have been crossed.

In communicating with my parents, Uncle Bill had given me the thirteenth lash. He had reached them, and gained their trust, before I could say a word, and it seemed more than I could live with. But sheltered in the walls of my home, present with those that loved me even when they didn't know my heart's pain, I healed. The power of grace and forgiveness in my life was far more powerful than the sting of a drumstick, the healing of God more lasting than the actions of an immature adult.

I learned that some pain cannot be measured. As I went on to become a nurse, I knew instinctively that though the Western world tries hard to measure pain with their linear scales and numbers, some pain is so deep that a number can never express its affect or impact. It's into this pain that the Spirit of God alone speaks. It's he who whispers, "I am with you, you are not alone." He who whispers the word "beloved," and though the shouting pain threatens to drown out the voice, the whisper is as powerful as a well-equipped army, as strong as the strongest of pain medications.

That winter, God's whispers healed me, and though afraid to go back to boarding school in the spring, I knew I could do it. There was no thirteenth lash. The punishment didn't win. Love and grace were infinitely stronger than the beating of a drumstick.

THE DRUMSTICK BEATING did nothing to improve my behavior, or correct my "direct disobedience." In fact, I grew far worse. My thirteen-year-old self was insufferable. While many people know this in the abstract from memories, I have proof in the form of a bright red diary – kept sporadically throughout the year from 1973 to 1974. Little did I know that events in Pakistan were shaping history and I would live to regret my egocentric thirteen-year-old self.

The diary is hilarious and pathetic, giving the reader a window into how much my life resembled a typical American teenager. Boys and girlfriends fill up a majority of the pages. There are references to fights between my mother and me, sibling love and squabbles, and trips to boarding school, Karachi, and other local places. Pages are written with my name plus the boy who was flavor of the month. "Marilyn and Tom forever." "Marilyn and Phil Forever." "Tom loves Marilyn." "Phil loves Marilyn." "Marilyn loves Phil." Here I was, in a land that I've missed every day since I left it, and all

I could write about is boys and adolescent heartache. I would rewrite the words to Christian songs, removing the names Jesus and God and putting in the names of my current beau. In fairness to my teenage brain, this says as much about the shallow theology of the songs as it does about the brain of an adolescent.

Occasionally the diary shows a spark of empathy – at the death of a friend's father, at the near death of my Pakistani girlfriend, Angel – but overall its interest to me is in its normalcy. This is the fascinating thing about a life between worlds. It is at points as normal as any thirteen-year-old growing up in their passport country and at other times could no more resemble "normal" than a man walking on air.

The diary also tells a story of faith that oscillates through its pages. One day I am a Christian and want to please God; the next day I am angry with the world and particularly cross at God. One entry tells a story of a teenager with her mind on eternity and a sensitivity to the spiritual, the next discards all that with the stroke of a pen, writing instead about boys and cigarettes, about getting in trouble with house parents and annoying parents.

Grades 7 and 8 found me ready to try anything that was off limits. K-2 unfiltered cigarettes found their way from the local vendor to the perfect spot under my mattress, where I hid them until other friends could come over and enjoy the excitement of forbidden, if ghastly-tasting, fruit. These were so terrible that they were an excellent public health intervention, guaranteed to turn a teenager away from smoking quickly and forever. The marijuana that grew behind Holy Trinity Church in Murree was also a hidden offense, though none of us knew how to use it properly. It held little appeal other than being off limits. A bigger problem was the ease of buying illicit drugs over the counter. These were guaranteed to give you a high, then a low, and, if caught, suspension from school. We used them with no knowledge of their potency and a dangerous belief in our immortality. That I was saved from myself is clear, and I shudder to think of what could have been the outcome of my actions. The same strength that was a gift in surviving and thriving in boarding school was a weakness when it manifested itself in the strong will of a young teenager bent on breaking rules.

The summer after I turned thirteen a few of us got into everything there was to get into. We were in junior high and didn't have the sense to recognize that all things should not be experienced. Had we been children of diplomats and caught using the drugs we were using, it would have been the end of our parents' diplomatic careers. The missionary community was more forgiving. I learned just how forgiving when I made a visit back to Pakistan just before my senior year of nursing school. I was invited to dinner at the apartment of the boarding administrator, Marge Montgomery. Marge and her sister Rosie Stewart were fixtures at the school. With their kindly smiles and set ways, Marge made sure bills were paid, schedules made, and boarding staff happy. Rosie was the piano teacher, teaching chubby and clumsy fingers to play Chopin's Polonaise in A and Beethoven's Für Elise, occasionally discovering real talent among us. Auntie Rosie's patience with non-practicing, untalented children was legendary.

As I sat in their home at the age of twenty, full of life and energy, articulate about God's role in my world, Rosie shook her head in amazement and said to me and Marge with wonder, "Isn't it amazing how some of the worst kids turned out the best?!" It wasn't until that moment that I was truly aware of how far I had come and how much trouble I had given my parents, my boarding staff, and my teachers.

❖

ADDED TO THE discomfort of my junior high years was the ever-present competition in sports. Murree was not kind to unathletic children. Sports played a big role in the school community in determining "popularity potential." In the fall, when leaves were changing from green to gold there was field hockey for the girls and flag football for the guys. As November came, and the cold, stone classrooms held the smell of kerosene from tiny heaters that worked overtime to offer at least a bit of heat, athletes kept warm on the sports fields playing soccer. And in the spring, there were basketball teams for both girls and boys.

As far back as I can remember, whether the game was Capture the Flag or Steal the Bacon, I was last to be picked for any team. When I was little it was tolerable, but as I entered into junior high, I dreaded standing in line and waiting . . . waiting . . . waiting as girls and boys were one by one picked to join a team. It inevitably came down to one or two of us and the silent prayer, "Please God, let them pick me, don't let me be last, not this time God . . ." The older I got, the more I realized there were probably competing prayers prayed in those dreadful moments, and I wondered how God decided the outcome.

Was it like picking a daisy and pulling off the petals the way a preteen decides whether the boy in question "loves me or loves me not?" Was it all about picking the winning petal?

Sometimes my prayer was answered. Other times the person standing with me was picked, and I could hear the audible sigh the minute her name was called. I dared not glance up to see her look of pity as she awkwardly ran to take her place. It is easy to write and laugh about this now. No matter how good anyone at Murree was at sports, none went on to compete professionally; they were good, but they weren't that good. Their achievements were limited to our small school "nestled 'neath the great Himalayas." Faded black-and-white photos showing teams lined up in crisp uniforms are all that's left of their athletic prowess.

I once made it onto the girls' soccer team. In my junior year of high school the Walsh girls were unable to attend an inter-school tournament at the end of the semester. Sheryl and Shelley Walsh lived in Bangladesh, and they had already booked flights back home. The Walsh twins were a reminder that life is not fair. They were beautiful, smart, kind, and athletic. They captured the imagination of every boy at Murree and the envy of many of us girls. That year, I got to take their place on the soccer field and go to the tournament. I played my hardest but, by all accounts, the trade was unfair.

The inability to cross the athletic line, a line that held such prestige at my school, brought much pain and adolescent angst. I learned later that many of us had deep feelings of insecurity in these areas, all unspoken for fear we were the only ones. With so much else to worry about – friendships, life in dormitories, homesickness, coping with competing cultures of boarding school, home, our passport countries, and our adopted country – athletic angst only rose to the surface during those days when we had gym class. Otherwise, the feelings were suppressed into backspaces of the mind and memory, coming out through rueful laughter in later years.

My bright red diary tells of a faith that ebbed and flowed through the shifting hormones of adolescence. One week I write, "I can never be a Christian. It's all fake." The next week I write, "I know I want to follow God. It's just really hard sometimes." The ups and downs of my faith were correlated with whether the current boy I liked liked me back, or whether my best friend and I were fighting or not. In truth, faith had been such a constant part of my life that it was impossible to think of it as something separate and abstract. It was like the faith of the Muslims that surrounded me – a way of life as opposed to a separate entity. You didn't separate your faith from all of life.

Faith in my younger years consisted of nightly devotions and praying for our parents far away from our boarding school, doing "God's work." Funny that my parents never put their work that way. It was boarding school that attached "God" to the "work," not Mom and Dad. Maybe that's why their faith became winsome to me instead of joyless and legalistic.

Faith was weekly Friday chapel services bringing in speakers and singing. Faith was Sunday morning church held in our large school auditorium during the school year, in small Pakistani churches during our school vacations, and in Holy Trinity Church, the large and noble church built by the British in the 1800s in the town of Murree during summers. Faith was baptist singspirations as a child and Sunday night singspirations in junior high.

Old hymns still echo through my mind:

There is power, power, wonder-working power,
In the blood (in the blood) of the lamb (of the lamb).

Marvelous grace of our loving Lord,

Mercy there was great and grace was free.
Pardon there was multiplied for me,
there my burdened soul found liberty, at Calvary.

These were the songs sung by missionaries gathered together in the summer twilight. They lived in a country that alternated between hospitable and hostile, and they lived a life far removed from the churches and families they loved. These times were times that revived their souls and brought comfort in this land they loved and served in the best way they knew how. It was these songs that soaked into the marrow of their children, many of whom would go on to leave their Baptist roots but hold dear their parents and the foundation of their adult faith.

In those younger years, I knew surely and simply that I loved God. And I knew that He loved me. There were no questions. There were no whys. There was God and there was Me. We two were on a journey. Later, when the whys and the questions came, I would cry out in pain over betrayal and in agony over the unfairness of life. But faith in the early years was simple and solid, heard from my parents, echoed in my school, rooted in my life. It was not complicated by what-ifs and whys.

The climate where this faith flourished was in a missionary sub-culture. But the outside world echoed with faith as well. There were no atheists. God was alive and well. Whether in the mosque or the church, he existed, and he ordered the lives of those around us. Whether you were Muslim or Christian, faith was a way of life, not an appendage.

Long before I ever heard church bells ringing, the call to prayer had rooted its way into my conscious and subconscious mind. I cannot remember a time when I didn't love the call to prayer that echoed across cities, towns, and villages five times a day. I didn't even know what the words meant until I was in high school, but they brought comfort and security. As soon as I heard the call to prayer, I knew I was home. The call to prayer ordered our day from sunup to sundown. I never found this incongruous to our Christian faith. I overheard my mother telling a Muslim friend one day, when asked when she prayed, that she woke up at the first *azzan* and prayed then and through the day.

It was true. I could never wake up earlier than my parents. They were awake at the first *azzan*, partaking of their bread of life. This was their sustenance, their life-blood, what gave them purpose and reason for being miles away from family and all that was familiar.

Early on, I have memories of Dad taking us kids to large mosques in the city of Hyderabad during Eid celebrations. I was eyewitness to thousands of faithful Muslims gathered at the mosque to pray in unison, each movement, from standing to kneeling, full of meaning and reverence. In public, we witnessed only men praying; women in this area stayed home and did their prayers. Indeed, if we visited someone's home and the *azzan* was heard, women, particularly the elderly, would excuse themselves to go and pray. Mom and I would cover our heads with our *dupattas* during this time out of respect for the faith of our Muslim friends.

So either I chose faith or faith chose me – as a child, it was impossible to know. If there was ever a time when I wanted to throw my faith away, it was during the year when the baby died and I got beaten by a drumstick. That was the closest I came in childhood to tossing it off the Murree hillside, watching it go to the bottom of a rocky crevice in the mountains where it would surely die, like all the people in the buses that would go over these cliffs. The death of the baby, betrayal and beating by a houseparent, and the inappropriate touch of a young man were all events that built up, and I can trace the words in my diary to those specific events. Though I never wrote about the events themselves, the ups and downs of my faith journey tell the story.

But my faith didn't die. Instead it grew in the shadows, continuing to emerge in unlikely moments, surprising both me and others with its tenacity.

CHAPTER 5
LOVE OF FLYING

Harry kicked off hard from the ground. The cool night air rushed through his hair as the neat square gardens of Privet Drive fell away.... He felt as though his heart was going to explode with pleasure; he was flying again, flying away from Privet Drive as he'd been fantasizing about all summer, he was going home.... For a few glorious moments, all his problems seemed to recede into nothing, insignificant in the vast, starry sky.

JK Rowling, *Harry Potter and the Order of the Phoenix*

❖

I LOVE AIRPLANES. From the cardboard meals eaten in tight quarters, to the extreme fatigue as I make my way to the tiny bathroom at the end of a long transnational flight, I love flying and everything that goes along with it. Planes and travel make me feel alive, humble me, and bring indescribable excitement. I become like a little girl.

The story of how the Wright brothers changed the world forever is well-known. Not so well-known is how flying became affordable for the average person, including our family. In 1914 a "seaplane" began service across Tampa Bay, but commercial flying was not embraced quickly. During World War I, aircraft were associated with military operations, not transportation. The advent of "air mail" in 1917 changed this when the United States government began using planes for mail, and "via airmail" was stamped across envelopes throughout the country. Then in 1969 Pan Am, short for Pan American Airlines, the unofficial U.S. flag carrier, inaugurated the Boeing 747, a massive four-engine aircraft that could carry as many as 450 people and was twice as big as any other jet. The 747 would become an iconic part of my experience.

In my early childhood, it was customary to dress up when flying. Just as Mom had worn pearls and a sophisticated suit when boarding ships in her early years of travel, we put on our best clothes to fly around the world. I still have an aversion to traveling in sweat pants.

These major transatlantic or transpacific flights happened every four years, but when they came, my parents made the most of them. We never travelled straight back to the United States. We always took the long route, stopping in Bangkok, Hong Kong, Japan, and Hawaii when we went the West Coast route, or various countries in Europe or the United Kingdom when we went the east coast route. Either way, by the time I left home I had been in more countries than I could count, had eaten brioche with strong coffee in small *pension*s in Austria, had milked goats in Germany, and had shopped for electronics in Hong Kong. I had also seen major cathedrals, mosques, and landmarks in every country we visited. The richness of these experiences was often lost on me. It was a normal part of our lives, and I did not yet fully appreciate how vast and amazing our world is, how tiny we are in comparison.

My romance with flying began with furloughs. I thought I loved furloughs, although, in reality, before we returned to the United States in 1974, I had experienced only two, one when I was four going on five, the other when I was nine going on ten. I liked the flying to and from, the shopping, the food. I loved relatives, and Christmases with Grandma K, aunts, uncles, and cousins. I liked that I was different, special. But in the summer of 1974, when we began a year-long furlough that would stretch into two, I was fourteen, an age of dramatic, day-to-day changes. One day I was the most secure adolescent found anywhere on the globe, in any country or culture, the next day I was a crying mess of emotions who fit in nowhere, least of all my passport country.

Stan graduated from high school that summer, and the day after graduation Mom, Dad, my younger brother Danny, my cousin Barbara, and I headed off on a weeklong journey to the United States via Pakistan International Airlines. In Vienna, we stayed at a *pension*, eating brioche and drinking strong coffee each morning, and visited the famed Lipizzaner stallions. In Germany, we stayed with a delightful German family on acres of beautiful farmland, visiting Koln and Frankfurt along the way. We were treated with food and hospitality, and welcomed as part of the family. It was on this trip that I milked a goat, discovered that I didn't like warm

milk straight from the source, and learned my only German –
Mein auto ist kaput! (My car is broken!). I also tasted my first
liqueur-filled chocolate, which, for a missionary kid who had
never tasted alcohol, felt scandalous. I ate more than a few
chocolates that day, feeling sweetly devious and grown-up. In
Zurich we stayed just streets away from the family of a boy in
my class, my first true love, and traveled with his family into
the Alps via a cog railway.

Meanwhile, my brothers were having adventures
more dangerous than milking goats and drinking liqueur-
filled chocolates. Stan and Tom headed overland through
Afghanistan, Iran, and Turkey, planning to arrive over a
month later. In the 1970s, this overland route was well-
travelled, and boys who grew up at Murree had a strong
sense of adventure, knew how to travel independently, and
needed few luxuries. The excitement was in the journey.

My own journey ended at Logan International Airport
in Boston, where a large crowd had gathered to meet us with
Ed and his fiancée, Sharon, at the front. We were nervously
excited about meeting Sharon. She would be the first addition
to our family through marriage, and we were anticipating a
large wedding on the campus of Gordon College in August.

The trip back to the United States and the summer of
family fun held no hint that the two years ahead would be
some of my most difficult. In Pakistan I identified as an
American. I wanted miniskirts and rock music and took an
increasingly superior attitude towards my Pakistani friends.
I was at times completely unbearable. I may have been a
missionary kid, but I was the one of the superior boarding
school education and air travel to America every fifth year.
Everything changed that furlough.

I began grade nine in Winchendon in the fall of 1974. To
say I was scared is a disservice to my adolescent emotions. I

was terrified. My older cousins lived next door, but I was still the little cousin without status or popularity. My currency had not been established. Two weeks before school began, my brother Tom headed off to football camp. After we visited him I began to dread what was coming. He looked miserable, and something inside of me died for him. How bad was it? He was a senior in high school, away from all he knew and loved. He was away from his best friend, his classmates that he had grown up with, his beloved Murree, and away from teachers who admired and respected his brain. He would have to forge his way in a new, alien world in an impossibly short span of time. I left that visit with an inexpressible dread in my heart; I felt that I would soon experience hell.

While visiting Tom at football camp I decided Jesus needed to return before I began high school in an American public school. There was no way Jesus would make me go through that sort of agony and terror. I began to pray. The movie *A Thief in the Night* was released that year, telling the story of the end of the world and those left behind on earth because of their unbelief. I had already memorized the song "I Wish We'd All Been Ready," a lament for those who would miss the rapture only to be left behind at horrible football camps and in American public high schools. I knew *I* was ready, and that was all that mattered. I didn't care if the rest of the world went to hell, I just knew that hell for me was starting school and if Jesus was worth anything he'd better show up. I shared this with Stan just two days before school started. He looked at me confidently and said, "He won't come back; he wants you to go through this." Such callousness offended me; I vowed not to speak to him for some time.

Early on a September morning just after Labor Day, I headed off to school. My memories of the day are fuzzy.

At the large double doors to the school I heard words that I had never heard spoken aloud before. Words like these had sometimes been whispered in the hallowed halls of my Christian boarding school, but this was a full assault on my tender, virgin ears. I was shoved aside as I tried to make my way into the crowded halls.

The morning was a blur. I found my way to homeroom and realized I didn't know the words to the American Pledge of Allegiance. The class stood together and faced the flag. My eyes darted to my left and to my right to see what my classmates were doing. We were in alphabetical order, and I would soon learn that Brenda Botti was on my left and Steve Carter was on my right. Both would soon become good friends, but right then they were scary strangers, far more confident than me. Both were looking at the flag and had their right hands placed across their chests. I nervously did the same. An adult voice was broadcast through a scratchy intercom and the words began: "I pledge allegiance to the flag of the United States of America...."

All the mouths surrounding me were uttering the same words. Red-faced, I began murmuring something. I don't know what it was, but it wasn't the Pledge of Allegiance. The pledge, which normally takes barely a minute, seemed to last for a lifetime. A lifetime of insecurity. A lifetime of not belonging. My heart beat so fast that I was sure people could hear it. I was uncomfortable in my clothes – clothes that had seemed fine that morning but suddenly felt tight and ill-fitting. My face was red and my mouth was dry with nervous emotion. Finally, the Pledge ended and chairs scraped along the floor as people sat down.

This scenario would be repeated for my own children when we moved to the United States from Cairo, Egypt, many years later. My middle son would write, "I knew about flags, but I didn't know about allegiance." So it was with me. On my fifteen-year-old stage, this was my opening act and I felt small and insignificant, insecurity flooding over me in waves. My ears burned as I assumed everyone around me was talking about me. It wasn't just paranoia. It was a small town that didn't see many new kids. They *were* talking about me. I was late to every class and ready to cry by ten in the morning.

In third period science class I met someone who I was convinced would make my life miserable for the rest of the year, maybe even the rest of my life. The girl sitting behind me was my exact opposite – sophisticated, pretty, and, above all, thin. Looking at her was enough to make me believe in the Greek gods – capricious, malicious, and gorgeous. She was everything that I was not. The mean girl seemed to take an instant dislike to me, slowly eyeing me, top to bottom. She ended her critical survey with my toes, which were brightly painted with shiny red polish. No one in 1970s New England wore toenail polish, least of all someone in grade nine. She stared. Then she turned to her friend, the girl beside her, to discuss this strange alien creature who had entered their classroom.

I couldn't wait to get home. *This* was America. This place – this cold, chaotic, small-minded place where the natives laughed at a teenager with red toenail polish – represented what was known on the world stage as the greatest country on the globe. This was a jungle. Years later the movie *Mean Girls* told the story of a teenager who moved to the United States from Africa where she had lived with her anthropologist parents. The movie portrayed the teenage world in the United States as a world of wild beasts – tigers, lions, and laughing hyenas – disguised as teenagers. My first day at an American high school felt like that.

I missed my small school in Pakistan so much that it hurt. Boarding school may have been hard, but this was impossible. I would not go back to the jungle the next day. I couldn't go back. And where on earth was Jesus? I had asked so little of him. He was proving completely untrustworthy, and I would have none of it. I went to bed heavy of heart and angry at Jesus. It was a bad mixture.

Mom's insistent voice was my alarm clock the next morning, and I knew there was no way around this fire. I had to walk through it, regardless of the burns I would sustain. For three days I suffered. Then on day four my fate suddenly changed. The pretty, sophisticated, thin girl talked to me. When I shuffled into science class, eyes on the ground, defeated as only a fourteen year-old can be defeated, the beautiful, blonde, mean girl caught my eyes and said: "Hey you! You were my best friend in Miss Crowley's four-year-old kindergarten!"

"I was?" I said with a small voice.

"Yes." After day three of terrorizing me, she went home and told her mom about the interaction. Her mom looked at her and said, "Marilyn? Marilyn Brown? She was your best friend in kindergarten!"

Her name was Christie, and in that science class a life-long friendship began. Christie is still sophisticated, thin, and beautiful, but after those initial days of terror and intimidation, it all changed. Behind that face was someone who could laugh and have fun, who was loyal to the bone, who loved and welcomed me.

My time in Winchendon extended from grade nine and into grade ten. I became a varsity cheerleader and a carnival queen for my class. I smoked pot. I tasted beer. I was a third culture missionary kid trying to make sense of the world around me in whatever way I could. But furlough was not for me. I was to go back to Pakistan in the July before grade 11 and shake the dust of a public American high school off feet that were still adorned with their bright red toe nail polish. I would go back to *tongas*, buses, and trains; my passage through Pakistan would continue. I could not have been happier.

VISITING CHURCHES WAS mandatory for the missionary on furlough. My parents were determined to keep as much of a sense of consistency and normalcy as possible during these year-long furloughs, so they carefully decided when and where we would go as a family, and when and where my father would visit churches alone. This was critically important to our family, and I am grateful for their wisdom.

In Pakistan we were often a novelty. As a little white missionary kid, and later an older white missionary kid, I was stared at constantly. I had no color. I looked different from all those around. I sometimes hated the attention, hated being stared at, wanted to lash out at those who stared, to mock them. Other times, I welcomed the attention. It made me feel special. It made me feel superior to those around me.

In Pakistan I was set apart as a privileged little white girl. On home leave, visiting small New England churches, I was also different. And being stared at in churches by American villagers turned out to be far worse than being stared at by Pakistani villagers. Rural Pakistani children gawked at us out of curiosity; at youth groups in New England we faced equally curious stares, but I found them harsher. This was the place I was supposed to belong, this was the place where my parents had been born and raised. Mom and Dad called New England "home" so, in my reasoning, it should have been easier. But it wasn't. Instead, attending strange Sunday School classes or youth groups in New England was like being paraded as a new animal in a zoo. My face burned at the audible whispers.

"Are they missionary kids?"

"I don't know."

"Look at her red toes."

Once again, the red toes had given me away. Oh why, why hadn't I learned the first time? Thankfully, winter would soon be upon us, and my red toes would soon be hidden in thick boots and socks.

I had learned how to work with stares and attention in Pakistan. I had learned how to discern when the stares were rude and demanded response, and when they were just curious. I knew what to say and how to live. But I had no idea how to respond to Christian youth groups in the United States. My favorite visit was to a church in New Hampshire, where a girl took me under her wing. She treated me like I was completely normal, took me to a store, and taught me how to shoplift. She left me with the best memory I have of visiting a church.

Small town New England in the 1970s was largely Catholic. I didn't know then that the kids in these youth groups were facing their own struggles of being Protestant in a Catholic area. Even if their ancestors had come on "the Boat" (vernacular for the Mayflower), they still faced battles to belong. When you're a teenager, your own ego goes into protective mode, and what better way to protect myself than to be arrogant and dismissive. If I dismissed them, then I was in control. Far better that than have them dismiss me.

At the Bethany Bible Chapel in Winchendon, I had good friends. Melanie Epps had reached out to me in the first few days of arrival. Bruce Beckwith was a friend and a crush. Gail, Marylou, and others had become friends and confidantes. The Chapel youth group had grown exponentially when my brother Tom and I arrived. Kids found out that we were there on Sundays, so they came on Sundays. We went apple picking and had game nights; went hiking in the fall and occasionally attended sports games together. Largely it was a social group, and I don't remember leaning on it for any sort of spiritual guidance. That could be because I wasn't looking for spiritual guidance. I was merely trying to find a place to belong.

Outwardly I made friends and I was popular and involved. Inwardly I was aching. I ached with longing for the old church building that housed our Murree classrooms, that froze in the winter and echoed with the sound of monsoon rains in the summer. I ached for familiar people and faces, for those who had known me since birth. I had experienced many times of homesickness in the past, but that was within Pakistan. This was different. I was experiencing the first of many episodes of geographic longing. It was also my first experience of recognizing the giant chasm between worlds, a chasm separated by more than an ocean. It was a chasm of culture and food and people and faith, and I was suspended somewhere in the middle of the chasm.

I did not know how to live in America. I was forever a foreigner in a place where I thought I should feel more at home. My parents did not know how to parent in America. They were unprepared for the challenges of homecoming dances, dating, boyfriends, class rings, and cheerleading. This was a new journey for all of us. My parents had launched two of their children. Ed was married and finishing up college ,and Stan was in college. Tom was a senior in high school, navigating his own tough waters and away from all that he knew and loved. Dan was still in elementary school. I, meanwhile, was oblivious. And I was not an easy teenager.

My tongue often ran away without my brain, and I never worried about consequences. I had somehow survived that first day of American high school, but that year and the following one became years of angst and rebellion.

I NEVER BECAME used to visiting strange churches that supported our family. Theoretically I was supposed to belong in these churches. Weren't my parents part of this? And by default, shouldn't I have been part?

Another factor was at play here. These were the churches that gave money so that my parents could be in Pakistan. They were not anonymous buildings or faceless people; they were part of what my parents called the "Body of Christ." I didn't really know what that meant. This was a body, I had been taught, in which people care for one another in tangible, practical ways. This meant more than bringing finger sandwiches and lemonade to funerals and making quilts at missionary circles; it was supposed to mean caring for people beyond your comfort level. This was supposed to be a group of people that supported and believed in what my parents were doing in Pakistan. My parents had talked about the many ways they had been loved by this group of people, but in my current adolescent state, I couldn't hear it.

A few years ago, in an attempt to capture my feelings and memories of this group, I wrote an imaginary letter to these supporting churches:

You tried so hard!

You went through your children's clothes, certain that you could find something, anything really, that you could send to the children of missionaries. You pictured the huts we lived in, the threadbare tunics we wore, the lack of stores and supplies. You thought we would never know the difference between Levis and no name jeans.

You advertised and arranged special drop off times so those clothes could make their way from your basements to our homes, our bodies.

You packed up oatmeal, and flour, thinking that surely we would use these products and be so excited when they arrived. It never entered your mind that chocolate chips and taco mix were what we craved.

You really did send tea bags to the part of the world that invented tea.

You sent pants with no zippers and old-fashioned dresses, all with love and a pure heart. And we mocked with hearts that were mean and not pure.

And I thought you were well-meaning and clueless. And I laughed.

And then I began meeting some of you. And you really didn't know. You really were giving us gifts from your heart. You were taking time and energy that could have been used in a hundred other ways to care for us so far away.

You put little stitches on big warm quilts and sent them our way so we could be warm. And with each stitch you prayed for us. You prayed. And prayed. And prayed.

When my mother and I went over a cliff in the mountains, with only a barbed wire fence separating us from certain death – you were praying. When my brother got in a near-fatal accident in Turkey, you were praying. When we faced illness, and sorrow, and separation, you prayed. When babies died, and boarding school was too hard, and people hurt us, you prayed.

You were so much better than me – with my arrogance and my "well-meaning-but-clueless" song and dance. You prayed with a fervor and love that I never had. You knew what it was to care for people you had barely met.

I still have two of your quilts. And when I look at them I think of how much I judged – and how wrong I was. And I thank you in my heart.

My response to New England churches and youth groups was the beginning of my disconnect from "American Christianity." This disconnect has haunted me, and I have vacillated between guilt, anger, and resignation. I could accept cultural differences in other places. But legally and spiritually I was *supposed* to belong in the United States, and especially in American Evangelical communities of faith. They were *supposed* to be safe, but in my mind, they had failed. So I never allowed myself to fully enter these communities. I was unable to shake off the experiences of my youth. I remained the 'animal in a zoo' well into my adulthood. I would finally find my home within Eastern Orthodoxy, an ancient faith that has survived centuries, passed down through icons, the church fathers, and the Scriptures.

But that would be a much later chapter in my story.

As the two-year furlough came to an end, I couldn't wait to get back to Pakistan. The thin blue aerogrammes again flew back and forth between Pakistan and Winchendon, my soul poured out to my friends back in Pakistan. I tried to make it seem like all was wonderful, stories that told of a popular, cute, cheerleader who had adjusted beautifully. And in a way I had. I had many friends. Everyone knew the girl from Pakistan. I was an enigma in this small town that lived under the shadow of a giant rocking horse.

If one story captures all of the angst and discomfort of my teenage years in the United States it is the story of how I became "Carnival Queen." I was in Grade nine, and it was winter. The high school had an annual winter carnival that included snow sculptures, special events, a bonfire, and a grand finale in the form of a winter dance. Every grade was allowed to pick a "queen" who would then go on to compete with other nominees. She would be crowned during the winter dance, to the envy of all her friends. I was picked to be the Carnival Queen in our class. It was a bit like Prom Queen. I have a feeling that two of my guy friends filled in extra ballots to be sure that I won, but the way I won didn't matter. The fact is that I, a nobody little missionary kid from Pakistan, was picked to be Carnival Queen.

There was only one problem: I was not allowed to date, and I most certainly was not allowed to go to school dances. I was in a dilemma. I was convinced that my parents would see the value of this nomination and relax the house rules for just one night, but, alas, it was not to be. Dad was traveling and Mom was solo parenting. The decision was final. I would not go to the dance. I would not be crowned Carnival Queen of the whole school.

Or would I? My ability to deceive was not just limited to hiding novels under the bedclothes. Come the proverbial hell or high water, I would be at that dance. I went off to youth group that night, sullen and angry, but determined. At the appointed time, my friend showed up to youth group and picked me up, and we went to that dance. It was a terrible time. A guilty conscience combined with being the only

Carnival Queen who was not in a formal gown proved to be a miserable mix. I did not win the school nomination. I snuck home heavy of heart, angry at my parents, and angry at the entire student body of the high school. I fell into an anxious sleep, dreaming of the comfort of my school setting in Pakistan, where Carnival Queens and school dances were nonexistent and where I was the Princess of Quite-A-Lot without even trying.

Added to the social discomfort was the fact that I did not like myself. I was uncomfortable in my skin. Besides having a constant inner ache, I became fat, a closet eater. I pilfered food from the refrigerator and stole leftovers from dinner plates. I gained thirty pounds, and every pound showed on my five-foot, three-inch frame. I counted the days until I would leave, and I grew fatter. Like Eustace in C.S Lewis's *Voyage of the Dawn Treader,* I was self-centered, proud, and whined about everything. And just as Eustace became on the outside what he already was on the inside, his body transformed into a huge, scaly dragon, so too my internal reality shaped what I was on the outside.

For Eustace the story did not end there, and neither would it for me. Eustace was transformed back to a boy through the work of Aslan and became a different person. He was stripped. Layers and layers of dragon skin were peeled away until his soft, boy skin was once again revealed:

> The very first tear he made was so deep that I thought it had gone right into my heart. And when he began pulling the skin off, it hurt worse than anything I've ever felt. The only thing that made me able to bear it was just the pleasure of feeling the stuff peel off.
>
> C.S. Lewis, *The Voyage of the Dawn Treader*

When I look back, I don't always want to remember those years. I prefer to remember what it was like when I was able to feel myself transformed, when I would have the *"pleasure of feeling the stuff peel off."*

But furloughs are a part of the whole, a big piece of the story lived between two worlds. I didn't transform in the United States. It never seemed possible. It was in Pakistan that I could transform, from caterpillar to butterfly, from dragon to girl, from self-centered and miserable with ill-fitting skin to open and willing to learn, comfortable with who I was. So I grew up and I grew fat. And I counted the days until I would return to the security of Pakistan.

In Pakistan, we were part of a community. Though imperfect and flawed, we shared all of life together in a place where we were all foreigners. We were deeply close, connected in a way that goes well beyond normal neighborhood relationships. We were part of a small group that lived counter-culture in both our adopted country and our passport countries. We lived apart from blood relatives, and so those around us became relatives in proxy. We inherited each other's houses, cars, clothes, families, and dolls. So it would be easy to leave blood relatives and my life in the United States. Pakistan was my home, the place where I belonged.

So I remained an awkward, overweight teenager, desperate to figure out who and what I was. I did not find hope for my identity in the churches that gave sacrificially to our family. I did not find it in the youth groups that were minorities in their own right in the midst of Catholic New England. And I did not find it in popularity and activity at Winchendon's Murdock High School. I found it when I returned home to Pakistan. I knew that I didn't want to live like I had for those two years. I was sick of being fat. I was sick of trying so hard to be popular. I was sick of not belonging. I was desperate for home. I was sick of life being all about me.

When we left Winchendon on our journey back to Pakistan by way of California, I breathed an exultant sigh of relief.

WHEN I WALKED off the plane onto Pakistani soil, a burden lifted. I could begin again. I could leave the past two years behind. In the United States my faith went into a holding pattern, unable to be fully born until I returned to a place of security and belonging. Here the extra weight I carried from two years of poor eating and insecurity could be shed, along with my Eustace Scrubb skin. The cut would be deep, but oh, so freeing.

Perhaps that is why I remember my junior and senior years of school with such fondness. I continued to invite punishment for breaking rules, smoking, and boy problems. But these were years of growth and contentment in my inner core. I came away with a tremendous self-confidence that still surprises me given who I had been the two years before.

I arrived back fat. Mom will probably chide me as she reads this and claim that I was not fat. Indeed, some cousins at the time consoled me by saying, "You're not fat, you're just fluffy!" But I knew differently. I had become a big girl. A pretty face was overshadowed by large thighs and big breasts. Being big came from heredity accompanied by a large side-dish of hotdogs, burgers, and ice cream – too much food and too little exercise. People described me the way fat girls have been described through the ages. "She has such a pretty face!" Other phrases were unspoken. "She's fat. What's wrong with her? She must not exercise enough. Why doesn't she lose weight?"

At Murree, no one could ever be fat. Horrible food, a lot of walking, and regular cases of pinworms produced a population of children that did not struggle with weight. I was the exception. Genes had blessed me with a healthy appetite and tendency toward plumpness, and it became one of the pains of my childhood. Being called "fatty" was the ultimate insult. The sting of those words from my brother's friends has stayed with me through the years, even after I arrived and stayed at a normal weight for a long time. But nasty people will get their comeuppance. I peruse pictures of these men who called me fatty, now bald and middle-aged and unable to hold in bellies that once were muscular and young. "Who looks better now?" I want to shout. Instead, I laugh silently, aware that the sting of name-calling in adolescence fades, but never really goes away.

When I arrived back in Pakistan from the U.S. in 1976, I knew instinctively that when I began walking the high hills of Murree I would take off weight, and take off weight I did. Although the chubby image remained etched in my mind, before long I had shed pounds and inches. But it was about far more than weight loss. It was about belonging. I was back where I belonged. I had spent two years trying so hard, trying to fit, trying to say and do the right things.

And now I was back. I no longer had a frenzied desire to fit in. I was back with my tribe and I belonged. Belonging had never tasted so sweet. My attitude toward Pakistan would also change during these years. The sense of curiosity and empathy for my adopted culture that was developing in my younger years grew exponentially. I wore exclusively Pakistani clothes and tried to learn more about Pakistan. While volunteering at Shikarpur Christian Hospital during winter vacation, I made friends with many of the Punjabi nurses, enjoying tea times and occasional sleepovers at their hostel. They were all far from their homes in the Punjab, and most were only a couple of years older than I was. We would sit together during the tea time break at the hospital, eating greasy *parathas* and sipping hot chai. There was good-natured teasing toward me, and I was the brunt of a good many jokes – some I understood and others fired off in rapid Punjabi so I didn't have a clue what was really being said. It helped that I had grown secure enough to laugh with them at my own language and cultural mistakes. Somehow it was so much easier in Pakistan than it had been a year earlier in the United States. Mom and I continued to visit women in their homes, our relationships growing stronger with each visit.

THAT FALL, I entered my junior year with enthusiasm, joy, and a boyfriend. Skip had come to MCS by way of Iran, and I loved him as much as any sixteen-year old can love a boy, perhaps even more. We laughed and talked for hours, holding hands in the dark on Saturday night walks along the road between our school and the tiny village of Jhika Gali. We began those Saturday evenings watching ancient 8mm movies from the National Film Board of Canada whose appeal was that they allowed us to clasp hands in sweaty, teenage passion under the cover of darkness. After the movies, we walked the mile to Jhika for *chai*, omelets, and *parathas* at our favorite tea stalls.

I also inherited a best friend. Nancy, best friend of my younger years, had gone to the United States for her senior year of high school. Before I even arrived back in Pakistan, she had introduced me through letters to Elizabeth. Beautiful Elizabeth was half-Scottish, half-Irish with blue eyes and a personality that could rule the world. We shared laughter and food from home, and if there was trouble to be found, we embraced it. We lived life in living color, ever fun and exciting, never troubled or dull.

Elizabeth was more of an athlete than I. Her legs were longer and she had a natural ability in field hockey and soccer. My passport to popularity would come later in the year through acting and, the following year, through cheerleading. Short cute skirts, pyramids, and catchy rhythms appealed to my love of dancing and love of drama. I loved being a cheerleader. My junior year I had just arrived back from my two years in the United States, and I didn't dare put my body on the court to be watched, much less evaluated by boys whose brothers had called me fatty. But in my senior year after a weight loss of 25 pounds I joined the cheerleading squad. I was thrilled the day I tried out in our large auditorium and made the cheerleading squad. I loved every minute of my cheerleading days.

Despite Elizabeth's athletic ability, both Elizabeth and I shared a hatred for gym class. Our gym uniforms were ugly green chemises worn over jeans or white pants. Sweat suits look like evening gowns in comparison to what we lovingly called the "greenie." The school recognized the need for physical activity but knew that it had to be done in a way that was sensitive to the conservative culture that surrounded us. The "greenie" was the solution. MCS girls of the 60s may not have been thrilled with the outfit, but in the 70s we rebelled. We sewed on ruffles and sequins, and experimented with various shades of green. The result was a variety of green chemises, still serving the purpose but with person-specific bedazzling that lent them a personality all their own.

A day came in spring of junior year when Elizabeth and I did not want to go to gym class. In truth, we never wanted to go to gym class. An opportunity came one day when we knew that Debbie, our beloved house parent, would not be in her apartment. Here was our opportunity. Our teacher, Mr. Murray of the Scottish brogue and kilt, would not be able to contact Debbie to let her know we were missing. So we went to her apartment to make fudge, planning to return to our room to eat it while our classmates sweated through gym class. The plan was foolproof, or so we thought, until Debbie walked into her apartment. We gave each other an "oh crap!" look but played it cool. And then Debbie said, "Aren't you girls supposed to be at gym?" We had the grace to blush, and our guilty faces told the rest of the story. Debbie sent us on our way, but we didn't go to gym. We took the fudge to the prayer room in the basement of the hostel dorm, certain that no one would find us there. Twenty minutes later, Debbie stormed in to say the most vicious thing she could have said to us: "I'm disappointed with you girls!" We all loved Debbie, and none of us wanted Debbie disappointed in us. We took to the field with chocolate-faced guilt, the fudge sitting like stone in our stomachs. It was not one of our finer moments. It is a credit to Debbie's huge heart and spirit of forgiveness that she loves both of us to this day, and considers us dear friends.

While outwardly we were the rule breakers, in private moments both of us recognized that faith was a primary ingredient of our lives. We might not always live like it in public, but in private, we knew that we loved God and we knew that God loved us. We were quick to disobey, but equally quick to confess and ask forgiveness. Beyond the surface were hearts that were soft to God and to others.

ELIZABETH AND I both grew more familiar with the principal's office and, by default, the principal during that year. I was already well-acquainted with Mr. Roub. He was principal of my elementary, middle, and high school from the time I was six until the time I graduated. There may have been a year or two in there where he was on a well-deserved furlough and another favorite, Mr. Nygren, took over, but overall it was Mr. Roub.

Chuck Roub was a big man with a booming voice, strong presence, and a heart that embraced his staff and students. He was a leader in every sense of the word, and he used his leadership skills to serve the mission community with integrity and grace.

Through the years our small school faced almost all of the challenges that a large high school in the United States would. Although home churches and mission agencies may have wanted to deny it, we encountered drugs, smoking, revolts and rebellions, staff/student tension, suicide attempts, deaths, eating disorders, and more. All these took place in a complicated context, a small, Christian sub-culture in the middle of a Muslim country. It took incredible wisdom and sometimes just pure grit and determination to work at the school and believe in its mission. Mr. Roub had all of that and more.

Because he was in our mission agency, I often called him Uncle Chuck. We were like extended family and the auntie and uncle labels were used all the time. In the absence of blood family, we didn't need a Mister or a Missus. We needed something more, and the auntie and uncle title put more responsibility onto us, and onto those given the title.

I grew up knowing Uncle Chuck as principal of our school and as friend to my dad. At one point when Dad was deeply discouraged about his work in Pakistan, he wrote a letter to his friend. Uncle Chuck boarded an overnight train that took eighteen hours to visit my dad for a few hours, just to encourage him, then he boarded the train back.

When my parents would come to Murree, they always visited, and often stayed, with the Roubs. This became more complicated in my junior year. I had all sorts of reasons to spend time in the principal's office. Smoking was one of them. As in most high schools, smoking was absolutely forbidden. But K-2 cigarettes, with a pristine picture of the famous K-2 mountain on the outside and ghastly, unfiltered cigarettes on the inside, were cheap and accessible.

But my conscience was strong, and one day I found myself in the Roub's living room making up a story about a friend who I knew was smoking. "What on earth should I do?" I asked. Uncle Chuck was a man of wisdom. He asked the right questions and quickly discovered that "the friend" was me. He gave me a punishment, but he did more. Like a priest, he absolved me, prayed with me and for me, and sent me on my way. I never smoked again, and this marked the last time I was ever in the principal's office.

EARLY FALL OF my junior year, I received a telegram from my parents. Telegrams were never good news. We received them, and sent them, during times of emergency and crisis. Just as a telegram had informed us of the news of Peter Hover's death so many years before, so did my last two years of high school include two telegrams with bad news. Though a year apart, they both came in the month of September.

The first brought gut-wrenching news that my brother Stan had been in a terrible car accident in Turkey. Stan and his friend and classmate Paul Johnson were taking a year off college, traveling overland. The last we had heard, all was fine. They were expected in Pakistan in early September. The telegram brought news that they were both lying unconscious in a hospital in Ankara, Turkey. Because of visa situations, it was decided that Connie and Larry Johnson would go to Turkey first to care for both of them. They would let Mom and Dad know if Stan needed them there. The news spread quickly through our community, and prayers were offered on their behalf constantly. Memories of the year that Stan broke his arm emerged, and I was scared. Would Stan live? Would he have permanent brain damage? What about Paul?

Connie and Larry arrived in Ankara a few days later and found Stan concious, while their son still lay unresponsive in a hospital bed. Three weeks later, he too woke. The boys began a long rehabilitation process. They both healed and arrived in Pakistan a couple of months later. Miraculously, there was only minor residual damage. Once again I was witness to the fact that accidents and bad news were a part of life. You didn't let the news paralyze you – you did what you had to do, even when it meant traveling far distances to help the person who needed you.

The second telegram came in September of my senior year from my brother Ed. Sharon, his wife of only four years, had been diagnosed with a malignant brain tumor. The telegram was short – telegrams never could give all the information you wanted – and he ended it with Romans 8:28. I had memorized that verse years before, and it was a text that the missionary community clung to during any tragedy. Somehow we all had to believe, "All things work together for good to them that love God, to them who are the called according to His purpose." How can you be twenty-five years old and be told that your wife has a malignant tumor and send a telegram to your parents with words of hope? I don't know. I wasn't the main character in that story. I was a bystander, receiving the news via telegram, thousands and thousands of miles away.

Ed was far away from us and from Pakistan as he went through that year. We heard news through the year – sometimes good, other times concerning. Surgeries and hospitalizations became part of his life, while on the other side of the world, I was finishing up high school. We would not see him until the summer that I graduated. Ed lost Sharon in the spring of 1981. He was twenty-eight-years old, throwing dirt into her grave even as his four-year-old daughter waited for him at home. All things work together for good.... all things work together for good. It was our own call to prayer, a call that we heard over and over through the years, until it was either accepted or rejected by the hearer.

PAINFUL GOODBYES BEGAN at the end of our junior year; seven of our class of sixteen left for their passport countries. I said goodbye to Tina who I had known since I was a little girl, to Margo who had become a dear friend, and to Elizabeth, my best friend and comrade. It had been a special year of bonding and boyfriends. Seven of us shared the same bedroom full of memories and secrets of the heart. I went into the summer of my senior year with a heart heavy with the burden of these goodbyes. It was a precursor to what the following year and graduation would be.

But I had been marked by resilience from the time I was six years old and crying tears into my pillow on the first day of boarding. This was just one more challenge on life's road. I would not let the loss of my best friends ruin my senior year. And I didn't.

I entered into senior year as queen of my world. Others had come before me, and others would come behind, but this year I was queen. The angst and rule breaking that characterized my junior year was gone. I found a place of security in my faith and my world. I had lost weight, I was a cheerleader, I was co-editor of the school newspaper, and I was popular. For a brief time, I owned the school. The year began with joyful expectation.

As the school year continued, I picked out my senior pictures and the yearbook quote from George Bernard Shaw that I chose captures the year: "*Life is no 'brief candle' for me. It is a sort of splendid torch which I have got hold of for the moment, and I want to make it burn as brightly as possible before handing it on to future generations.*" This was my time and I would make it count.

In late April around forty of us, accompanied by several staff, travelled to Kabul to represent our school at an inter-school fine arts convention. We would compete in debate, theater, music, and art, joining high schools from New Delhi, Islamabad, Lahore, Karachi and Kabul. I loved these fine arts conventions. Though I was left behind during athletic tournaments, acting and speaking were areas where I excelled.

This was not my first trip to Afghanistan. Our family had vacationed there periodically during my life. I remember tasting my first strawberry during a summer vacation, years before, juicy and red, like nothing I had ever tasted, instilling in me a love of this beautiful fruit. But this trip was different. I was older, my family was not with me, and this was our final school trip of that year. In a couple of months, I would leave Pakistan for the United States and a new life in college.

We boarded the bus early in the morning to begin the long trip down the mountain toward Peshawar. From Peshawar we wound upwards through the famed Khyber Pass, stopping for mouth-watering kebabs in Jalalabad. Late in the day, we arrived in Kabul and made our way to the homes of our expat hosts. We were housed around the city at the homes of various embassy and business expatriates. Our activities began the day after we arrived.

These interschool events were highlights of the year. We made new friends, expanding out of our small community to hear other ideas and thoughts. We performed plays and had debates, and learned new skills like calligraphy and water color. In the evenings there were special events and dances. Murree kids always had to sit at the sidelines during dances, painfully aware of our "weird" status. There was a school rule that prohibited dancing, some of us hated that rule and vowed to break it. I loved to dance and had already been punished in the past for breaking the rule. This was my senior year, and I was wise enough to decide ahead of time that when the final night dance came, I would keep my feet on the ground and kiss my boyfriend instead. It seemed a good compromise. There were no rules against kissing.

The decision that I had made so carefully and with so much thought would never be tested. On our second to last day in Kabul, in the midst of our performance of Thornton Wilder's *Our Town*, a play in which I was making my debut as the student director, school administrators entered the auditorium, interrupted the play, and herded us from the theatre on campus to the gymnasium. The gym was located in the center of campus and was less conspicuous from the main road. We were told that under no circumstances were we to leave the building; even permission to go the bathroom was restricted to two at a time. When my turn to use the facilities came, my high school friend, Sarah, and I peeked through a window and were shocked to see giant army tanks rolling through town. They were moving fast and purposefully, and we soon lost count of how many had passed. We knew something serious was happening and speculated quietly about what it might be.

An hour later, an important looking official came into the gym. He didn't have to ask for our attention. We were so quiet we could hear only our own breathing and, in the background, the sound of those heavy trucks barreling down the road. There had been a military coup. None of us would be going home as planned. All of us would be sent to the embassy houses closest to the high school until it was safe to travel. We were under strict curfew, and no one was to break that curfew. He finished speaking and we soberly lined up to go to various homes.

I was placed with several friends, and that was really all that mattered to me. All hell may break loose in Afghanistan, but be assured they better put me with my friends or they would have a far more difficult situation on their hands. Our sober and uncharacteristically obedient response ended as soon as we arrived at the house where we would be staying. It was party time.

We were unused to the joys of a commissary that supplied the latest in American foods even to a country as far removed as Afghanistan. Our hostess, Joan Fort, had the gift of hospitality and a well-stocked pantry full of cake mixes, chocolate, American peanut butter, and more. We became such good friends that when I returned to Pakistan, married with a baby, she and her husband, who had been transferred to Islamabad, immediately took all of us in. While Kabul was under military curfew and warplanes flew over and around us, we baked cakes and created a party.

That evening, more than twenty of us sat in the Fort's dining room and on their balcony, eating fried chicken and watching warplanes dive through the air. It was like a movie scene. I don't remember once being afraid. We were safe. We were secure. We were teenagers lucky enough to have won an extra vacation away from school, in a foreign country, eating

commissary food. The gods were to be praised. Who cared
that a country had been invaded, an ambassador killed, a
king deposed? To our everyday world, this meant nothing.

I cringe as I remember my callousness, my ignorance of
history and politics. This coup would be known in history as
the "Saur Revolution," the revolution that paved the way for
the Soviet invasion just one year later. A few years later, I was
to meet my husband and tell him tales of the Kabul Coup.
"It was awful," I would say. "There we were, over twenty of
us in the house, watching planes swoop overhead and snipers
shoot anyone who broke curfew." And then we found my
diary and the truth was revealed. For in the diary, there is
little about world events, and a great deal that speaks to the
teenager I was and what I truly cared about. I wrote about
my boyfriend, about my frustration with my boyfriend, about
my friends, and about the cake we made and ate. I wrote
almost nothing about the historical Kabul Coup.

As I think about third culture kids, and our lives between
worlds, this does not surprise me. Instead, I think about
what we saw as regular life – military coups, blackouts, wars
between nations, constant movement, train parties. For us
this was normal. Only much later would I grow to deeply
regret not putting something substantive and historical
inside the pages of the red-bound book modestly entitled
"My Diary."

FAITH IN HIGH school was marked by occasional 'revivals'
that swept through our small community, bringing waves
of tears and confession. We confessed going too far with
a boy, though none of us quite knew how far too far was.
We tearfully confessed hatred of classmates. We confessed

gossip. We confessed all of these things earnestly, heavy-hearted with soul-searching repentance.

At Sunday night "singspirations" we sang what passed for new and modern songs. "It Only Takes a Spark," we sang with gusto, "to get a fire going." "I Wish We'd All Been Ready," we sang, and quaked at the thought of being among those left behind at the Rapture. We sang "The Gospel in a Word is Love" in a round allowing the harmony to echo. We were experiencing the first rudimentary precursors to contemporary worship music, and the new tunes and hint of a beat seemed to us a huge advance over the hymns of our childhood. We were oblivious to the pitiful theology, which would not survive, while the hymns of my parents' generation continue to echo timeless truths of the faith. But we were good singers, we loved to sing, and our self-taught guitarists led our worship with sincerity, if not always skill.

My hormones shifted, my verbalized faith oscillated, but there was a constancy to what I believed. My doubts were frequent, my faith was immature, but the foundation that had been set many years before had an immoveable, stone-like quality. Inappropriate touch, homesickness, intimate acquaintance with loss, the humiliation of beating – none of this had crushed my faith. God had not beaten me. God had not disrespected my body. Bad things happened all the time – they happened to everybody. Who was I to be immune?

I did question. Why did Lizzy's dad die? Why did a little baby die in a freak accident? The questions built up through the years, but at that time, the answers did not seem difficult. I willingly and purposefully rebelled in words and actions, but I never saw this as discarding my faith and my need for God. This Christian faith seemed able to take me through sadness and insecurity, through a lifetime of separation from my parents. I had watched as others who had lost far more than I had continued to believe. Carol Hover never seemed to turn her back on her faith. The parents of that baby girl who was killed so long ago didn't turn their backs on their faith. Instead, it seemed to me, their faith in God, their belief in his love, seemed to grow stronger.

When the telegram came from my brother, telling us the news of Sharon's brain tumor, I clung to Debbie, my house parent. I don't remember specific things she said – but I do remember her presence. I remember that we prayed together. I remember that she never spoke banal platitudes, but she was a witness bearer to what I was thinking and what I was feeling. Who was I, I reasoned, to not believe in the ultimate goodness of God when my brother, who had far more to lose, would accept it? These were some of the questions I discussed with Debbie during my senior year.

I know now that something critical was happening within me. My faith was no longer a copycat version of those around me. It had become my own. I was learning that it wasn't enough to know what other people believed, I needed to know what I believed. Maybe that is part of the mystery of faith.

Do any of us really understand the anatomy of a faith? Certainly it is the cornerstone of Christianity. But can we do any more than admit that its most important ingredient is mystery? That I was sensitive to spiritual things from a young age was obvious. But what propels a person to make the leap from a child's faith to an adult faith? What convinces one that they need God for each breath they take, while another discards God along with her childhood toys? Centuries ago, people asked Jesus to give them a sign that he was the Son of God. He answered them in a metaphor. Some believed and some didn't. I had seen more than metaphors of the existence of God. I had seen living examples of faith. Nevertheless, the holy mystery of faith still puzzles and disturbs me. But at this stage of my life, as each day brought me closer to the end of childhood, my faith grew more and more crucial.

The Bible, previously displaced by novels under the bedclothes, was now by my bedside. Its pages became worn with page turning, and the 'red-letter boring' of the past was replaced by honest interest and searching. I kept a black-inked pen at the ready to underline verses and write in the margins. I scribbled questions in the margins, and my diary now recorded less of 'boyfriend' and more about the God-Man, Jesus. I began memorizing verses and reading books on prayer – *Daring to Draw Near* – and on the Psalms of Ascent – *A Long Obedience in the Same Direction*. I underlined them as much as I did my Bible.

My final months in Murree were filled with joy, peace, and security. I was preparing to graduate. I had been accepted into West Suburban School of Nursing in a suburb that bordered the city of Chicago. It was a school that several students from MCS had attended, and I was excited about my chosen profession. Spring that year in Murree was glorious, a succession of picture-perfect days of sunshine and daisies. All of life seemed good and God was ever-present. I had grown strong and confident in my life and my faith. I knew who I was. I knew where I was going. The angst of previous years was past. Though I would miss Pakistan dreadfully, I would make her proud. I would make Murree proud. I was a daughter of this school and this nation. I wouldn't let them down.

The strength I experienced during that time was a gift. A few years later I would face challenges to my faith and upbringing that I could never have foreseen. But that spring, all I knew was that the God who had sustained me when I was six years old, weeping into my pillow on a bunk bed, was becoming increasingly real to me. My faith, born so young, was growing.

In a few years I would go through a crisis, wondering if God really existed in the United States. But for now, I was learning more of what it was to know constant faith through shifting hormones and circumstances.

This I knew, and I knew it well: when you're six and you wake up at five in the morning, away from home and unconditional love in a dormitory of seven other little girls, just as young and equally homesick and insecure, there is no one to comfort you. When you are twelve, and your backside aches for a week because of the beating of a house parent, there is no person to comfort you. When you question why dads and babies die in the middle of the night, there is no person to answer you. When you are sixteen, and you feel misunderstood by all those around you, unable to articulate your heart, there is no person to comfort you. When you are eighteen, and your heart is breaking at the thought of leaving all you know and all you love, there is no person to comfort you.

My faith was more than theology – it was a living, breathing entity. It wrapped me with a profound sense of comfort and love, and I knew beyond any previous doubts that God was real. I knew in the marrow of my bones, and the depths of my soul, that there was something greater than boarding school loss, stronger than the grief of goodbyes, deeper than the pain of misunderstanding. I knew that redemption was not just a theological idea, but that somehow it was more real than anything on this earth.

Faith was the story written on my life, and my life was witness to a greater reality. Day by day, I was learning more and more as my childish faith metamorphosed into an adult faith. I was learning that my story was witness to the God who made me in his image, ordained my days. He was the one who knit me in the womb, who saw my comings and goings, who knew my thoughts before they came to be. Like icons, their golden glow radiating off of church walls, my life was to reflect something bigger than boarding school, more important than identity and belonging.

Later in life, I learned to appreciate the use of icons as aids to worship in Eastern Orthodox tradition. I would learn that icons were windows to Heaven, the eternal reality. I would grow to love the rich colors of iconography. Later in life, I would learn that icons teach history, doctrine, morality, and theology. I would learn that they remind us "what we are and what we should be." I would learn that icons challenge us as we look at the lives of the Saints, the lives of those who chose to follow their God, their Savior. I would learn that icons bear witness to stories. I would learn that icons allow us a glimpse of the Kingdom of God.

But that was later. For now, my life itself was the icon. I was part of something bigger than myself, something better than all that surrounded me, something eternal. This was my faith story – a journey to something infinitely greater than myself.

THE LAST WEEK of my senior year we passed yearbooks around, struggling to write what our hearts were feeling with cheap pens next to black and white photographs. I reserved the best spaces for best friends and boyfriends, and retreated to quiet spaces to read their words. When I would re-read them in the future my heart would ache with longing. The week was a flurry of activity – concerts, awards ceremonies, dinners, and free time of lounging with our friends on picnic tables outside of the school. But amidst the flurry, we knew that this was all ending, and nothing could stop it.

The week culminated on a clear, starry summer night as ten of us walked slowly, one by one, down the aisle of the school auditorium. I knew every feature by heart. I had invited Jesus into my heart in this auditorium – several times. I sang in choir here, played piano for school concerts, giggled with friends, held a boy's hand, practiced cheerleading. It was this auditorium where we read our mail and watched basketball games. I had been in plays on this stage, playing the part of Toinette in Molière's *The Imaginary Invalid*. This was where we had practiced *Our Town* for hours before heading to Kabul and the famous Kabul Coup. This was the center of our school, and its high ceiling and huge stone walls held the memories of a million events.

Elgar's "Pomp and Circumstance" echoed off the old walls of the building, saying to all those present: Here they are! It's their turn – their turn to graduate, their honor, the class of 1978. We had been to many graduations before, but this was ours. There were speeches, piano duets, and singing. As I sat on stage, I looked out on my community. I looked out and saw people who had written on my life. I saw my parents and my youngest brother. I saw my adopted aunts and uncles, my teachers and my mentors. I saw my friends and those who would come after me. In that moment, I saw only the good. The hard memories were not a part of this event, they weren't invited. The ceremony ended and our names were called individually. We stepped forward to receive diplomas with wild applause. Principal Chuck Roub presented "The Murree Christian School Class of 1978" and the processional began that would take us down the aisle and out of the church. We were finished. We would be leaving MCS and all that we knew.

Up in the cafeteria, a reception of punch, cake, and cookies had been set out, hosted by mothers of the incoming senior class. Giant crepe paper flowers in the class colors were hung from the ceiling. The reception line snaked from the cafeteria through the staff lounge, a space forbidden to students except on this one day of the year. These were my classmates' parents, and my parents' friends. They had seen me grow from bratty little girl to almost woman, watched me transform from turbulent pre-teen to happy teenager. They slipped envelopes into my hand – dollar checks, rupees in cash – knowing what was to come and how much I would need every penny. These were my people, my community. Each hug was long and hard in wordless goodbyes. Many of them I was never to see again.

The magnitude of what I was leaving was not completely lost to me that night. Even in the midst of the goodbyes, I felt my throat catch. But as I look back I am overwhelmed by it. We left behind our entire lives the night of graduation. We said goodbye to all we knew. For the rest of our lives we would struggle to answer the question, "Where are you from?" We would rage at those who attacked our adopted country, even as we raged at Pakistan herself. Some of us would be accused of crying "every time a cow died in Pakistan." Others stoically moved forward, silent about the impact of being raised in another world.

In *Some Far and Distant Place*, my friend Jonathan Addleton writes poignantly of graduation night. It was another class, an earlier year, but the emotions were the same.

> By late evening, the crowd began to thin and, after a time, only we graduates and our families remained, talking quietly among ourselves. It was over, it was really over—there would never be a night quite like

this, not for us anyway, an evening so full of promise and yet so tinged with all the sadness and inadequacies of adolescence. There was so much I wanted to say, so much I longed to do; but, as happened so often, I held back, keeping emotions inside that at this, of all possible nights, should have been on open display for all the world to see. I felt empty when I said my final goodbyes to people among whom I had spent almost my entire life, leaving in most cases without so much as a handshake. (Jonathan Addleton, *Some Far and Distant Place*)

As for me, I went back that night to the cottage where we had set up our home for the past few weeks of summer. Suitcases and bags sat on beds and chairs throughout the cottage. It was beginning to echo with the empty place we would leave behind, and it smelled musty and damp, the effects of monsoon season already begun. Crying had to wait, there was still packing to do. But how do you pack up a life?

I stayed up to gather the remainder of my possessions, putting them into an old green suitcase, and finally fell asleep to the sounds of monsoon rain on the tin roof. The next day I would leave Pakistan and never sleep in this house again, never walk up the hill to catch the school bus. The final chapter of life as a child in Pakistan had ended. I was the baby turtle, making its way slowly to the sea. No one could do it for me. In order to survive and thrive, I had to do it by myself.

IF THE NIGHT of graduation had been near perfect, the morning was dreadful. We were all tired, both physically and emotionally. My parents were packing up and when they came back, I would not be with them. As my mom looked around Forest Dell, she told me later, "I was completely undone. I didn't know how I could do this. I didn't know how I could leave you behind." I knew none of this.

We were invited to breakfast at Auntie Connie's cottage, just across from ours. Before we got there, a vicious fight over clothes began. I was on one side, Mom and Dad on the other. I wanted to wear my cute jeans with a short, embroidered shirt. Mom wanted me to wear something that covered my bum, invoking the general rule whenever we left the house. "Wear something that covers your bum!" was a phrase said in every home in our community. We not only heard it at home, we heard it in boarding school. A "covering top," it was called. When I had planned this outfit – and I had planned – I was thinking ahead to Karachi, England, and beyond. I felt Mom to be seriously short-sighted in thinking I should conform to the norm. There was nothing normal about this day. My brain did not control my tongue, and I said some mean, nasty things to Mom and Dad.

In retrospect, the fight seems inevitable. How can you pack up a life without a fight? It's an impossibility. Ten years later, I would remember this fight when my husband and I viciously tore into each other over a cookbook in a Karachi hotel room, at a time when we too were packing up a life. Packing your suitcase for a trip and packing up a life are distinctly different. In the one, you put clothes and necessities; in the other, you pack your heart. Exposed and vulnerable, your heart sits in the suitcase and the even the most benign action can damage it. In that fight, my heart was damaged, mostly because it was already so raw.

My dear Auntie Connie gave us a break from our emotional morning by serving us a beautiful breakfast, and we forged a fragile truce. My boyfriend, Skip, and his father, Norm, arrived a bit later, and we packed my life into a small van and headed down the mountain. Conversation was minimal, it was too difficult to talk. Norm dropped us at the entrance to Islamabad International Airport, and we began checking in. Too soon, it was time to say goodbye. The goodbye was far more difficult for me than for Skip. He still had another year. He was a Senior and would enter with all the enthusiasm and energy that I had had a year earlier. I was the one who was leaving it all behind. Mom allowed us a public hug, which was incredibly magnanimous of her given the conservative culture where we made our home.

But the hug ended, and we went through security to the other side. The hot tarmac smelled like tar in the beating sun. I took one last look back at the terminal before I walked up the stairs to the door of the plane.

We landed in Karachi a couple of hours later. Our flight to London was scheduled for the middle of the night, so we made our way to the home of our friends – the Montgomerys. Mom used to say that Bob and Ruth Montgomery were the salt of the earth. He was as gentle as she was brusque. They had lived in Jordan before moving to Pakistan, and our families lived side-by-side for several summers. Joy Montgomery was my "big sister" in boarding school, and she had held me many a night when stoicism broke, bringing on waves of homesickness and a flood of tears. We had known them for years and were always welcomed to their home.

Auntie Ruth greeted us with *chai* and food, and Mom told Dan and me to try and take a nap. As we lay in their guest room, I looked at the ceiling fan and drowsily talked about Skip, wondering if we would stay together, if he would get another girlfriend. With complete confidence, my young brother said, "You won't," and turned away. I was wounded, and angry at his confidence, mostly because deep down I suspected his reading of our future was absolutely correct.

As hard as I try, I can't remember our plane ride to London. Those hours have been blocked from my mind, much like an old letter damaged with water. No matter how hard you try to read it, the ink has run together so that it is only a blur and can't be deciphered. I do remember London itself. We stayed at the Foreign Missions Guest House, a bed and breakfast designed to give Christian workers a clean and affordable place to stay in London. We had stayed there in previous trips through London, and once again we indulged in the hospitality of this guest house in a city that was hardly affordable on a missionary salary. The public dining room was always full of other travelers like ourselves, enjoying good British tea and cold British toast.

At the end of our time in London, I would travel on to Scotland to visit friends in Glasgow and Fraserburgh, while Dan and my parents returned to the U.S. On the day that our journey together ended, Dad wanted to make sure I had everything I needed. Impatiently I assured him that I was a grown up, I could take care of myself. In Heathrow Airport I hugged all three, then hugged them again. Last-minute advice from my parents felt superfluous. After all, I reasoned, I went to boarding school at six years old. I had been groomed for this moment my entire life. A final kiss and I turned and began making my way toward my gate alone.

As I walked away, their beautiful faces etched in my mind, their goodbye kisses fresh on my cheeks, I didn't look back. I couldn't.

❖

Amidst all this madness, all these ghosts and memories of times past, it feels like the world around me is crumbling, slowly flaking away. Sometime, when it's this late at night, I feel my chest swell with a familiar anxiety. I think, at these times, that I have no more place in my heart for Pakistan. I cannot love it any more. I have to get away from it for anything to make sense; nothing here ever does.

But then the hours pass, and as I ready myself for sleep as the light filters in through my windows, I hear the sound of those mynah birds. And I know I could never leave. (Fatima Bhutto, *Songs of Blood and Sword*)

My childhood in Pakistan was an extraordinary gift – a gift that is foundational to who I am today. What would I do if I could go back to those days? What would I have done differently? With 20/20 vision how would I have lived? If I could write a letter across time to that girl, the one who left Pakistan so many years ago, here is what I might say:

You are leaving Pakistan tomorrow. In the morning, you will have one of the worst fights of your teen years with your parents. You will only stop fighting because your boyfriend and his father are coming to pick all of you up in a van and take you down the mountain to the airport. You don't yet know that as you leave the soil of Pakistan your heart will hurt so deeply that you won't even be able to cry.

And here is what you will wish about your life in Pakistan, a life lived between worlds, between East and West, between Christian and Muslim, between

Pakistan and America, wishes that you have grown into based on greater understanding and maturity.

You will wish that you had taken Urdu seriously. You had such a good ear for this language and a strong foundation. You will wish that you took advantage of this and gained the fluency that was a possibility at an early age.

You will wish that you learned more about the music of Pakistan, that you understood the ghazals written with beautiful poetry.

You will long to relive some of your friendships with Pakistanis, recognizing in the future the arrogance of your childhood as a little white girl growing up in the East.

You will ache to go back and apologize – to houseparents whom you were rude to, to classmates who have left the faith, to others hurt by your choices.

You will wish you had spent more time in the inner courtyards of your Muslim friends, chatting, cooking, and learning, learning, learning.

You will wish many things; you will regret other things.

But there are some things that you will never regret.

You won't regret that early in life you learned of a God who laces your memories with grace, who takes boarding school tears and turns them into joy in the morning.

You won't regret that you learned of this God through your parents, through your houseparents, through your adopted aunties and uncles, through Pakistan, a land you love.

You will understand that, though you were shortsighted, you know the God who delights in healing our eyesight, in restoring poor vision.

With all you now know, can now see, you won't regret that you are a third culture kid, with all the complexity and joy that goes with it. And you'll realize that 20/20 vision is reserved for God alone.

I LEFT THE soil of Pakistan in the summer of 1978. At the time, there was little research on the impact of a mobile life on children. The term "third culture kid" was just beginning to be used. The only task ahead of me was to go back to my passport country, assimilate, and succeed. I wasn't sure what that meant or what success would look like. Since I was going to nursing school, I suppose I assumed that it meant I was supposed to become a nurse. Oh, and get married. I was definitely supposed to get married.

I never thought that moving to the U.S. would be an adjustment. It was never mentioned at MCS. "Reentry" seminars had not yet made their way into the missionary or expatriate vocabulary.

I had certainly seen others leave. They usually came back with new clothes and stories to tell of their passport countries. I was mostly interested in the clothes. But I had never paid attention to the experience as a whole. I was absorbed in my world in Pakistan, and would not have paid attention had someone attempted to tell me what it was like to move to a country that we knew only through infrequent visits.

I had never heard of frozen sadness, of ambiguous loss; I had never heard of the grief sustained through the years through frequent goodbyes and distance away from parents at young ages while at boarding school. The research around third culture kids would not become mainstream until many years later.

But I know what it is now. It is sadness, frozen in time. At one point, I longed to express my grief, but it felt foolish. What was there to grieve? I loved the unique experiences that defined my childhood. Plus, my experiences were years ago. I have a different life now. I have moved forward. In more honest moments, I realized there was grief, but it was hidden. I realized that being able to see the people and places I loved, even if it was just one more time, would be a gift. But I also realized that sometimes that is not possible. I couldn't go back to what was. I would always have an echo of *saudade*, that wistful longing for what no longer exists. Perhaps that is when I recognized that closure would be impossible. Instead, I would learn to be okay with ambiguity, be at peace with paradox.

And somehow along the way, being at peace with paradox happened. I grew to love living between. Many years later I would attempt to express it in writing.

Any third culture kid who lives effectively in her passport country has a moment of truth when she realizes it's okay to live here, it's okay to adjust, it's okay, even if she never feels fully at home, never feels a level of comfort in who she is in her passport country. To adapt doesn't mean settling for second best. To adapt is to use the gifts she developed through her childhood in order to transcend cultures and to find her niche in both worlds.

In all my years since, no one has ever asked what I left behind. Many have asked, "What was it like?" "Were you happy?" Hundreds have asked the dreaded "Where are you from?" No one has asked what I left behind. But maybe, a friend of mine suggests, that is the most important question of all.

So when she comes to you, don't ask her where she's from, or what's troubling her. Ask her where she's lived. Ask her what she's left behind. Open doors. And just listen. Give her the time and space and permission she needs to remember and to mourn. She has a story — many stories. And she needs and deserves to be heard, and to be healed, and to be whole. (Nina Sichel, *"The Trouble with Third Culture Kids,"* Morning Zen Blog, June 20, 2014)

What did I leave behind? Everything. I left everything behind – homes and friends, sounds and smells, places and sights, all that defined my childhood.

There were only three portable things that I carried with me when my passage through Pakistan ended: my passport, my memories, and my faith. The passport would expire, replaced by one with new pages, and with it a portion of my life would be gone. The memories would fade, though some would revive through reminiscing and writing. Only my faith would remain. Like all humans who embark on a journey of faith, there are markers along the way, and we move forward, sometimes willingly, other times hesitantly. Sometimes we are screaming, and other times we are silent. Sometimes we believe, and other times we deny. All the while, the Author of our story, the Writer of our faith, continues to draw us ever to himself. And so it is with me. The story is not over; the journey continues. The mystery of faith is not over. Some days, it feels as though it is still just beginning.

CHAPTER 6
GOING HOME

We leave something of ourselves behind when we leave a place, we stay there, even though we go away. And there are things in us that we can find again only by going back there.

Pascal Mercier, Night Train to Lisbon

I HAD FORGOTTEN how long the driveway to the Holland Bungalow in Shikarpur was. Turning off from the busy road, we entered the gate of the compound. Once inside the grounds were calm and peaceful, just as I remembered. We walked past homes of three Brahui families who had lived there for years, then on to the large bungalow where I had lived my last two years of high school. The property had the look of neglect. The grounds were thick with brush and desert plants, and a bougainvillea plant was growing, wildly happy with no human to tame it. Layers of dirt had settled over the windows and thresholds of every door, and dusty footprints showed that a few others had walked these rooms recently. I peered into my childhood bedroom, a smile on my face. The same bedspread that I had when I left at age eighteen was still on the bed. I gasped in astonishment. If this was not proof that this was home, nothing ever could be. Memories flooded my mind and heart. I couldn't stop smiling.

I was sixteen and my older brother Stan had gone into my room and locked me out. "Dear Diary," he yelled out in a high voice, egging me into a scream of protest. He yelled, I screamed, and suddenly Ali Madad, our faithful, handsome chowkidar, bolted up the path with a gun poised – whoever was hurting Marilyn would pay! Mom's embarrassment at her miscreants was acute. With guilty faces and eyes, she made us go and confess that we had just been fighting. Ali Madad, gracious man that he was, laughed and forgave us, partially because his affection for our family, particularly my brother Stan, was great.

I was seventeen, playing my guitar for hours on the verandah during school vacation, picking out chords to a Queen song. I was seventeen, sleepily getting ready to go work at the Christian hospital as a volunteer caring for moms and babies who had no other means of care. I was in the kitchen and Arbab came with a beautiful meal of *saag* and *maani*, the aroma of spices making my eyes water. And then I was eighteen, saying goodbye for the last time. The memories tripped over my brain like a waterfall flowing over rocks, desperate to find their way to the open fall.

I was on my way to visit Arbab, my childhood friend. I had last seen her twenty-three years before, when my firstborn was a four-month-old baby.

As we approached her home at the back of the large compound, Arbab came running out, tears in her eyes. She began blessing me, over and over she uttered words, *"Allah mahabbat, Allah jo shukr ahay, Bismillah,"* She hugged and blessed, her hand on my head. It was a greeting of biblical proportions.

We sat on the *charpai*. I could not have stopped smiling if I had tried. My heart was so full of the best sort of memories, of hope, of thanks for my past, and of thanks for this trip – an undeniable and gracious gift.

The visit ended soon after the evening call to prayer. I wished so much that I had brought something, anything, to show my love, but in my haste I had come empty-handed. Arbab hugged me as though she could never let go, and I hugged her back the same way.

The ride back was silent except for the clip-clop of the horse's hooves as it pulled the *tonga*. Tomorrow I would head back to Karachi to catch a plane to Abu Dhabi, then board a fourteen-hour flight back to the United States. Our time was over too soon, but jobs, demands, husbands, and children awaited my sister-in-law and me back in the United States. We packed up under the harsh glare of a fluorescent light, a fan overhead, and music from the Hindu temple just steps away from the back gate blaring through our open door.

As the late night call to prayer echoed across Shikarpur, I lay down to sleep, my heart burning with those conflicting emotions of deep happiness and extreme loss. I fell asleep under the whir of the fan, a deep dreamless sleep where all of life made sense.

CHAPTER 7
MAPPING YOUR TCK JOURNEY

*You either walk inside your story and own it, or stand
outside your story and hustle for your worthiness.*

Brené Brown

❖

*We tell ourselves stories in order to live. ... We look for
the sermon in the suicide, for the social or moral lesson in
the murder of five. We interpret what we see, select the
most workable of the multiple choices.*

Joan Didion, *The White Album*

I BEGAN TO write my story over eight years ago. I
put together pieces of memory, patched them with adult
understanding, and wove them together into words that
ultimately turned into chapters of this book. As I wrote, I
began to understand more about how important stories
are to our understanding of others and ourselves. I thought
more specifically about the third culture kid's journey, the
stories behind the arrivals and the departures, the narrative
that captured the sweetness of hello and the bitterness of
goodbye.

If you have reached this point of the book, then you have
traveled with me in my story, you have read many chapters
of my childhood. As with any of us, my story has many more
chapters that I haven't included here. I could write chapters
about my transition from college to adulthood, chapters about
raising my own family in Pakistan, Egypt, Massachusetts,
Phoenix, Boston, and Cambridge, and chapters about
arriving in the United States with twenty-six suitcases and
an Egyptian Siamese cat.

For all of us stories build and grow day after day, year
after year. Woven through the years in both these narratives
are good times and hard times, richer times, poorer times,
times of sickness and the times of health. Our lives are made
up of much joy, grief, anger, peace, strife, reconciliation, and
laughter. In our story there has always been laughter.

A few years ago, two researchers out of Emory University
developed a tool called "Do you know?" Children were asked

to respond to twenty questions about their families. The results were astonishing. They found that the more children knew about their family the higher their self-esteem and their ability to withstand stress and function normally. The more children knew about their family, the more likely they were to be happy and healthy. In fact, the results state that knowing family stories was the "best single predictor of children's emotional health and happiness." When children knew their family stories, they knew that they were part of something that mattered. They realized that it wasn't just about them, it was about something bigger.

We all need to know that we are a part of something larger and greater than we are. In *Being Mortal*, Atul Gawande says "In the end, people don't view their life as merely the average of all its moments—which, after all, is mostly nothing much plus some sleep. For human beings, life is meaningful because it is a story."

This final chapter is my invitation to you, my readers. It is an invitation to begin to write your story, to make a visit to your memory archives and to think about what has gone into your journey. When you write your story, don't worry about grammar, syntax, spelling, or punctuation. Just tell your story as you remember it, walk in the archive for a time and enjoy the sweet nostalgia of memory. Learn to tell your story. Your story is uniquely yours and cannot be taken away. Stories define us, they tell the listener or reader how our experiences made us who we are today. Telling our stories invites questions, and questions invite more of the story.

The following pages are for you to use as resources in telling your own story. From a poem called "I'm from" to a TCK dictionary, you will find words and reflections that take you from my specific story to a more general third culture kid perspective. TCKs don't all share the same story. Rather, there is a perspective that can strengthen and connect the individual to a bigger story, one person at a time.

With all my heart, I believe that as we learn to tell our stories, we begin to understand not only the complexity of our experience, but the complexity of the human experience and ultimately, the human heart.

"I'm From..."
By Robynn and Adelaide Bliss

When my daughter Adelaide was a sophomore in high school, the Language Arts teacher gave her students what on the surface seemed a simple assignment. She wanted them to write a poem introducing themselves to her and to the class. Five short stanzas. Two lines each. Begin each stanza with, "I'm from..." Apparently the teacher's included lines like, "I'm from the yellow kitchen, blue popsicles and red posies. I'm from the white house, the fenced yard, the barking beagle".

It's a good assignment.

Theoretically.

Unless where you're from is convoluted and you've inherited some confusion on that particular subject. Unless it is too long of a story to be captured neatly in five short stanzas. Then it isn't such a great assignment.

Adelaide cranked out a rough draft. The teacher read it over Adelaide's shoulder. She cautioned her against being too vague. It wasn't specific enough. It didn't describe where Adelaide was from. She should give it another go.

Over the weekend, sprawled on her bedroom floor, Adelaide read her first draft out loud. I loved it. Tears sprang to my eyes. My young daughter had captured the ambiguities of a globally scattered childhood succinctly. She discerned her own angst. She understood mine too.

We talked about what she should do. I didn't want her to make any changes and yet she needed to meet her teacher's expectations. Eventually she tweaked it some. But it was her original first draft that I connected with.

> I'm from the wide airplane wings
>> Swooping me up and setting me down.
> I'm from the navy blue passport
>> Filled with endless destinations.
> I'm from the suitcases not always full
>> Yet always tucked away in the corner.
> I'm from the experiences, the people, the places
>> From North America to Europe to Asia.
> I'm from never knowing where I'm from
>> But always feeling at home.

What might it look like to write your own "I'm From.." poem? Pick up a journal and begin your story with a poem like this one.

THE THIRD CULTURE KID DICTIONARY

Words are important. We use them every day, all day. They describe what we want, what we think, how we feel, and a myriad of other things. Language and words are amazing communication tools.

Take the term TCK or third culture kid. Many don't know the definition of this term. While there are multiple definitions, my favorite is from the Sociologist David C. Pollock:

> A Third Culture Kid (TCK) is a person who has spent a significant part of his or her developmental years outside the parents' culture. The TCK frequently builds relationships to all of the cultures, while not having full ownership in any. Although elements from each culture may be assimilated into the TCK's life experience, the sense of belonging is in relationship to others of similar background. (David C. Pollock, Ruth E. Van Reken, and Michael V. Pollock. *Third Culture Kids: The Experience of Growing up Among Worlds.*)

Some words describe the TCK journey better than others. Some of these words don't exist in the English language, so for the English speaker we rely on words from other places, other languages. I have compiled twenty words that I believe best describe the TCK experience. Some are funny, some are sad, but all help us as we struggle to articulate our particular journey.

Adopted Country. The countries that take us in and raise us as one of their own, yet we know we don't ultimately belong to them.

Adult Third Culture People. Our parents, or other people who have chosen to make another country their home for a long period of time. Unlike the TCK, whose developmental years are formed through living in a country other than their passport country, this person is a fully developed adult when they make this decision. Thus there is a difference in perspective.

Belonging. The sense of being a part of something; belonging is something we long for and wish for but that seems to elude us, always remaining just outside of our grasp.

Code-switching. The process that goes on internally while we interact with people from other countries and cultures to determine how to best communicate with them.

Cultural Confusion. What happens when we are faced with pop culture or culture cues that we are supposed to understand from our passport culture, but realize we are clueless as to their meaning.

Fernweh. From German. Distance Pain. The sense or feeling of wanting to be somewhere else. A reverse homesickness, a longing for a place that isn't where you are right now.

Goodbye. The word which we don't like to say, the action which we don't like to do.

Hiareth. Welsh word with no English equivalent. A homesickness tinged with grief or sadness over the lost or departed. Wistfulness or longing for something of the past that no longer exists.

"Home". The ambiguous place where either our cat lives or our suitcase is unpacked. Not necessarily a geographic location but a place defined by memories, events, people and places that span the globe.

Identity. A government document issued by our countries of citizenship that indicates all the countries we have visited or lived, otherwise known as a passport.

Invisible Immigrant. Understanding the migrant experience to another country yet being seen outwardly as one who is originally from that country; that sense of having much in common with the immigrant experience and yet looking so much like those around us that we are assumed to be one of the crowd. Our immigrant sensibilities are invisible.

Language of Elsewhere. A language without grammar, syntax, past tense, present perfect, or superlatives. The language of 'other' best spoken with tea, coffee, talk, meals, reaching out, asking questions, sometimes shopping, and most of all-time.

Nostalgia. A longing for the past that we have created, the one that helps us escape our current reality; a suffering caused by an unappeased yearning to return.

Saudade. Portuguese. A "vague and constant desire for something or someone that does not or cannot exist. Not a discontent but a vague and indolent longing."

Killing the Saudade. The act of spending time with those who understand your 'saudade' and reminiscing or participating in some activity reminiscent of your past (e.g. eating a meal at a restaurant that serves food from your adopted country). This can kill those feelings – for a while.

Sun-drenched Elsewheres. The opposite of a sedentary life; those places that we are haunted by and dream of going to.

Third Culture Kid Envy. The sense of ill-will that rises in us like bile when others are traveling to or writing books about those places that we consider our own.

Third Culture Kid Bigotry (or Prejudice). The unfortunate "I am better than you" that can arise as a result of feeling 'other' and manifest itself in various ways. Occurs primarily in our passport culture.

Third Culture Kid Grief. That grief that is a result of too many goodbyes, too much change, and unspoken sorrow.

Tribe. Our people, our group of other third culture kids from varying countries and nationalities that share a common language and experience.

As you think of your story, what would you add to these words? What other words are important to your TCK lexicon?

You Know You Married a TCK When....

Marrying a third culture kid comes with challenges. It is a cross-cultural marriage, but is not always recognized as such. The following list details things that have actually happened in my marriage.

You know you married a TCK when.....

You're listening to NPR and she shouts "I know that reporter".

You're playing Trivial Pursuit and she gets stuck on pop culture but gets every country question correct.

You have to teach her idioms again. And again. And again.

Every three months she has to either get across an international border or rearrange the furniture.

You try to convince her that she cannot bargain for fresh produce at the fixed price grocery store.

She nods and laughs at a joke, but you know by the look on her face that she does not understand a word of it.

You find her in tears after trying to order coffee in her passport country.

She gets ragingly envious when you have an overseas trip — and she doesn't get to go.

You know that the only restaurants she will want to go to on Valentine's Day are ethnic restaurants.

One of her favorite places is the international terminal at the nearest airport.

Every immigrant she meets becomes her best friend.

She dissolves in tears when she hears news reports of tragedies from her adopted country/countries.

Her decorating style mixes samovars with reindeer, white lights with Egyptian perfume bottles, and Turkish bowls with books.

She is fiercely protective of her TCK "tribe." You criticize her tribe, you criticize her!

She has no problem sending her kids across the ocean to countries with uprisings and revolutions but sits up half the night worrying about them driving your car down the street to a friend's house.

She gets completely paralyzed in the cereal aisle of a grocery store Or the bread aisle. Or the chips aisle. Or pretty much any aisle, but especially the cereal aisle.

The Language of Transition

I do want to make sure we have a language for transition and crossing cultures and homesickness and living in a state of between-ness. I did not have that growing up and have found the TCK vocabulary helpful as an adult.

Elizabeth Trotter

Like my friend Elizabeth, I did not grow up with a language of transition. My husband, who grew up as a military kid, did not have a language of transition either. Whether you use the term third culture kid or not, having a language of transition is critically important.

The language of transition means knowing the importance of goodbyes. We honor the goodbyes. That may look different for every member of the family, and that's where it gets tricky. Honoring the goodbyes means we won't make our kids get rid of all their treasures. Yes, I get the problem of space. But that stuffed lamb means more to your little girl than you can possibly understand during the chaos of moving. The dollhouse? Do NOT give it away! Honoring the goodbyes means making space for different members of your family to grieve their lasts: the last trip to that favorite restaurant, to school, to church, to the playground. Honoring the goodbyes means making sure that final meal is with people you love deeply.

The language of transition means knowing the word "Saudade." Saudade is a 12th-Century word from Portugal, thought up by the diaspora who longed for the soil of Portugal, but had no vocabulary, no language of transition to express it:

> "The famous saudade of the Portuguese is a vague and constant desire for something that does not and probably cannot exist, for something other than the present, a turning towards the past or towards the future; not an active discontent or poignant sadness but an indolent dreaming wistfulness." *(A. F. G. Bell. Portugal of 1912)*

These are feelings so deep that you can scarcely give words to them. Your throat catches. You experience an intense, but wordless, longing and desire. How do I know this? Because I have experienced it, first hand. What we long to describe is *Saudade.* It also means we know how to *"kill the saudade,"* how to find ways to contain the longing so it doesn't destroy us. Finding the restaurants or the people who know the world that we came from, getting together for an evening of food and talk – these are ways that we kill the saudade – sweet and necessary activities while in transition.

The language of transition includes building a RAFT. Knowing the importance of **Reconciliation, Affirmation,**

Farewell, Think destination. Ruth Van Reken and Dave Pollock developed this acronym in a chapter of *Third Culture Kids: Growing Up Among Worlds*. The entire chapter is devoted to transition and dealing with leaving one place and starting in a new one. It is a constructive and practical look at leaving well, at closure, and at saying our goodbyes in peace.

The language of transition means having a vocabulary for cross-cultural adjustment. For a child, much of the art of crossing cultures is learned from the parents. If parents are struggling and resisting the host culture, the kids will pick that up and internalize it. The language of transition means that as adults we will educate ourselves on culture shock and cultural adjustment and work to pass that on to our kids. It takes action on our part. Rudyard Kipling's famous lines come to mind:

> And the end of the fight is a tombstone white
> with the name of the late deceased
> And the epitaph drear: "A Fool lies here
> who tried to hustle the East."
> Rudyard Kipling, *The Naulahka*

While that may seem like a harsh ending to a life, the meaning could not be clearer. Cross-cultural adjustment is imperative and having the words to express that and wisdom to understand it is part of the language of transition. I would also add that cultural humility is a necessary ingredient to the work of cross-cultural adjustment.

Finally, the language of transition means learning to understand the idea of living between worlds. "Every good story has a conflict. Never being fully part of any world is ours. This is what makes our stories and memories rich and worth hearing. We live between worlds, sometimes comfortable in one, sometimes in the other, but only truly comfortable in the space between. This is our conflict and the heart of our story." (Marilyn Gardner, *Between Worlds*) Learning to be comfortable in the space between is part of the language of transition.

Like learning any language, we don't master the language of transition overnight. Rather, it takes time, effort, laughter, and tears. We make mistakes, we get up, and we move on, but developing a vocabulary of transition is an important step along the way.

Building a Raft

In their landmark book *Third Culture Kids: Growing Up Among Worlds*, Dave Pollock and Ruth Van Reken devote a chapter to transition and how to deal with leaving one place and starting in a new one. The chapter is a constructive and practical look at leaving well, at closure, at saying our goodbyes in peace. While transitions are never easy there are concrete steps we can take to make them as smooth as possible, always bearing in mind that no matter how well we prepare some situations will arise that are completely out of our control. The authors suggest four steps that make up the acronym RAFT. They are: **Reconciliation, Affirmation, Farewell, Think destination.**

Reconciliation is the first step in building a RAFT. It is important to leave in peace; when we leave in peace we can begin in peace. By contrast when we leave with unresolved conflict we carry that conflict with us to the next place. Reconciliation means leaving in peace as far as is possible. When we've struggled mightily in a place this is difficult. I remember leaving Massachusetts and the small town on the

North Shore of Boston where we lived. We loved our house, and throughout our time living there we had laughed hard, cried a lot, partied much, and grown in extraordinary ways. But we struggled with the choking provincialism of the area, and we felt other's eyes upon us, criticizing at every turn. It was not easy to leave that town in peace, and so I didn't. Thanks to some beloved friends in a nearby town, we were able to return and create new memories, but I still wish I had been able to leave with greater peace. This is the move that comes to mind when I think about the first log of the raft. Reconciliation is an obvious first step – if we are able to reconcile well then we can better move on to the other three logs.

Affirmation means acknowledging those we love and letting those who have become our dear friends know how much we love them and how much we will miss them. Affirmation is about talking to a teacher and saying "Thank you! Thank you for your role in my kid's development." Affirmation is about saying thank you to coffee shop baristas and favorite bakery vendors, people who worked in church nurseries and pastoral staff. It's about affirming the time we had in a place and the people who knowingly or unknowingly helped us create a home.

Farewell calls us to honor our goodbyes. Saying goodbye is critically important. We grieve as we say goodbye because we are losing places and people that we love. Each goodbye is a little like death, it's saying goodbye to permanence and to relationships as we know them. Those relationships will change, they have to change. Comfort and hope will have their place, and they are part of the process, but sometimes we need to just sit with our grief before being forced to move on. The global transnational family has developed an amazing capacity to adapt, to move forward, but sometimes we need to just stop where we are and honor that moment.

Think Destination is the last of Pollock and Van Reken's recommended logs. This can be either tremendously difficult or really easy. When our family left Cairo we thought our hearts would break, the collective grief in our family was palpable and as long as we live I don't think any of us will forget our last night in that city of eighteen million people. A last meal eaten with laughter and joy; saying goodbye to dear friends Jenny, Len, Yasmine, Neelam, and Tariq as they sang to us a hymn of blessing; hugging tight, not knowing when or if we would ever see each other again – these friend who knew our lives in Pakistan and Egypt. Finally we walked down the road toward our home just steps from the Nile River with the smell of jasmine in the air. How could we think destination? How could we think ahead when we were leaving so much? And yet we did. We thought destination as we sorted and packed and began reestablishing connections back in our passport country. We thought destination as we sent out emails asking people for advice on housing, schools, churches. We thought destination as we prayed and planned, even while tears formed at every thought and our hearts began to bleed in anticipation of that final goodbye when we would look out the plane window and feel grief too deep for words, too heavy for tears. At the time I didn't know the RAFT acronym. The first edition of *Third Culture Kids: Growing Up Among Worlds* was not released until three years later. The research was still being conducted, interviews with third culture kids and adult third culture kids were not yet complete.

A few years later when we left Massachusetts for Phoenix this last step, 'thinking destination,' was easy – I could not wait to exchange ice and snow, the dog days of New England winters – for the desert sun and vast blue sky. During that move, other logs on the RAFT were more difficult.

Each move we make varies. Intuitively I think many of us know this RAFT, we know that this RAFT is critical to take us over the sometimes calm, sometimes rocky, always unpredictable thing called 'transition'. But to see it in print, validated and researched, gives many of us a life line to draw from, a method to keep us afloat.

THOUGHTS ON ENTRY AND REENTRY FOR THE THIRD CULTURE KID

Every summer I begin thinking about change and transition, about reentry and culture shock. With the first warm breezes of the season, I am transported to places and times where this was my reality. And I begin to hear stories from others who are going through these transitions. The stories are told in photographs and short, often humorous, statements, hiding the tremendous impact of transnational moves.

When I began looking into information on reentry, I came across refugee resettlement and orientation programs for refugees entering a country. I was struck by how much the advice resonated with me as a third culture kid. While on one level the TCK and the refugee experience are worlds apart, the goals and the realistic expectations in refugee orientation programs are remarkably helpful. Because orientation for the refugee is not just about theory and information, it is designed to give the refugee "the opportunity to develop realistic expectations regarding their resettlement, to consider different situations that might arise in a new country, and develop skills and attitudes that will

facilitate their adjustment and well-being" (http://www.
culturalorientation.net/providing-orientation/about)

The first thing I realized is that a Third Culture Kid, like
the refugee or the immigrant, doesn't 'reenter'. Instead we
'enter' a world that is not familiar, a world that calls up all
of our flexibility and ingenuity to adjust. It may seem like a
small thing, but the difference between those words is huge.

So I began developing my own list for the third culture
kid tribe. I offer it here with hope that both those who enter
and those who re-enter may find a nugget of truth.

Adopt realistic time expectations. Entering a new world is a
journey and it rarely happens in three months or six months.
We are moving to a new country, a new world. As such it
deserves all the attention we would give to going into a totally
different culture. Transitioning to a new life in our passport
country is far bigger than spending a summer vacation there.
Give yourself a minimum of two years, but don't be surprised
if it takes five.

Accept that we are shaped by a combination of worlds. As
TCKs, our worlds are woven together in a semi-formed
tapestry. Many of us feel like completely different people
when we're in our passport countries. We are not chameleons
and we are not impostors; rather we're trying to make sense
of our worlds and figure out what cultural adaptation looks
like as we effectively transition to our passport countries. Yes,
there is loss of identity. But as we work through these losses,
our identities as those who can live between worlds emerge
stronger than ever.

Understand culture shock. We don't go through reverse
culture shock – we go through culture shock. Reverse culture
shock means we know a culture, have been away from it, and
are returning to differences we didn't expect. In our case,
we don't really know this culture we are entering. We may

think we know it, because our passports tell us we should, but we don't. And while reverse culture shock is described as "wearing contact lenses in the wrong eyes", culture shock is having a completely new prescription.

Give voice to a longing. Struggling to give voice to our longings is enormous. Somehow it doesn't feel valid. But giving voice to our longings is legitimate. Our world as we know it has ended. We may be able to visit our home, our adopted country, but we know that we must have a valid and legal way to stay there should we wish to go back. We will have times of intense longing and wistfulness for what no longer exists. Giving voice to 'saudade' helps take away its power and ability to control. The longings are there, they are valid, but if they control us we will despair. Our longings can be expressed through writing, through connecting to other TCKs, through the visual arts, through theatre, through faith, and through friendships.

Understand how our worldview was shaped. While our parents went overseas with already developed worldviews and through their interactions in their host countries had their worldviews affected, ours began developing in our host country. Our first memories may be the sound of the Call to Prayer or a dusty road and traffic jam involving a buffalo, two donkey carts, and our parent's jeep. They may be of a crowded and colorful bazaar filled with colorful fabrics and bangles. Our experiences shape our worldview this will probably differ markedly from those of our parents and those of our peers in our passport countries. Having realistic understanding and expectations on differing worldviews helps us to not expect or demand that others understand us.

Accept that faith can be complicated. For many of us, faith is paramount to who we are. But it gets tangled up in our adjusting to life in our passport countries. It's particularly difficult if we feel we can't question God, express disbelief or doubt, or change denominations because it feels disloyal to our parents. This can inhibit our honesty as it relates to our faith journeys. Perhaps doubt was never a part of our faith journey before, but now that our world has changed the doubts surface. A question emerges: "Will the faith that sustained me through my journey thus far be big enough to get me through this crucial juncture?" It's an important question and often we need to find people beyond our parents who can hear and understand us, speaking truth into our faith and our doubt.

Look for cultural brokers. Often there emerges someone who doesn't share our background but who understands in a way that defies our understanding. This is a gift. This is the person who explains life to us, and walks beside us. This is the one who looks through our high school yearbook and says "Now who's this with you? And did you go on that camping trip where you got in trouble for sneaking over to where the boys were sleeping before or after this picture was taken?" This personal interest helps us understand what friendship, listening, and cultural brokering look like. So learn from them. Look to them. But don't put undue burdens on them.

Recognize the significance of place. Place is significant physically, emotionally, and spiritually. At the core of our identity as humans is a need for 'place'. Call it 'belonging', call it 'home', call it anything you like, but all of us are integrally connected to place. We are incarnate beings and so when those places are taken away, we suffer from a "disruption" of place. It is clear that the TCK has a disruption of place – often multiple times in their lives. If the disruption goes beyond our ability to adapt it becomes a pathology. The late Paul Tournier, a gifted Swiss psychologist, calls this a *"deprivation of place"*. He says that to be human is to need a place, to be rooted and attached to that place. Many of us downplay this connection to place by over spiritualizing it or underestimating its importance. We need not dismiss it, we need not idolize it; we must only acknowledge it and recognize it as valid.

Acknowledge the yearning heart. All of us have a heart that yearns for belonging, for acceptance, for love. This is the human condition. It is a fundamental truth and it is not unique to the third culture kid. What is hard is tying this in with all of our TCK experiences, life story, and worldview. It is easy for us to mistake our yearning for only that which we left, instead of remembering that we had a heart that yearned before we ever left for our passport countries. If we can grow in an understanding of our hearts, what is global and universal in our yearning, and what is specifically tied to being a third culture kid, we are in a good place. A desire for place is universal, a desire for our *particular place*, whether it be Buenos Aires or Bolivia or Cairo or Lebanon, is specific to our TCK background.

Accept and offer grace. In the midst of all of this, it is so easy to want grace, and so hard to give grace. Yet all of this is about grace. The grace that we were given by our host country, the grace of others who walked beside us as kids, the grace of our parents in caring and loving even when they don't fully understand. Those of us who 'get' grace will find it easier to give grace. Can we give grace to those who we feel dismiss us, hurt us, misunderstand us, or don't like us? Can we give grace to the people who we misunderstand, who we don't like, who we dismiss?

None of this is a formula and it is not a list of stages. Although there are similarities that bind us together as TCK's, ultimately we each have our own unique story.

Walking through the entry process and emerging on the other side is one more chapter in that story, one more pattern in the ever-evolving tapestry of our lives.

Normalizing Departure

Six years ago my mom told me that from age six through age eighteen I never slept in the same bed more than three months at a time. I don't even remember what we were talking about, but I do remember the moment. The fuzzy fog of self-accusation that had enveloped me suddenly changed into clear and complete understanding.

It always felt like it was my fault that I didn't feel like I belonged. If only I tried harder. If only I reached out more. If only I wasn't so sensitive.

If only . . .

With my mom's revelation, the "if only" suddenly became a "no wonder!" complete with all the emphasis an exclamation mark can give.

No wonder I always felt temporary.

No wonder I grew restless every few months, rearranging furniture, changing pictures on the wall, looking for a new job.

No wonder I thought I could feel my inner scream of rebellion when people around me were unwilling to face change.

Our life as third culture kids had rhythms of movement. You never questioned those rhythms, they were like the seasons of the year, and you don't question seasons of the year. Instead, you meet them and embrace them. Then, just when you've grown tired and have had enough of winter, you see the burst of spring through forsythia and daffodils poking through old, gray snow.

Like the seasons, arrivals and departures were normalized. We came, we left, and in between we lived. Our resilience was amazing but along the way we didn't always face the grief that had collected, didn't always realize that there were some coping mechanisms that would need to be confronted, things that prevented us from fully engaging in life with the people around us.

Deepak Unnikrishnan, an Abu Dhabi based writer, recently wrote an article called "Abu Dhabi: the city where citizenship is not an option." Other than airport layovers on the way to Pakistan, I've never been to Abu Dhabi, yet it's been a long time since I read an article that so completely described the third culture kid experience and the normalization of movement that others find so difficult to relate to.

Like me, Deepak grew up in a place that was not his 'passport' country. There are no long-term options for citizenship in the United Arab Emirates, and so children like Deepak, who then become adults, know that at some point they will leave. They had to have a reason to stay.

> . . . at 20, with the help of a loan from my parents, I found myself leaving for the US. I don't recall having a conversation with anyone about how I felt. My parents, like others of their generation, normalized departure. But they didn't tell us what to do with the memories, or how to archive them. (https://www. theguardian.com/cities/2017/dec/13/abu-dhabi-citizenship-uae-foreigner-visa-india)

Deepak questions the words that are available to those of us who are trained to leave our homes behind. "Expatriate isn't right. Neither is migrant. And guest worker just feels cold, almost euphemistic," he says.

As I think about this I realize why I continue to hold on to the identity and importance of the term "third culture kid." Because that is the identity I believe the author is looking for. We are trained to leave our homes behind. We know we won't stay, we know we can't stay. It is we whose memories matter so deeply, whose memories need to be archived so that we can hold on to pieces of place. It is we who continue to embrace this identity, even as we move into more permanent seasons and places in our lives.

As kids we are involuntary transients; as adults sometimes the easiest path to take is to become voluntary transients, procreating involuntary transients along the way. We continue patterns of normalizing arrivals and departures, understanding the sweetness of arrivals and the bitterness of goodbyes. We are expert packers and planners, holding our arrival and departure manifestos in our hearts and heads.

But sometimes, we need to plant our feet solidly into the soil around us and stay a little longer. Sometimes we need to realize it's okay to write our names in the land of our passport countries, even as we hold on to archived memories to give us strength.

For most of us, being raised as foreigners meant our stay in [insert country] was free of permanence. For some, a temporary stay meant a year or two; for others, time dragged on indefinitely, but always, always, the time would come to say goodbye. Our parents may have chosen to remain, but we would leave. We were raised to be different, we were raised knowing we wouldn't stay, knowing that as soon as we finished school we would leave and probably not come back. (Nina Sichel, *Unrooted Childhoods*)

It May Take Some Time to Breathe

I recently arrived back from an overseas trip. As soon as the plane landed, I felt a familiar tightening in my chest. I have lived in Cambridge now for eight years, yet I still feel what is almost like a panic attack come over me as I walk from the plane, through the long gateway, into the terminal. It's hard to breathe.

I was in the house only five minutes when I began to make bread, desperate to belong, aching to make this not feel like I'm in a strange, alien land where I will never truly belong. This is ridiculous. I've lived here eight years, longer than I've lived anywhere. Why do I feel this way?

When the bread is done, I find I can catch my breath and relax, I take in gulps of air and breathe. Breathing is somehow part of belonging.

I was born to belong. You were born to belong. We were all born to belong.

To belong – to be attached or bound by birth, allegiance, or dependency – usually used with to, as in "they belong to their homeland."

Our creator built into us a longing and connection to place. Look at the Incarnation – God linked to time and place through the person of Christ. So displacement, whatever form it takes, causes a certain amount of pain. We were born to belong.

Paul Tournier speaks profoundly about belonging: "He who once had the experience of belonging to place, always finds a place for himself afterwards; whereas he who has been deprived of it, searches everywhere in vain."

You have to have a place before you can leave a place. You have to have a self, before you can give of yourself. You have to have a home before you can leave a home.

Home, belonging, place—the words are connected, woven together, tapestry-like. We try to separate them, only to weave them together once again.

During a recent trip, I heard story after story of leaving home, of displacement. I am acutely aware that this catching my breath, this reaching and aching to belong is not just a third culture kid phenomenon. Home and belonging are hard concepts to grasp for many in our world. The immigrant, refugee, third culture kid, expat — all experience a painful though expanded view of home. I also feel the inadequacy of words to describe home and belonging. Though there is much written about this, and much of it is good, I still find I need better words. There is something missing.

I felt this way until I read this short haiku written by a friend of mine. He was able to accomplish in six short lines what few can ever accomplish.

> home's the skin we live
> in, moving its shedding; you
> now new and tender
> they say you leave your
> heart, i say your lungs; it may
> take some time to breathe

> Neil Das, *Haiku on Moving*

That's it. You leave your lungs. So I stop and give myself time to catch my breath, time to bake bread, time to breathe.

More Resources
By and For Third Culture Kids

Third Culture Kids: The Experience of Growing Up Among Worlds Third edition. David C Pollock, Ruth Van Reken, and Michael Pollock.

This new edition gives even more resources, new material on grief and transition, and a look at the broader category of cross cultural kids. This book is a must-have on your book shelf if you are raising TCK's or cross cultural kids.

Misunderstood: The impact of growing up overseas in the 21st Century. Tanya Crossman.

An excellent addition to TCK literature. Tanya gives us detailed narratives and interviews from hundreds of third culture kids. This should be on every parent and every school's bookshelf.

❖

Belonging Everywhere and Nowhere: Insights into Counseling the Globally Mobile. Lois Bushong.

Lois explores how to effectively counsel those raised outside their passport countries. She is an adult TCK and brings compassion and understanding into the journey.

Emotional Resilience and the Expat Child: Practical Storytelling Techniques That Will Strengthen the Global Family. Julia Simens.

Julia is a counselor who has navigated many relocations. This book is a workbook to work through as a family and helps children and adults develop their personal narrative.

Unrooted Childhoods: Memoirs of Growing up Global. edited by Faith Eidse and Nina Sichel.

A series of essays from both well-known and not so well known third culture kids including Pico Iyer and Isabel Allende. I love this book for its complexity, variety, and truth.

Safe Passage, how mobility affects people & what international schools should do about it. Douglas W. Ota.

Ota knows what it is to live between worlds and experience grief: "Moving is one of life's greatest challenges. The largest study in educational research history demonstrates that moving harms learning. But moving not only challenges students. The experience of lost identity extends across the lifespan, also affecting parents and school staff. Firmly grounded in psychological theory and cutting-edge neuroscience, Safe Passage maps the challenges and charts a course for individuals, schools, and accrediting bodies to navigate them. Although primarily focusing on international schools, the hopeful message within this book reaches into any school, university, or organization where human beings come and go."

Writing Out of Limbo: International Childhoods, Global Nomads and Third Culture Kids. Gene H. Bell-Villada, Nina Sichel, Faith Eidse, and Elaine Neil Orr

Writing out of Limbo is written in the style of a text book, and it is great resource to have in an organization's library to offer to parents and kids.

Letters Never Sent, a global nomad's journey from hurt to healing. Ruth Van Reken.

Letters Never Sent is Ruth's personal story from ages six to 39: "Ruth van Reken describes herself as 'a person in process' – someone whose life is made up of the continuous interplay between her inner and outer journey. For more than twenty-five years, Ruth has traveled to over 45 countries sharing what she has learned while 'listening to life' about the often paradoxical nature of growing up globally. What she has learned resonates with expatriate children and adults from all sectors – corporate, diplomatic, military, missionary, immigrant and refugees."

B at Home: Emma Moves Again. Valerie Besanceney.

This is a delightful children's book that deals with the fear, excitement, and other emotions of being uprooted as a child: "Emma is only ten years old, but has already moved twice. Now, her parents are telling her the family is moving again. She's furious, sad, nervous, and a little excited, all at the same time. Unsure of how to tackle these conflicting emotions, she turns to B, her faithful teddy bear. While trying to come to terms with the challenges of another move, what Emma really wants is just to 'be at home'. As the journeys of Emma and B unfold, home changes once again, but home also begins to take on a new meaning that Emma can take with her wherever she goes."

Arrivals, Departures and the Adventures In-Between. Christopher O'Shaugnessy.

Christopher is an amazing story-teller and uses that gift well in this book. "Once, down a dark alleyway, a struggling TCK bumped into a mysterious Zen master, a grinning comedian, and an author of thrillers. That alleyway and those personas reside at O'Shaughnessy's center. Get ready to grab your seat to steady your heart and to avoid falling over with laughter." (Douglas W. Ota)

Slurping Soup and Other Confusions. Tonges et al.

This book is a collection of 23 real-life stories from TCKs followed by activities to go along with the stories. An excellent resource for parents and kids in transition.

The Global Nomad's Guide to University Transition. Tina L. Quick.

For years I've heard about Tina, but this September I had the privilege of meeting her. She is absolutely lovely. Her book is a treasure for university students and their parents. So many of us didn't realize we were different from our peers in our passport countries until we entered university.

The Art of Coming Home. Craig Storti.

This book dives into the reentry process for those coming back from overseas postings. Not TCK specific but has some excellent advice.

The Anika Scott Series. Karen Rispin.

These are five novels for middle schoolers and teens: Anika Scott is 12 years old and lives with her family in Kenya. It's not easy to be 12 and it's not easy to navigate a life between worlds. The reader joins Annika on her adventures and journey in Kenya as she learns more about herself, God, and the world she lives in.

Notes from No Man's Land. Eula Biss.

In this set of essays Eula Biss addresses race, identity, and belonging through looking at her own family and through history. This book is full of insight and wisdom on what it means to belong, to be home, to have privilege, and to live in a diverse country.

Global Mom: Eight Countries, Sixteen Addresses, Five Languages, One Family. Melissa Dalton-Bradford.

Melissa Bradford shares a journey of global motherhood that includes adventure and profound loss. This book addresses parenting, moving, and grief intertwined in a global journey. Melissa is amazing.

Cat Tales. Pauline Brown.

When the Brown family adopted a kitten to keep out uninvited guests like mice and rats, they had no idea how many adventures that Old Black Cat would get herself and her family into. From camping in the foothills of the Himalayas, to holding up a train in the busy city of Lahore, OBC and her family find themselves in many hilarious and tricky situations. These delightful, true tales follow their travels through Pakistan as they learn to trust God more with every adventure.

Between Worlds: Essays on Culture and Belonging;. Marilyn Gardner.

Between Worlds is my first book. The essays explore the rootlessness and grief as well as the unexpected moments of humor and joy that are a part of living between two worlds.

Between Worlds charts a journey between the cultures of East and West, the comfort of being surrounded by loved ones and familiar places, and the loneliness of not belonging. "Every one of us has been at some point between two worlds, be they faith and loss of faith, joy and sorrow, birth and death. *Between Worlds* is a luminous guide for connecting—and healing—worlds." (Cathy Romeo)